MW00791231

Colloquial
Serbian

THE COLLOQUIAL SERIES
Series Adviser: Gary King

The following languages are available in the Colloquial series:

Afrikaans	German	Romanian
Albanian	Greek	Russian
Amharic	Gujarati	Scottish Gaelic
Arabic (Levantine)	Hebrew	Serbian
Arabic of Egypt	Hindi	Slovak
Arabic of the Gulf	Hungarian	Slovene
Basque	Icelandic	Somali
Bengali	Indonesian	Spanish
Breton	Irish	Spanish of Latin
Bulgarian	Italian	America
Burmese	Japanese	Swahili
Cambodian	Kazakh	Swedish
Cantonese	Korean	Tamil
Catalan	Latvian	Thai
Chinese (Mandarin)	Lithuanian	Tibetan
Croatian	Malay	Turkish
Czech	Mongolian	Ukrainian
Danish	Norwegian	Urdu
Dutch	Panjabi	Vietnamese
English	Persian	Welsh
Estonian	Polish	Yiddish
Finnish	Portuguese	Yoruba
French	Portuguese of Brazil	Zulu (forthcoming)

COLLOQUIAL 2s series: *The Next Step in Language Learning*

Chinese	German	Russian
Dutch	Italian	Spanish
French	Portuguese of Brazil	Spanish of Latin America

Colloquials are now supported by FREE AUDIO available online. All audio tracks referenced within the text are free to stream or download from www.routledge.com/cw/colloquials. If you experience any difficulties accessing the audio on the companion website, or still wish to purchase a CD, please contact our customer services team through www.routledge.com/info/contact.

Colloquial
Serbian

The Complete Course for Beginners

Celia Hawkesworth
with Jelena Ćalić

Routledge
Taylor & Francis Group

LONDON AND NEW YORK

First published 2006
by Routledge
2 Park Square, Milton Park, Abingdon, Oxon, OX14 4RN

Simultaneously published in the USA and Canada
by Routledge
711 Third Avenue, New York, NY 10017

Routledge is an imprint of the Taylor & Francis Group, an informa business

© 2006 Celia Hawkesworth

All rights reserved. No part of this book may be reprinted or
reproduced or utilized in any form or by any electronic, mechanical, or
other means, now known or hereafter invented, including photocopying
and recording, or in any information storage or retrieval system,
without permission in writing from the publishers.

British Library Cataloguing in Publication Data
A catalogue record for this book is available from the British Library

Library of Congress Cataloging in Publication Data
Hawkesworth, Celia, 1942–
    Colloquial Serbian: the complete course for beginners/
    Celia Hawkesworth; in association with Jelena Ćalić.
    – 1st edn.
        p. cm – (The colloquial series)
    Includes index.
    1. Serbian language – Textbooks for foreign speakers –
English.   2. Serbian language – Spoken Serbian.
    I. Ćalić, Jelena.   II. Title.   III. Series
    PG1239.5.E5H298   2005
    491.8'282421 – dc22   2004029633

ISBN: 978-1-138-94979-9 (pbk)

Typeset in Times by
Florence Production Ltd, Stoodleigh, Devon

Contents

Acknowledgements

I would like to thank the friends and colleagues who have helped with the various stages of the evolution of this book, which has grown out of the earlier volume *Colloquial Croatian and Serbian*. Nada Šoljan, Damir Kalogjera, Ljiljana Gjurgjan, Višnja Josipović and Vesna Domany-Hardy all generously advised on its various different drafts. The present work is the result of a most enjoyable collaboration with Jelena Ćalić. Her advice and help on many aspects of life in Serbia and Montenegro, in addition to her skills as a teacher of the Serbian language, as seen in the exercises she has devised, have been invaluable. She has also provided the numerous illustrative photographs which enhance the text. I shall always be grateful to her for her hard work, patience and cheerfulness throughout the production of the book.

MAĐARSKA

HRVATSKA

Vojvodina

Dunav Novi Sad •

RUMUNIJA

Beograd ■

BOSNA I
HERCEGOVINA

Užice •

SRBIJA

Niš •

Novi Pazar •

CRNA GORA

Priština •

BUGARSKA

Podgorica •

ALBANIJA

MAKEDONIJA

0   40   80 km

0   40   80 mi

Introduction

Learning Serbian

Serbian, and its close relations, Bosnian and Croatian, belongs to the South Slavonic group of languages, along with Bulgarian, Macedonian and Slovene. Of all the Slavonic languages, the Bosnian/Croatian/Serbian linguistic complex is the easiest for English speakers to master, and it is considered one of the easiest of all the European languages for English speakers to pronounce. There is just one small hazard for those who have difficulty in producing a rolled 'r'. In some words 'r' has the value of a vowel and carries the stress. Innocent students should be prepared to be exposed to a series of tongue-twisters, such as **Navrh brda vrba mrda** 'On top of the hill a willow sways', or words such as **Grk** 'Greek', or the onomatopoeic **cvrčci** 'cicadas' (pronounced 'tsvrchtsi' with the stress on the 'r').

The alphabet consists of thirty phonemes: one letter for each sound. The pronunciation of these letters is constant, not varying with its position in a word. Each letter is pronounced, e.g. **pauk** 'spider' consists of two separate syllables. Notice the spelling of **Srbija**: without the **j** there would have to be a break between the two final vowels **i-a**. Also, the spelling is phonetic. That is to say, words are written just as they are spoken. In other words, the learner could gain full marks in dictation from the very beginning.

Dialects

Serbian has two main dialects, defined by the pronunciation of the letter 'e' in certain situations. As each written letter is pronounced, this difference in sound is reproduced also in writing. Thus, for example, the word for 'milk' is pronounced and written **mleko** in Ekavian and **mlijeko** in Ijekavian. The Ekavian dialect is used in the greater part of Serbia, while Ijekavian is used in some parts of Serbia, in Montenegro and by Serbs living in Bosnia-Herzegovina and Croatia. This book uses Ekavian throughout, but the two Bosnian characters who appear in the Dialogue 'Ekipa' speak Ijekavian.

Alphabets

The historical division of the South Slav lands between the Orthodox and Catholic spheres of influence has meant that the Serbian language may be written in either the Cyrillic or the Latin script. Both have been modified for the language's phonetic system, and transliteration letter for letter is possible from one to the other.

Stress and tone

Stress

There is no absolute rule for the position of the stressed syllable in a word, except that it is never the final syllable. In a polysyllabic word it is generally the pre-penultimate syllable – which in practice generally means the first syllable. This is a fairly safe principle for you to adopt. Listen carefully for words in which there is a long syllable in addition to the stressed syllable: it can sometimes sound as though there are in fact two stresses on a word, see the section on tone below. In certain words, the stress may shift from singular to plural or from one case to another, e.g. **vreme** 'time, weather' has genitive singular **vremena** and nominative plural **vremena**. This is something to listen for in the more advanced stages of learning the language. In this book the stress is marked by underlining in the new vocabulary as it is introduced and throughout some of the reading passages so that you do not have to think about it too much as you read. In a word of two syllables the stress is not marked, as it will always fall on the first.

Tone

The Serbian language has a system of tonal stress, which, on the one hand, is quite complex and, on the other, more marked among the speakers from some areas than others. This question may be largely ignored in the early stages except for one or two situations indicated below. Nevertheless, the student should be encouraged from the outset to listen carefully to examples of the spoken language and observe the variations in tone. Traditional textbooks identify four tones to indicate the rising or falling of the voice on (a) short and (b) long stressed syllables:

1 short rising ` **gospòdin** (Mr)
2 short falling ` **gòspoða** (Mrs)
3 long rising **víno** (wine)
4 long falling ˆ **dân** (day)

Naturally, these variations are more noticeable on long syllables. Occasionally they indicate a difference in meaning:

grâd	town	**gràd**	hail
pâs	belt	**pàs**	dog
lûk	arch	**lùk**	onion

One particularly obvious example is when unstressed verbal **sam** 'am' is used in conjunction with the adjective **sam** 'alone'. The statement **sam sam** 'I am alone' consists of two quite distinct sounds.

The recordings which accompany this book enable the learner to hear the language spoken by native Serbian speakers. Dialogues and other sections of text for which there are recordings are marked with the icon ⓝ.

Note: When writing Serbian, pay particular attention to the diacritic marks: **c**, **č** and **ć** are all different letters and to omit the diacritic will result in misunderstandings (as in English, if 't' is not crossed it can be read as 'l'). Also, when using dictionaries, be aware that **d**, **ð**, **l**, **lj** and **n**, **nj** are all *separate* letters: i.e. **ljiljan** 'lily' will not be found under **l** but under **lj**.

Using the book

The grammar presented here may appear complicated at first as it contains so much that is new to the English speaker. The student is advised to learn to observe the language in practice by close analysis of the reading passages, which have been designed to illustrate each point as it arises. Tackle only one topic at a time and refer frequently to the main text of each unit to observe each point 'in action'. Make sure that you have fully understood and absorbed each point before going on to the next. Use the exercises to test your understanding and return to the relevant section if you make a mistake or are at all uncertain. The exercises marked with a dagger (†) have answers given in the 'Key to exercises' at the end of the book.

There are two stories running through the book which may be used to monitor your progress: translate each instalment into English, checking your version with the translation at the back of the book, and, at a later date, translate it back into Serbian. If you make a mistake be sure that you understand how you went wrong.

By the end of the book you will have covered all the main points of the grammar and much essential vocabulary. You will then need to consolidate your knowledge and expand your vocabulary by further reading. You should be able to read newspapers with relative ease, as well as more complex texts with the help of a dictionary. Suggestions for further study are listed below.

Every effort that you put into learning the language will be richly rewarded as you find yourself able to communicate increasingly freely.

Good luck!

Suggestions for further study

History, culture and politics

Benson, Leslie, *Yugoslavia: A Concise History*, Palgrave, London, 2001
Glenny, Misha, *The Balkans 1804–1999: Nationalism, War and the Great Powers*, Granta Books, London, 1999
Gordy, Eric D., *The Culture of Power in Serbia: Nationalism and the Destruction of Alternatives*, Pennsylvania State University Press, University Park, PA, 1999
Iordanova, Dina, *Cinema of Flames: Balkan Film, Culture and the Media*, British Film Institute, London, 2001
Judah, Tim, *The Serbs: History, Myth and the Destruction of Yugoslavia*, Yale University Press, New Haven, CT and London, 1997
Pavlowitch, Stevan K., *Serbia: The History of an Idea*, New York University Press, NY, 2002
Thomas, Robert, *Serbia under Milošević: Politics in the 1990s*, Hurst, London, 1999
Wachtel, Andrew, *Making a Nation, Breaking a Nation. Literature and Politics in Yugoslavia*, Stanford University Press, Stanford, CA, 1998

Dictionaries

Ignjatović, Zdravko *et al.*, *ESSE English–Serbian Serbian–English Dictionary*, The Institute for Foreign Languages, Belgrade, 2002
Benson, Morton, *Standard English–Serbo–Croatian, Serbo–Croatian–English Dictionary*, Cambridge University Press, 1998
Hlebec, Boris, *Osnovni englesko–srpski, srpsko–engleski rečnik*, Zavod za udžbenike i nastavna sredstva, Belgrade, 2003

Internet sources

General, tourism

www.mfa.gov.yu	Ministry of Foreign Affairs
http://www.serbia-tourism.org/	tourist info on Serbia
http://www.visit-montenegro.cg.yu	tourist info on Montenegro
http://www.beograd.org.yu	tourist info on Belgrade
http://www.beograd.com/	links to general sites

Culture

http://www.msub.org.yu/main.htm	Museum of Contemporary Art, Belgrade
http://www.narodnopozoriste.co.yu/	National Theatre, Beograd
http://www.jdp.co.yu/	Jugoslovensko dramsko Pozoriste, Beograd
http://www.kinoteka.org.yu/	National Film Archive

Media

http://www.mediacenter.org.yu	links to media sites
http://www.politika.co.yu	*Politika* newspaper
http://www.b92.net	Radio B92
http://www.setimes.com	*South East European Times*

Pronunciation and alphabets

🎧 (Audio 1: 1)

Latin		Cyrillic		Approximate pronunciation	Example	Cyrillic order
A	a	А	а	a in father	mama 'mum'	А
B	b	Б	б	as English b	brat 'brother'	Б
C	c	Ц	ц	ts in cats	otac 'father'	В
Č	č	Ч	ч	ch in church	čaj 'tea'	Г
Ć	ć	Ћ	ћ	tj in capture	kuća 'house'	Д
D	d	Д	д	as English d	da 'yes'	Ђ
Dž	dž	Џ	џ	J in John	džemper 'jumper'	Е
Đ	đ	Ђ	ђ	roughly dj	đak 'pupil'	Ж
E	e	Е	е	e in bed	krevet 'bed'	З
F	f	Ф	ф	as English f	fotografija 'photograph'	И
G	g	Г	г	as English g	govoriti 'to speak'	Ј
H	h	Х	х	ch in loch	hvala 'thank you'	К
I	i	И	и	e in he	ili 'or'	Л
J	j	Ј	ј	y in yes	jaje 'egg'	Љ
K	k	К	к	as English k	karta 'ticket', 'map'	М
L	l	Л	л	as English l	lep 'beautiful'	Н
Lj	lj	Љ	љ	ll in million	ljubav 'love'	Њ
M	m	М	м	as English m	molim 'please'	О
N	n	Н	н	as English n	ne 'no'	П
Nj	nj	Њ	њ	n in news	konj 'horse'	Р
O	o	О	о	o in not	ovde 'here'	С
P	p	П	п	as English p	pesma 'song'	Т

Latin		Cyrillic		Approximate pronunciation	Example	Cyrillic order
R	r	Р	р	rolled	**r**o**diteǉi** 'parents'	Ћ
S	s	C	c	<u>ss</u> in ble<u>ss</u>	**s**e**stra** 'sister'	У
Š	š	Ш	ш	<u>sh</u> in <u>sh</u>y	**šlǉva** 'plum'	Ф
T	t	T	т	as English <u>t</u>	**trg** 'square'	Х
U	u	У	y	<u>ou</u> in should	**u**č**iti** 'to learn'	Ц
V	v	B	в	as English <u>v</u>	**v**i**no** 'wine'	Ч
Z	z	3	з	as English <u>z</u>	**za**š**to** 'why'	Џ
Ž	ž	Ж	ж	<u>s</u> in plea<u>s</u>ure	**ž**i**vot** 'life'	Ш

1 Upoznavanje

Meeting

In this unit we will look at:

- the verb **biti**
- personal pronouns: 'I', 'you' etc.
- nationalities
- basic word order
- formation of questions
- introducing yourself

 Dialogue 1 (Audio 1: 2–3)

Džon i Anđela Braun putuju u Beograd

John and Angela Brown are travelling to Belgrade. As the plane touches down, Angela's neighbour speaks to her. What is his name?

(A)

MILAN: Dobar dan.
ANÐELA: Dobar dan.
MILAN: Ja sam Milan Jovanović.
ANÐELA: Ja sam Anđela Braun, a ovo je moj muž, Džon.
MILAN: Drago mi je. Dobro došli u Beograd!

Vocabulary

a	and/but	**dan**	day
dobar (m.)	good	**dobro došli**	welcome
drago mi je	pleased to meet you (lit. 'it is dear to me')	**ja**	I
		je	is
		moj	my (m.)
muž	husband	**ovo**	his (n.)
sam	am	**u**	to, into

(B) Cyrillic

DŽON:	Vi ste Srbin, zar ne?	Ви сте Србин, зар не?
MILAN:	Da, ja sam Srbin, a vi?	Да, ја сам Србин, а ви?
DŽON:	Mi smo Englezi.	Ми смо Енглези.

Vocabulary

da	yes	**Englez**	an English person
mi	we	**smo**	are (1st pers. pl.)
Srbin	a Serb (pl. **Srbi**)	**ste**	are (2nd pers. pl.)
vi	you (2nd pers. pl.)	**zar ne?**	aren't you?
			(isn't it? etc.)

Language points 1

Greetings

Dobar dan 'good day' is used as the basic greeting for most of the day. The phrase for 'good morning' – **dobro jutro** – is used only up to about 10 a.m., and that for 'good evening' – **dobro veče** – after about 6 p.m. Informal greetings are: **zdravo, ćao.**

Personal pronouns

	Singular		*Plural*	
1st	**ja**	I	**mi**	we
2nd	**ti**	you (familiar)	**vi**	you (formal, polite)
3rd	**on**	he	**oni**	they (m. or mixed gender)
	ona	she	**one**	they (f.)
	ono	it	**ona**	they (n.)

Notice the two different words for 'you'. **Ti** is the familiar singular form, used for family, contemporaries, close friends, colleagues, children and animals. **Vi** is used for more than one person and also as a more formal way of addressing one person to show distance and respect for age or social status. Like nouns and adjectives, the pronouns have different forms depending on their function in a sentence. You will learn these later.

Because the verb endings in Serbian clearly denote the person of the subject, personal pronouns are not used when they are the subject (in what is called the nominative case), except for emphasis. Compare:

Kako se zovete? (no personal pronoun)
What are you called?

Zovem se Milan. Kako se vi zovete?
I'm called Milan. What are *you* called?

Ne razumeju engleski. Da li on govori srpski?
They don't understand English. Does *he* speak Serbian?

Dialogue 2 (Audio 1: 4)

Questions

(A) – Zdravo Anđela, kako si?
 – Dobro, hvala, a kako si ti?
 – I ja sam dobro, hvala.

(B) – Govorite li srpski?
 – Nažalost, još ne. Ali učimo!
 – Bravo!

Vocabulary

kako si?	how are you?	**dobro**	well
hvala	thank you	**govoriti**	to speak
srpski	Serbian	**nažalost**	unfortunately
još ne	not yet	**ali**	but
učimo	we are learning		

Vocabulary building

Nationalities 1

Read this list of nationalities and try to work out what they are. Once you are confident that you recognize all the Latin script names, cover them up and try to read them in Cyrillic:

Srbin	Hrvat	Bosanac
Englez	Irac	Škotlanđanin
Velšanin	Francuz	Amerikanac

Србин	Хрват	Босанац
Енглез	Ирац	Шкотланђанин
Велшанин	Француз	Американац

Note: These nouns all have feminine forms as well. Try to read them in Cyrillic:

Српкиња	Хрватица	Босанка
Енглескиња	Иркиња	Шкотланђанка
Велшанка	Францускиња	Американка

Language points 2

The verb biti *'I am'*

This is the first verb you must learn. It has two forms: a long stressed form and a short unstressed (*enclitic*) form. The short form is the more common, while the stressed form is used in certain specific situations.

In Serbian there are several short forms of the kind known as 'enclitics'. These are words which carry no stress and are pronounced as though they were part of the preceding word. Consequently, they cannot be placed first in a sentence or clause.

The short form of biti

(I)	**(ja)**	**sam**
(you)	**(ti)**	**si**
(he/she/it)	**(on/ona/ono)**	**je**
(we)	**(mi)**	**smo**
(you)	**(vi)**	**ste**
(they)	**(oni/one/ona)**	**su**

Ja sam Englez.
I am English.

Ona je Srpkinja.
She is Serbian.

Vi ste Srbin.
You (formal) are Serbian.

Mi smo studenti.
We are students.

Exercise 1†

(a) Fill in the gaps with the appropriate form of **biti**:

1 Ja ___ Engleskinja. Moj muž ___ Škotlanđanin.
2 Oni ___ Amerikanci, a mi ___ Englezi.
3 Vesna i Neda ___ Hrvatice. One ___ studentkinje.
4 Vi ___ Bosanac?
5 Oni ___ dobro.

(b) Choose the correct pronoun:

1 ___ ne govorimo srpski.
2 ___ si Francuz.
3 ___ ste studenti?
4 Anđela i Džon su muž i žena. ___ su Englezi.
5 Zovem se Milan. ___ sam iz Beograda.

Language points 3

The long form of biti

Once you have learned the short forms, you can move on to the long forms. You will see that the endings are the same but they have an additional syllable (**je**). They are generally used *without the personal pronoun*.

(I)	**jesam**	(we)	**jesmo**
(you)	**jesi**	(you)	**jeste**
(he/she/it)	**jest(e)**	(they)	**jesu**

Remember: the short forms are the norm, the long forms are used only in certain specific situations:

1 In questions which follow this model:

stressed verb + interrog. particle **li** + subject

Jeste	**li**	**(vi)**	**Englez?**
Jesu	**li**	**(oni)**	**Srbi?**
Jesi	**li**	**(ti)**	**Francuz?**

2 In single-word answers to such questions as:

Jeste li Englez? Jesam.   Are you English? Yes, I am.

3 For special emphasis:

> **Jeste li umorni? Ja jesam, ali Anđela nije.**
> Are you tired? Yes, *I* am, but Angela is not.

Note: In the case of the third person singular *only*, it is possible to use the short form when asking questions with the interrogative **li**:

> **Tvoj muž je Irac, je li?**

Exercise 2†

Answer the following questions using the long forms:

1 Je li Neda Srpkinja?   _____
2 Jesu li Dado i Denis Bosanci?   _____
3 Jesmo li mi Srbi?   _____
4 Je li moj muž Irac?   _____
5 Jesi li ti Amerikanac?   _____

Language points 4

The negative form of biti

(I)	**nisam**	(we)	**nismo**
(you)	**nisi**	(you)	**niste**
(he/she/it)	**nije**	(they)	**nisu**

Try reading these in Cyrillic: **нисам, ниси, није, нисмо, нисте, нису**

Ja нисам уморан.   **Он није Србин.**   **Ми нисмо студенти.**
I am not tired.   He is not Serbian.   We are not students.

Exercise 3†

Use the negative form of **biti** to complete the following sentences:

1 Mi _____ studenti.
2 Oni _____ muž i žena.
3 Ti _____ Englez.
4 On _____ moj muž.
5 Ja _____ dobro.

Dialogue 3 (Audio 1: 5)

Tanja and Ljiljana meet in a Belgrade street.

Тања:	Здраво, Љиљана!
Љиљана:	Ћао, Тања!
Тања:	Како си?
Љиљана:	Добро, хвала. Како си ти?
Тања:	Нисам лоше.

TANJA:	Hi, Ljiljana!
LJILJANA:	Hi, Tanja!
TANJA:	How are you?
LJILJANA:	Fine, thanks. How are you?
TANJA:	Not bad.

Exercise 4

Fill in the gaps in the following dialogue with suitable words:

– Z_____ , ja ____ Marko. A kako se ___ zoveš?
– Z_____ , ___ se zovem Džon.
– D___ mi je.
– ____ ___ ___ .
– J_____ li ti Englez, Džon?
– N_____ . Ja ___ Amerikanac. A ___ Marko?
– ___ ____ Srbin.

Language points 5

Word order

There are several small unstressed words which the foreign learner can find tiresome to start with. They include the short forms of **biti**, which we have learned, the short forms of the personal pronouns, the interrogative particle **li** and the reflexive particle **se**. They must be placed immediately *after* the *first* stressed word or phrase in a sentence or clause. We will return to this later.
    Examples:

Ja *sam* umoran.
I am tired.

Mislim da *ste* umorni.
I think that you are tired.

Nisam umoran, gladan *sam.*
I'm not tired, I'm hungry.

It follows that, where unstressed forms are concerned, word order is quite strict and that it is affected by the presence or absence of the personal pronoun.
Compare:

Mi *smo* **gladni.**   We are hungry.
Gladni *smo.*

The meaning here is identical, except that the use of the personal pronoun tends to make the sentence emphatic.

Zovem se Marija.   (neutral)
Ja se **zovem Marija.**   (emphatic)

For example, someone else has been addressed as Marija and the speaker is pointing out that *she* (the speaker) is Marija and not the other person.

Exercise 5

Put the sentences in the jumbled-up dialogue below in the right order:

Mi smo dobro.
Zdravo Vesna.
Kako ste?
A ti?
Ćao, Džon. Ćao Anđela.
Nisam loše.

Language points 6

Formation of questions

As in English, in speech questions may be expressed through intonation alone:

Vi ste Englez?   You're English?

In the written language, however, and more formal speech, one of the other forms must be used.

1 Questions may be introduced by an interrogative:

> *Interrog.*   *Verb*
>
> **Zašto   učite srpski?**
> *Why* are you learning Serbian?
> **Ko   ste vi?**
> *Who* are you?
> **Šta   radiš ovde?**
> *What* are you doing here?

2 When a sentence does not contain an interrogative word, the
particle **li** is used (a particle is a short, indeclinable part of
speech). This is placed immediately after the main verb, which
must then be the first word in the sentence:

> *Verb*   *Interrog. part.*
>
> **Dolazite   li   često ovamo?**
> Do you come here often?
> **Čeka   li   vaša žena?**
> Is your wife waiting?

3 Another way of using the particle **li** is to combine it with the
conjunction **da**. In this case the main verb may be placed
anywhere in the sentence:

> *Question marker*
>
> **Da li   govorite srpski?**
> Do you speak Serbian?
> **Da li   razumete engleski?**
> Do you understand English?

Note: Method (3) is far more common in Serbian, while (2) is
favoured in Croatian.

4 Negative questions are introduced by **zar**:

> *Particle Negative verb*
>
> **Zar   ti nisi Englez?**
> Aren't you English?
> **Zar   studenti ne razumeju?**
> Don't the students understand?

See 'Grammar summary' for three other patterns, section 7 (p. 307).

∩ Reading passage 1 (Audio 1: 8)

K_ulturni život u Be_ogradu (1)
Cultural life in Belgrade

*This story follows the experience of Ben Wilson, a journalist from
London, who is on an assignment from his paper to give a compre-
hensive picture of cultural life in and around Belgrade. Who is
waiting for him at the airport?*

Ben Vilson je iz Lond_ona. On je n_ovinar po zan_imanju. Sada je u
Beogradu. Njegov pr_ijatelj Dejan čeka na _aerodromu. Ben _izlazi.

– Ej, zdravo, Bene, dobro d_ošao!
– Hvala, D_ejane![1] Bolje te n_ašao!

Dejan vodi Bena do automob_ila i oni _odlaze u Zemun.

1 This is the vocative case, used when addressing people. It is becoming less frequent,
but listen out for such changes to the endings of people's names.

Beogradski aerodrom

Vocabulary

aerodrom	airport	**automobil**	car
bolje te našao!	used as a response	**čekati**	to wait
	to **dobro došao**	**do**	to, up to
	(lit. 'better to	**iz**	from
	have found you')	**izlaziti**	to come/go out
na	at, on	**njegov**	his
novinar	journalist	**odlaziti**	to go, leave
prijatelj	friend	**sada**	now
u	in	**voditi**	to lead
zanimanje	occupation,		
	profession		

Note: You will see in the text that some words have altered endings. We shall learn these in the coming units.

Exercise 6

(a) Answer the following questions:

1 Da li je Ben iz Londona?
2 Da li je on sada u Parizu?
3 Ko čeka Bena na aerodromu?
4 Gde odlaze Ben i Dejan?

(b) Match the following questions and answers to make a dialogue:

CARINIK: Dobar dan, gospodine Vilson.
Vaš pasoš, molim.
Sve je u redu. Dobro došli u Beograd.
BEN: Izvolite.
Hvala.
Dobar dan.

Vocabulary building

Nationalities 2

For the time being you will need to learn each of these individually: there are set patterns and with time you will recognize them. In many cases the name of the country is the feminine form of the adjective, which also gives the name of the language, but the nationalities have to be learned. Try to read the lists in Cyrillic below.

Country	Language	Nationality (m.)	Nationality (f.)
Енглеска	енглески	Енглез	Енглескиња
Србија	српски	Србин	Српкиња
Црна Гора	српски	Црногорац	Црногорка
Хрватска	хрватски	Хрват	Хрватица
Босна	босански	Босанац	Босанка
Словенија	словенски	Словенац	Словенка
Македонија	македонски	Македонац	Македонка

Language in action

Questions and answers
Pitanja i odgovori

Predrag is showing Tom round his home town.

Tom:	Šta je ovo?	*What is this?*
Predrag:	Ovo je pošta.	*This is a post office.*
Tom:	Šta je to?	*What is that?*
Predrag:	To je pozorište.	*That is a theatre.*
Tom:	Da li je to kafić?	*Is that a café?*
Predrag:	Ne, to je knjižara.	*No, that's a bookshop.*
Tom:	Gde je apoteka?	*Where is the chemist's?*
Predrag:	Tamo, preko puta.	*There, across the road.*

New words

pošta	post office	**pozorište**	theatre
kafić	small café	**knjižara**	bookshop
apoteka	chemist		

Culture point

Drago mi je and **milo mi je** mean 'I am glad' or 'I am delighted'. These expressions are used frequently when people are introduced to each other. A third person need not make the introduction: strangers will introduce themselves, telling you their name, or just their surname, as they shake your hand.

Exercise 7

(a) Fill in the missing information:

Country	Nationality		Language
	Male	Female	
_____	Hrvat	Hrvatica	hrvatski
Engleska	Englez	_____	engleski
Francuska	Francuz	Francuskinja	_____
Srbija	_____	Srpkinja	srpski
Nemačka	Nemac	Nemica	_____
_____	Amerikanac	Amerikanka	engleski
Italija	_____	Italijanka	italijanski
Rusija	Rus	Ruskinja	_____
Španija	Španac	Španjolka	_____

(b)[†] Fill in the gap with the appropriate word:

1 Ja sam Anđela. Džon je moj _____ .
   (a) prijatelj (b) muž (c) automobil (d) novinar
2 On ne _____ srpski, ali malo razume.
   (a) govori (b) uči (c) radi (d) misli
3 Nisam dobro. Malo sam _____ .
   (a) nažalost (b) bolje (c) drago (d) umoran
4 _____ se ona zove?
   (a) Šta (b) Ko (c) Kako (d) Zašto

(c) Make dialogues out of the following jumbled sentences:

(1) A: ti Kako Zdravo se ? zoveš.
    B: Tanja. mi Drago je.
    A: sam. novinar Ja ? ti A
    B: studentkinja. Ja sam

(2) A: Dejan. Kako? zoveš ti se sam Ja
    B: Ljiljana.
    A: mi Drago je
    B: ti si Šta po zanimanju?
    A: sam inženjer Ja.

Reading passage 2 (Audio 1: 9)

Екипа (1)

The gang

*This story describes the life of a group (**екипа**) of young people in Belgrade. It is printed in the Cyrillic script to offer you an extra challenge in the early stages of your mastering it. Good luck!*

Маја се јавља пријатељу Луки мобилним телефоном.
Maja telephones her friend Luka. What does Luka suggest they do?

Здраво, Лука, шта радиш?
Ништа. Ти?
Ништа.
Ајдемо у клуб!
Важи!

Vocabulary

ајдемо!	let's go!	**важи!**	OK! Agreed!
јављати се	to contact, get in touch with	**клуб**	club
		ништа	nothing
радити	to do	**шта**	what

2 Putnici idu u hotel

The travellers go to the hotel

In this unit we will look at:

- main conjugations of verbs
- verbal aspect
- reflexive verbs
- adverbs

 **Dialogue 1** (Audio 1: 10)

Razgovor na aerodromu

Conversation at the airport

John and Angela discuss the best way to get to their hotel. Does Milan live in Belgrade? How does he suggest that they go to the hotel? Why is a minibus such a good idea?

MILAN: Vi ste prvi put u Beogradu?
ANĐELA: Jesmo. Da li vi živite ovde?
MILAN: Ne, živim u Nišu, ali ostajem nekoliko dana u Beogradu.
DžON: Možete li nam reći kako da odemo u grad?
MILAN: Možete da idete autobusom ili taksijem. Ali ja vam preporučujem kombi.
ANĐELA: Šta je to?
MILAN: To je mali autobus koji vozi do hotela i privatnih adresa, što je vrlo zgodno. Plus, nije tako skup kao taksi.
DžON: Hvala, to zvuči odlično!

Vocabulary

ali	but	autobusom	by bus
kombi	minibus	koštati (koštam)	to cost
mali	small	moći (irreg. mogu,	to be able
		možeš, može,	
		možemo, možete,	
		mogu)	
nekoliko	a few	odličan, -čna	excellent
ostajati	to stay	otići (odem)	to go (away)
(ostajem)			
ovde	here	preporučivati	to recommend
		(preporučujem)	
prvi	first	put	time
reći (reknem)	to say	skup	expensive
tako	so	taksijem	by taxi
voziti	to drive	zgodno	convenient
(vozim)			
zvučati	to sound	živeti (živim)	to live
(zvučim)			

Language points 1

Verbs 1: Main conjugations

There are several classes of regular verbs. See 'Grammar summary', section 4 (p. 302) for a complete list of these. For the time being it will be enough to learn the three main sets of endings, which are classified according to the first person singular ending in the present tense. These endings are **-am**, **-im**, **-em**. Once you know the first person singular of any regular verb, the other persons of the present tense can be deduced.

-am
This is the most straightforward set of endings. The infinitive of these verbs ends in **-ati**: **imati** (**imam**) 'to have'; **morati** (**moram**) 'to have to, must'.

-im
This set of endings is usually derived from an infinitive ending in **-iti**: **govoriti** (**govorim**) to speak; but they may also be derived from **-ati**: **držati** (**držim**) to hold; or **-eti**: **voleti** (**volim**) to love, **želeti** (**želim**) to want.

-em
This is the most frequent set of endings and is derived from many different infinitives.

Note: The first person present of every new verb you come across should always be learned.

	morati *to have to*	*govoriti* *to speak*	*razumeti* *to understand*	*zvati (se)* *to call/* *be called*
(**ja**)	**moram**	**govorim**	**razumem**	**zovem** (**se**)
(**ti**)	**moraš**	**govoriš**	**razumeš**	**zoveš** (**se**)
(**on/ona/ono**)	**mora**	**govori**	**razume**	**zove** (**se**)
(**mi**)	**moramo**	**govorimo**	**razumemo**	**zovemo** (**se**)
(**vi**)	**morate**	**govorite**	**razumete**	**zovete** (**se**)
(**oni/one/ona**)	**moraju**	**govore**	**razumeju**	**zovu** (**se**)

🎧 Dialogue 2 (Audio 1: 11)

Two passengers are talking at the airport as they wait for their plane to depart.

Биљана:	Идем на кафу, а ви?
Весна:	Идем прво да купим новине.
Биљана:	А ја морам да нађем дјути-фри: желим да купим цигарете.
Весна:	Ја желим да купим виски и коњак.

Vocabulary

идем на кафу	I'm going for a coffee		
прво	first		
да	to, in order to		
купити (купим)	to buy	**новине**	a newspaper
наћи (нађем)	to find	**желети (желим)**	to want

Exercise 1

```
Narodna Banka Srbije
Menjacnica AERODROM
Beograd 59
Tel: 601-555 lok 3270
*=================================================*
    Datum: 30/11/2004 17:39:32
    SB: 001140152041130100110043
    -------------------------------------------
    Osnova: Otkup efektive
    Valuta: 826-GBP
    Iznos:                          40.00
    Kurs: 109.31580              4372.63
    0.0000% prov.                   0.00
                        =======================
    Ukupno:                      4372.63
    796-------------
*=================================================*
```

Potvrda o promeni novca

(a)[†] Put the verbs in brackets into the correct form:

1 Ti odlično _____ srpski. (govoriti)
2 _____ vam da idete taksijem. (preporučivati, ja)
3 Šta da _____ ? (kupiti, ja)
4 Oni ne _____ automobil. (voziti)
5 Kada _____ u kafić? (ići, ti)

(b) Fill in the gaps in the dialogue with appropriate verbs:

A: Halo, taksi!
B: Izvolite, kuda želite da _____ ?
A: _____ da idem u centar, na Trg Republike.
B: Dobro, nema problema.

Trg Republike Republic Square (lit. 'The Square of the Republic')

(c)[†] Fill in the gaps with the missing pronouns:

1 _____ ne razumemo srpski.
2 Da li _____ govoriš engleski?
3 _____ razgovaraju.
4 _____ ne znam gde je taksi.
5 _____ mora da nađe poštu.

Language points 2

Verbs 2: aspect 1

This is largely a new idea for native English speakers, although English continuous and simple tenses reflect something of what is involved. We shall return to it in greater detail later. For the time being, you should know that most Serbian verbs have two forms, known as the *imperfective* and the *perfective* aspects.

It is possible to express a great range of different meanings by modifying the form of the verb, introducing ideas of repetition, partial action etc. The basic division is into:

1 action which is thought of as continuing, incomplete, 'ongoing': *imperfective*;
2 action which is thought of as complete or limited: *perfective*.

For example:

stvarati (imperfective): to be creating

the noun derived from this verb, **stvaranje**, means the *process* of creating, e.g. **stvaranje sveta** 'the creation of the world' (the act of creating);

stvoriti (perfective): to create and complete the action

the noun derived from this verb, **stvorenje**, means a 'creature' (the completed thing created), e.g. **ljudsko stvorenje** 'a human being'.

In Dialogue 2 there is an example of the use of the perfective aspect, **da kupim cigarete**. The speaker is thinking of a completed action of buying rather than the process of shopping. In this case the imperfective has a longer form, **kupovati** (**kupujem**), and is roughly equivalent to 'to be buying'. Another example, using the verb **piti** (**pijem** 'to drink') would be **Idem da popijem kafu**. The speaker is thinking of drinking up the whole cup and then doing something else. The imperfective means 'to drink' in a general way, e.g. **piješ li pivo?** 'Do you drink beer?' or 'Are you at the moment drinking beer?'.

 Reading passage 1 (Audio 1: 13)

Kulturni život u Beogradu (2)

As Ben and Dejan drive to Zemun, on the edge of Belgrade, where Dejan lives, they discuss what Ben wants to see while he is in Serbia. What does Ben want to do? Is he interested in travelling through Serbia?

Dok se voze u Zemun, razgovaraju. Dejan želi da zna šta Ben treba da vidi dok je u Srbiji. Dejan pita da li Ben želi da putuje po Srbiji ili želi da ostane u Beogradu. Ben želi da upozna kulturni život u Srbiji. Ali on misli da se mnogo toga dešava baš u Beogradu. Dejan se slaže i kaže da može da napravi lep program. Ben je vrlo zadovoljan.

Vocabulary

baš (emphatic particle)	just, right	**da li**	whether
dok	while	**dešavati se** (**dešavam**)	to happen

ili	or	**kazati (kažem)**	to say
kulturni	cultural	**lep**	nice, beautiful
misliti (mislim)	to think	**mnogo toga**	a lot of things
napraviti	to make (of)	**ostati**	stay, remain
(**napravim**)		(**ostanem**)	
pitati	to ask	**po** (+ loc.)	through, round
	(a question)	**putovati**	to travel
razgovarati	to talk,	(**putujem**)	
	converse	**slagati se**	to agree
treba	one (etc.)	(**slažem**)	
(impersonal)	should	**upoznati**	to get to know
videti (vidim)	to see	(**upoznam**)	
vrlo	very	**zadovoljan**	pleased
znati (znam)	to know		

Language points 3

Word formation

The verb ici 'to go'

You will have noticed from the examples in the Verbs 2 section
that one means of making a perfective is by the addition of a prefix.
The verb **ići** and its derivatives offer a useful example of the way
in which the addition of a prefix modifies the meaning of a verb.
Ići itself is bi-aspectual and the only neutral verb of motion. All
its derivatives convey some further information about the nature
of the movement:

> **od** 'away from' + **ići** = **otići** (**odem**)
> 'to go away, leave'

> > **Moram sutra da odem.**
> > I must leave tomorrow.

Once the new meaning has been established, a new imperfective
must be formed to express that meaning:

> **otići** (pf.) **odlaziti** (imp.)

> > **Odlazim u podne.**
> > I am leaving at noon.

Verbal prefixes

Here are some prepositions which can be used as prefixes: **u** 'in, into'; **do** 'up to'; **na** 'on, onto'; **iz** 'out of'; **s** 'down from'. Other common prefixes are not prepositions: **po** (a very common perfective prefix with no intrinsic meaning); **pre** (denotes 'over'); **pro** ('passing by'); **raz** ('dispersal').
Examples of verbs of motion deriving from **ići**:

do   **Dolazite li često ovamo?**
      Do you come here often?

      Moraš doći da vidiš kola!
      You must come to see the car!

u   **Ulazi polako u vodu.**
      He goes slowly into the water.

      Dete ne želi da uđe u kuću.
      The child does not want to go into the house.

na   **Ona uvek nalazi dobre restorane.**
      She always finds (lit. 'comes on') good restaurants.

      Ne mogu da nađem adresu.
      I can't find the address.

s   **Da li silazite ovde, gospodine?**
      Are you getting off here, sir?

      Siđi kod pošte.
      Get off by the post office.

The verbs in the following pairs of sentences are formed with other prefixes from the list above. Try to see whether you can work out what they mean. To make this more interesting for you, the sentences are printed in Cyrillic.

Гледају како брод одлази.
They watch the boat _____

Зар мораш тако брзо да одеш?
Must you _____ so soon?

Излазимо сваки дан у 8 сати.
We _____ every day at 8 o'clock.

Не жели да изађе из базена.
He doesn't want to _____ of the pool.

Воз полази у 10 сати.
The train _____ at 10 o'clock.

Морамо одмах да пођемо!
We must _____ immediately!

Никада не прелазе сами улицу.
They never _____ the road by themselves.

Пређите сада, светло је зелено!
_____ now, the light is green!

Пролази често поред њеног прозора.
He often _____ her window.

Овај дан мора брзо да прође!
This day must _____ quickly!

Do not attempt to learn all of these forms straight away. Remember the effect of the addition of prefixes to form perfectives and use these sentences for later reference.

Exercise 2†

(a) Choose the verb with the correct form to complete the dialogue:

1 Želim da _____ novac. (promenim/promenite)
  Moram da _____ dinare za taksi. (imam, imaš)
  Gde se _____ (nalazi, nalaze) menjačnica?

2 Tu odmah preko puta. Zar ne _____? (vidiš, vidim)

      promeniti to change   **preko puta** opposite

(b) Choose the correct form of the verb (the first one is perfective, the second is imperfective):

1 Ben želi da _____ Beograd. (upoznati/upoznavati)
2 Dejan često _____ po Srbiji. (otputovati/putovati)
3 Kad je u Beogradu, Ben uvek _____ kod Dejana. (ostati/ostajati)

4 Mislim da se mnogo toga _____ baš u Beogradu. (desiti se/
   dešavati se)
5 Moram da _____ rečnik u knjižari. (kupiti/kupovati)

   rečnik dictionary   **knjižara** bookshop

Language points 4

Sentence building

Dependence of one verb on another

One verb can depend on another in two basic ways:

(a) Main verb + infinitive

> **Moram   otići.**
> I must leave.
>
> **Žele   kupiti vino.**
> They want to buy wine.
>
> **Volite li putovati?**
> Do you like to travel?

Note: This is the construction favoured in Croatian and in some
Serbian dialects (e.g. in Vojvodina).

(b) Main verb + **da** (conjunction) + present tense

> **Moram   da   odem**
> **Žele   da   kupe vino**
> **Da li volite da   putujete?**

Note: This construction is favoured in Serbian and is the one
you should use.

Exercise 3

Make sentences from the words given below:

1 morati, kupiti, rečnik, Anđela
2 želeti, videti, Beograd, Ben
3 voleti, putovati, po Srbiji, oni

4 ne želeti, ići, u poštu, Milan
5 morati, popiti, kafu, ja

Language points 5

Reflexive verbs

There are many reflexive verbs in Serbian. They consist of a verb, which is conjugated in the normal way, and the indeclinable reflexive particle **se**. **Se** is an enclitic and therefore subject to the same rules of word order as the short forms of **biti**. Where it occurs with other enclitics, it comes after all the others except **je** (third person singular of **biti**):

sećati se (imp.), **setiti se** (pf.) to remember

Rado se sećam
I like to remember (lit. 'I gladly remember')

Želi da se seti
S/he wants to remember

Some verbs are always reflexive, while others may be used reflexively or as ordinary transitive verbs with a direct object:

Zovem sina svaki dan.
I call (my) son every day.

Zovem se Monti Pajton.
I'm called Monty Python.

Zatvaram knjigu i gledam kroz prozor.
I close the book and look out of the window.

Knjiga se zatvara i pada na pod.
The book closes and falls on the floor.

Volim te.
I love you.

Mi se volimo./Volimo se.
We love each other.

Gleda more.
She is looking at the sea.

Oni se gledaju. Gledaju se.
They are looking at each other.

Exercise 4

Complete these pairs of sentences by putting the reflexive particle
se in the appropriate place:

1 Ben, slaže / Slažemo, dobro
2 Zove, Ana / Studentkinja, zove, Ana
3 Vidimo, tamo / Beograd, vidi, tamo
4 Pošta, zatvara / Zatvara, sada
5 Gledaju, Ivo i Mara / Mi, gledamo

Language points 6

Adverbs

You will probably be relieved to know that these cannot be
declined! Some must be individually learned (**ponekad** 'sometimes',
negde 'somewhere'), others are like the neuter nominative form of
adjectives (**dobro** 'well', **rado** 'gladly', **brzo** 'quickly').

Exercise 5

(a) Answer the following questions on the text at the beginning of
the unit:

1 Da li su Anđela i Džon prvi put u Beogradu?
2 Gde živi Milan?
3 Kako Anđela i Džon mogu da putuju u Beograd?
4 A šta im Milan preporučuje?
5 Da li je kombi tako skup kao taksi?

im   to them

(b)[†] Fill in the gap with the appropriate adverb from the list below:

odlično   ponekad   dobro   rado   brzo

1 Milan _____ dolazi u Beograd.
2 Zvuči _____ !
3 Da li se _____ sećaš prijatelja?
4 On vozi vrlo _____ .
5 Džon i Anđela govore _____ srpski.

(c)[†] Translate the following dialogue into Serbian:

ANA: I'm tired. And besides, I don't like travelling by bus.

MARKO: A taxi costs a lot, but ... OK, we can go by taxi.

ANA: That sounds good! I just want to buy newspapers and cigarettes.

MARKO: Fine, but we have to find the duty-free first.

∩ Dialogue 3 (Audio 1: 14)

Екипа (2)

Маја и Лука, Јелена и Филип се с̲а̲стају
у клубу

Maja and Luka, Jelena and Filip meet at the club. Why are Jelena and Filip celebrating? What does Luka say he will do?

- Ej, друг̲а̲ри! Како сте? – пита Лука.
- Супер! Сл̲а̲вимо! – одговара Јелена.
- Шта сл̲а̲вите? – пита Маја.
- Данас ми је ро̲ђендан – об̲ј̲ашњава Филип.
- Ч̲е̲ститамо! Ајде да н̲а̲ручимо пиће! Ја частим! – каже Лука.

Vocabulary

данас	today	ми (dative of **ја**)	lit. 'to me'
нару̲чити	to order	објашњ̲авати	to explain
(нару̲чим)		(објашњавам)	
одгов̲а̲рати	to reply	пи̲тати (**питам**)	to ask
(одго̲варам)		пиће	drink
ро̲ђендан	birthday	са̲стати се	to meet
сла̲вити	to celebrate	(са̲станем)	
(сла̲вим)		су̲пер	great
че̲ститати	to congratulate	ча̲стити (**частим**)	to treat
(че̲ститам)			(here 'pay')

3 Dolazak u hotel

Arrival at the hotel

In this unit we will look at:

- nouns
- the nominative case
- the vocative case
- simple letters
- adjectives from proper nouns
- double negatives

 **Dialogue 1** (Audio 1: 15)

Dolazak u hotel

Arrival at the hotel

The Browns arrive at their hotel. What does the receptionist ask for?
Do the Browns want to have dinner?

RECEPCIONAR: Dobar dan, izvolite!
DŽON: Mi smo Džon i Anđela Braun. Imamo rezer-
vacije.
RECEPCIONAR: Dobro došli! Samo da pogledamo ... Kako se
prezivate?
DŽON: Braun.
RECEPCIONAR: Aha, da. Dvokrevetna soba. Molim vaš pasoš,
gospodine Braun. Hvala. I vaš, gospođo Braun.
Izvolite, ovo je vaš ključ. Želite li da večerate?
ANĐELA: Rado, hvala! Ja sam baš gladna!

RECEPCIONAR: Nema probléma! Restoran je tamo, preko
                    puta. Kolega može da odnese vaš prtljag.
                    Želim vam prijatno veče!
DŽON & ANĐELA: Hvala!

Vocabulary

gospodin	Mr, sir	**gospođa**	Mrs, madam
izvolite	please, here	**ključ**	key
	you are	**kolega**	colleague
molim	please (lit. 'I pray')	**nema probléma!**	no problem!
odneti	to take (away)	**pasoš**	passport
(odnesem)		**preko puta**	opposite
prezivati se	to be called	**prijatan, -tna**	pleasant
(imp.)	**(prezime**:	**prtljag**	luggage
	surname)	**rado**	gladly
restoran	restaurant	**vaš**	your
veče	evening	**večerati**	to have
		(večeram)	dinner

Na hotelskoj recepciji

Language points 1

Nouns

Every Serbian noun has a gender – masculine, feminine or neuter – which determines its declension. In the great majority of cases, the gender is immediately obvious from the nominative ending of the noun (the form in which it appears in a dictionary).

Masculine nouns

Most masculine nouns end in a consonant. Consonants may be 'hard' or, less frequently, 'soft'. The soft consonants are given here in Cyrillic. Find the equivalents in the Latin script: ц, ч, ћ, џ, ђ, љ, њ, ш, ж. All other consonants are hard.

hotel	(hard)
avion	(hard)
prijatelj	(soft)

Some masculine nouns end in **-o** (or **-e** after a soft consonant). This is the case with several proper names, e.g. **Marko**, **Branko**, **Djordje** and a number of nouns which used to end in **-l**. This **l** recurs in other cases:

sto	table
na stolu	on the table

Masculine nominative plural ending: -i

hotel	**hoteli**
avion	**avioni**
prijatelj	**prijatelji**

Note: Most monosyllabic masculine nouns have an additional syllable in the plural:

sto	**stolovi**
voz 'train'	**vozovi**

If the final consonant is soft, then **-ovi** becomes **-evi**:

muž 'husband'	**muževi**
ključ	**ključevi**

Certain combinations of consonants and vowels involve consonant changes, for example the combination **k** + **i** becomes **-ci**:

putnik 'traveller'   **putnici**

Neuter nouns

Neuter nouns end in **-o** or **-e**; nominative plural ends in **-a**:

selo 'village'   **sela**
more 'sea'   **mora**

Feminine nouns

The great majority end in **-a**: **soba** 'room', **torba** 'bag'. A few feminine nouns end in a consonant. There are not many and they must be learned. They include a large number of abstract nouns, and all abstract nouns ending in **-ost**:

noć 'night'   **stvar** 'thing'
ljubaznost 'kindness'

Feminine plural
For nouns whose singular ends in **-a**, the nominative plural ending is **-e**:

torbe   **sobe**   **gospođe**

For nouns ending in a consonant, the nominative plural ending is **-i**:

noći   **stvari**

Dialogue 2 (Audio 1: 16)

Two travellers are discussing their luggage. There seems to have been a mix-up.

Тања: Извините, господине, да ли је то ваша торба?
Ненад: Јесте. Зашто питате?
Тања: Мислим да је то моја торба.
Ненад: Мислим да грешите.
Тања: Али, погледајте: ово је моје име!

Ненад: Ох, у праву сте! Опр<u>о</u>стите! Онда је ово моја
                торба!
Тања: Тако је! Хвала вам!
Ненад: Хвала вама!

TANJA: *Excuse me, sir, is this your bag?*
NENAD: *Yes. Why do you ask?*
TANJA: *I think it's my bag.*
NENAD: *I think you're mistaken.*
TANJA: *But look: this is my name!*
NENAD: *Oh, you're right! I'm sorry! Then this is my bag!*
TANJA: *That's right! Thank you.*
NENAD: *Thank you!*

Exercise 1

(a) Which of these nouns are masculine, feminine or neuter? Write
them in columns, according to their gender and give their plural
forms as well:

> **prijatelj grad prezime** (pl. **prezimena**) **kuća mesto
> more stvar dan** (pl. **dani**) **selo kafić pozorište
> pošta ulica taksi hotel soba ime** (pl. **imena**)

(b) Make sentences with the nouns below. Some are singular and
some are plural, so remember to adjust the possessive pronoun
and verb accordingly. Notice that the nominative endings of
the possessive pronoun **vaš** 'your', **moj** 'my' are the same as
those of the nouns: m. sing. **vaš**, pl. **vaši**; f. sing. **vaša**, pl. **vaše**;
n. sing. **vaše**, pl. **vaša**.

> *Example*: **Izvinite, gospodine, da li su ovo vaše torbe?**
>   (**torbe**)
>
> **ključ torba knjige ime pasoši prijatelj
> kišobran prtljag rečnik karte**
>
>   **kišobran**   umbrella   **karta**   ticket

(c)† Put the verbs in brackets into the correct form:

  1 Džon i Anđela _____ u hotel. (stizati)
  2 Anđela _____ baš gladna. (biti)

3 Ona želi da _____ . (večerati)
4 Džon _____ (kazati): Ali Anđela, mi _____
   umorni. (biti)
5 Anđela _____ (kazati): Ja _____ (morati) prvo da
   _____ . (jesti)

      jesti (imp. **jedem**)   to eat

Language points 2

The nominative case (name/subject case)

The main uses of the nominative case are:

1 For the subject of a sentence or clause:

   Milan Jov_a_nović putuje u Beograd.
   Milan Jovanović is travelling to Belgrade.

   Vi pijete šljivovicu, a *on* pije pivo.
   You are drinking plum brandy, *he* is drinking beer.

   Mislim da *Nada* dolazi sutra.
   I think that *Nada* is coming tomorrow.

   Nažalost, *avion* kasni.
   Unfortunately, *the plane* is late.

2 For the complement of **biti**:

   Džon je *Englez*.
   John is English (lit. 'an Engishman').

   Kažu da nisi *Srpkinja*. Da li je to istina?
   They say you are not *Serbian* (lit. 'a Serbian woman').
   Is that true?

   Moj sin je *dobar student*.
   My son is a good student.

   Vesna je vrlo *lepa žena*.
   Vesna is a very beautiful woman.

Vocabulary building

Hotel accommodation

smeštaj	accommodation	**apartman**	(self-catering) suite
jednokrevetna soba	single room	**dvokrevetna soba**	double room
polupansion	half board	**punpansion**	full board

Exercise 2

(a)[†] Fill in the gap with the appropriate noun

novinari, aerodrom, knjižara, srpski, prijatelji, kombi, Amerikanac

1 Gde su vaši _____ ?
2 _____ se nalazi blizu grada.
3 _____ se nalazi preko puta pošte.
4 Da li ste vi _____ ?
5 Oni su _____ .
6 Koliko košta _____ ?

(b) Find the appropriate hotel accommodation for these people:

A Porodica Jovanović (mama, tata, sin, ćerka)
– žele da kuvaju sami

B Gospodin Nikolić
  – planira da provodi samo veče i jutro u hotelu

C Marko i Vesna
  – žele da se odmore

ćerka	daughter	**kuvati** (imp.)	to cook
sam	oneself	**provoditi** (imp.)	to spend (time)
jutro	morning	**odmoriti se** (pf.)	to rest

 ## Reading passage 1 (Audio 1: 17)

Kulturni život u Beogradu (3)

Dejan and Ben arrive in Zemun. Who does Ben meet when they get there? What does he give the children? What does Ben want to drink?

Uskoro stižu u Zemun, gde Dejan predstavlja Bena ženi Nadi i deci Ani i Janku. Ben vadi englesku čokoladu iz torbe i daje je deci. Nada kaže deci da moraju da kažu 'hvala'. Kažu: 'Hvala, čika Bene!' Dejan pokazuje Benu gde se nalazi soba za spavanje i kupatilo. Nada priprema večeru. Dejan pita Bena da li želi da pije vino ili pivo. Ben kaže da više voli vino, a moli i čašu vode.

Vocabulary

Benu	(dat. 'to Ben')	**davati (dajem)**	to give
deca	children (f. sing.	**deci**	(dat. 'to the
	collective noun,		children')
	sing. **dete**, gen.	**čaša**	glass
	deteta)	**čika**	uncle
i	and	**je**	it (object case
kupatilo	bathroom		of **ona**)
moliti (imp.)	to ask (favour,	**morati**	to have to
	service)	**nalaziti se**	to be found,
		(**nalazim se**)	situated
piti (pijem)	to drink	**pivo**	beer
pokazivati	to show	**predstavljati**	to introduce
(**pokazujem**)		(**predstavljam**)	

pripremati	to prepare	**spavanje**	sleeping
(**pripremam**)		**stizati** (**stižem**)	to arrive
uskoro	soon	**vaditi** (**vadim**)	to take out
večera	dinner	**vino**	wine
više voleti	to prefer	**voda**	water
za	for		

Exercise 3

Answer the following questions on 'Kulturni život u Beogradu' (3):

1 Šta Ben daje deci?
2 Šta oni kažu?
3 Šta Dejan pokazuje Benu?
4 Šta radi Nada?
5 Šta Ben više voli da pije?

Language points 3

The vocative case

In Dialogue 1, the receptionist said: '... **gospodine**' and '**gospođo Braun**'. This is the vocative case used for persons addressed in speech, or at the beginning of letters:

Dobar dan, gospodine Jovanoviću.
Good day, Mr Jovanović.

Draga gospođo Nado[1]
Dear 'Mrs Nada'

1 This is a useful stage between the formal **gospođa** + surname, and the more familiar use of the first name on its own. Of course there is no equivalent in English.

There are no vocative endings for neuter nouns or for the plural of any gender. So, only two sets of endings have to be learned.

Masculine
Hard consonants: **-e**   **gospodin, gospodine**
Soft consonants: **-u**   **prijatelj, prijatelju; Jovanović,**
                            Jovanoviću

Feminine[1]
Nouns ending in   **-a, -o**   **gospođa, gospođo**; **Nada, Nado**
Nouns ending in   **-ca, -e**   **gospođica, gospođice**; (Miss)
                                Ljubica, Ljubice

1 These may also be men's names with diminutive feminine forms: **Novica, Novice**.

Nouns ending in
a consonant: **-i**   **o, noći!**

Language in action

Examples of simple letters or email messages:

1 To friends, informal:

Dragi Ivane,
Ovde je prekrasno. Šteta što i ti nisi ovde!
Voli te Biljana

Dear Ivan,
It's lovely here. It's a shame you're not here too!
Love, Biljana

2 More formal, addressee slightly known:

Dragi gospodine Filipoviću,
Stižemo u ponedeljak. Radujemo se skorom viđenju.
Srdačan pozdrav,
Vaši Tim i Anna Smith

Dear Mr and Mrs Filipović,
We are arriving on Monday. We are looking forward to
seeing you soon.
Warm greetings/best wishes,
Tim and Anna Smith

3 Addressee unknown or known only officially:

Poštovana gospođo Ivić,
Slobodna sam da Vam se javim u vezi sa našim boravkom.
Molim Vas da nam rezervišete sobu za avgust mesec.
S poštovanjem,
Betty Jones

Dear [lit. 'respected'] Mrs Ivić,
I am taking the liberty of writing in connection with our stay.
Please would you reserve a room for the month of August.
Yours sincerely,
Betty Jones

Note: Notice that with women's surnames there is no vocative ending: it is impossible to mix feminine and masculine endings, so only the first part – **gospođa** or the first name – declines, the surname is unchanged. Notice also that in formal letters the pronoun 'you' is capitalized.

Exercise 4

(a)† Write the vocative forms of the following names:

Ivan   Marko   Milan   Zorica   Dragan
Maja   Svetlana   Đorđe   Vera

(b) Write the following letters:

1 Ben is writing to Dejan informing him that he is coming to Belgrade on Monday.

2 Anđela is writing to a hotel manager, Mr Popović, asking him to book a room for August.

(c) Now you phone a hotel and book a room:

RECEPCIONAR: Halo, dobar dan. Hotel 'Moskva', izvolite.
VI: *Say you want to book a single room.*

RECEPCIONAR: Pun pansion?
VI: *No, half board.*

RECEPCIONAR: Kada stižete?
VI: *On Monday.*

RECEPCIONAR: Koliko ostajete?
VI: Sedam dana.

RECEPCIONAR: Kako se zovete i prezivate?
VI: *My name is _____ . My surname is _____ .*

Language points 4

Word formation

Adjectives formed from proper nouns

All adjectives are written with a small letter, even when formed from proper nouns:

> **Ovo je beogradski aerodrom.**
> This is Belgrade airport.

> **Ovo je srpska zastava.**
> This is the Serbian flag.

> **Gledam londonske ulice.**
> I'm looking at London streets.

Exercise 5

Form adjectives from the nouns in brackets:

1 Danas u Beograd stiže _____ (Engleska) fudbalski tim.
2 _____ (Nemačka) predsednik ostaje ovde jedan dan.
3 Ovo je _____ (Francuska) vino.
4 Volim _____ (Bosna) humor.
5 Gledamo _____ (Španija) film.

> **predsednik**   president

Language points 5

Sentence building

Examples of questions and answers

Look at the following constructions. Notice the way the words for **ovo** 'this' and **to** 'that' do not change.

> **Dobar dan, da li je ovo vaš pasoš?** Da, to je moj pasoš.
> **Da li je ovo vaša torba?**   **Ne, to nije moja torba.**
> **Da li su to vaše stvari?**   **Jesu, hvala!**
> **Mama, ovo je moja devojka.**   **Je li? Drago mi je, dušo.**

Da li je ovo vaš sin?		Jeste, zove se Janko.	
A da li su to vaše ćerke?		Ne, to su moje unuke!	
Nije moguće!		Jeste, verujte mi!	
devojka	girlfriend	**duša**	soul, dear
ćerka	daughter	**unuka**	granddaughter
moguće	possible	**verujte me**	believe me

Double negative

The existence of two or more negative words in a sentence does not have the effect of making the sense positive. On the contrary, a negative pronoun or adverb (such as **niko** 'no one', **ništa** 'nothing', **nikad** 'never') require a negative verb:

Nemamo ništa da prijavimo.
We have nothing to declare.

Ništa ne vidim kroz prozor.
I see nothing through the window.

Nikad ne putujem autostopom.
I never hitch-hike.

Exercise 6

(a) Answer the following questions on Dialogue 1 at the beginning of the unit:

1 Da li su Anđela i Džon i dalje na aerodromu?
2 Šta Anđela i Džon daju recepcionaru?
3 Da li oni žele da večeraju?
4 Ko nosi njihov prtljag?

(b) Supply the missing half of the dialogue and then translate it:

DEJAN: Dobro došao!
BEN: ____ ___ _____ !
DEJAN: Bene, ovo je moja žena Nada.
BEN: ____ ___ ___ !
NADA: ____ ___ ___ ! Želite li odmah da večerate?
BEN: _____, _____ .
DEJAN: Izvoli, trpezarija je tu preko puta.

trpezarija dining room

(c)[†] Choose the right word to complete the sentences:

1 _____ što i ti nisi ovde.
   (a) drago; (b) lepo; (c) dobro; (d) šteta

2 _____ ništa da prijavimo.
   (a) imamo; (b) nemamo; (c) nismo; (d) jesmo

3 Ma nije _____ da si već gladna!
   (a) još; (b) skupo; (c) moguće; (d) rado

4 _____, da li znate gde je hotel *Moskva*?
   (a) izvinite; (b) pogledajte; (c) molim vas; (d) izvolite

5 Ja _____ volim crno vino nego pivo.
   (a) već; (b) prvo; (c) više; (d) još

⌒ Dialogue 3 (Audio 1: 18)

Екипа (3)

Dado and Sanja arrive at the club. Who are they? What does everyone want to drink?

– Филипе – каже Ј<u>е</u>лена – ово су моји нови пријатељи.
– Здраво, ја сам Сања, а ово је мој брат Дадо.
– Драго ми је. Изволите, с<u>е</u>дите – каже Филип.
– Мајо, има ли места до тебе?
– Св<u>а</u>како. Седи ту, Сања.
– Јесмо ли сви за црно вино? – пита Лука.
– Јесмо, хвала ти, Лука! – одговарају сви.

Vocabulary

брат	brother	**до**	beside (here)
има ли?	is there?	**место**	place, space
мој	my (m. sing.;	**нов**	new
	моји, m. pl.)	**свакако**	certainly
сви	all, everyone	**седети (седим)**	to sit
тебе	you (long form	**ти**	you (dat. of **ти**)
	of gen. of **ti**)	**ту**	here
црн	black (of wine		
	= red)		

4 Odlazak u grad

Going into the city

In this unit we will look at:

- accusative case
- accusative case after certain prepositions
- genitive case
- **nema** + genitive
- prepositions
- questions and answers

 ## Dialogue 1 (Audio 1: 19)

Džon i Anđela idu u turističku agenciju

John and Angela go to the tourist office. What do they want to see?
How do they go to Kalemegdan? What is Kalemegdan?

ANĐELA: Dobro jutro, želimo da idemo u grad i da vidimo glavne znamenitosti Beograda.

AGENT: Dobro, gospođo. Imate odavde autobus koji vozi do Brankovog mosta. Staje ispred hotela.

DŽON: Da li je Brankov most blizu Kalemegdana? Želimo da odemo na Kalemegdan.

AGENT: Jeste. Odatle lako možete da stignete peške do parka. Samo pitajte za Knez Mihajlovu ulicu. To je veoma lepa ulica, gde nema vozila.

ANĐELA: Divno! Hvala!

AGENT: Nema na čemu! Lepo se provedite!

PLANINE   ZIMA 2004/2005

ZLATIBOR je planina izuzetne lepote koju krase prijatna klima, blago podneblje, prostrani proplanci, bujni pašnjaci ispresecani planinskim potocima i prošarani borovima po kojima je ova planina i dobila ime. Prosečna nadmorska visina je 1000 metara, a okružuju je visovi: Čigota (1422 m), Murtenica (1480m), Tornik (1496m), Viogor (1281m) i niz drugih manjih brda. Zlatibor je udaljen od Užica 25 km.
Hotel **PALISAD** ***
Nedaleko od jezera, u prijatnom ambijentu borove šume, smešten je kompleks PALISAD. Sve sobe su sa kupatilima i telefonima. Za vreme boravka gosti se mogu zabaviti u salonima za dnevni boravak u čijem se delu nalazi aperitiv bar i TV sala, posetiti restoran i poslastičarnicu, kupovati u brojnim buticima, a veče provesti u dansing baru sa muzičkim programom.

CENE ARANŽMANA SA SOPSTVENIM PREVOZOM - 7 POLUPANSIONA

Polasci	Decembar		Januar		Februar		Mart
	18.	8.	15, 22.	29.	5, 12.	19, 26.	5,12,19,26.
Hotel							
PALISAD-A deo	14.550	15.300	14.850	15.750	15.750	14.700	14.550

Napomene:
• Usluge polupansiona obuhvataju: doručak (švedski sto), večeru (pansionska) i noćenje
• Boravišna taksa i osiguranje **nisu** uključeni u cenu i plaćaju se na recepciji hotela

Turistička reklama

Vocabulary

blizu (+ gen.)	near	**Brankov most**	Branko's Bridge
divno	wonderful	**glavni**	main
imati (**imam**)	to have	**ispred** (+ gen.)	in front of
jutro	morning	**Kalemegdan**	park at the
Knez Mihajlova	Prince Mihajlo		confluence of
	Street		the Sava and
koji	which		Danube
lepo se provedite!	have a good	**nema na**	you're welcome!
	time!	**čemu!**	
nema	there is not	**odatle**	from there
odavde	from here	**peške**	on foot
stajati	to stop, stand	**stići**	to arrive, reach
(**stajem**)		(**stignem**)	
ulica	street	**veoma**	very
vozilo	vehicle	**znamenitost**	sight

Language points 1

The accusative case (the direct object case)

This case is used if the question 'what?' (**šta?**) or 'whom?' (**koga?**) can be asked after the verb in a sentence:

> **Ima veliki crni kišobran. Šta ima? Kišobran.**
> He has a big black umbrella. He has what?
> An umbrella.

> **Vidim more. Šta vidiš? More.**
> I see the sea. What do you see? The sea.

Note: You will see that this has the same function as English 'I, me', 'he, him' etc. For example, 'He sees me', 'I see him' etc.

Formation of the accusative (singular)

Masculine inanimate nouns and neuter nouns

The accusative is the same as the nominative:

Nominative	*Accusative*
Ovo je kišobran.	**Imam kišobran.**
This is an umbrella.	I have an umbrella.
Ovo je naliv-pero.	**Vidim naliv-pero.**
This is a fountain pen.	I see the fountain pen.

Masculine animate nouns

The accusative of masculine nouns denoting animate beings is like the genitive ending. We shall come to this later in the unit.

Nominative	*Accusative*
Ovo je moj sin.	**Vidim sina.**
This is my son.	I see (my) son.

Feminine nouns

(1) Ending in a consonant. The accusative is the same as the nominative:

Nominative	Accusative
Ovo je lepa noć.	**Volim noć.**
This is a lovely night.	I like the night.

(2) Ending in -a. The accusative ending is made by removing the final **-a** and replacing it with **-u**:

Ovo je moja ulica.	**Volim ovu ulicu.**
This is my street.	I like this street.
Ovo je moja torba.	**Da li imate torbu?**
This is my bag.	Have you got a bag?

Exercise 1

(a)† Fill in the gaps with the appropriate singular form of the noun in brackets:

1 Volim _____ . (Beograd)
2 Imamo _____ . (problem)
3 Vidim _____ i _____ . (Dejan, Janko)
4 Iz naše sobe vidimo _____ . (Kalemegdan)
5 Ko ima _____ ? (ključ)
6 Džon pita _____ (Anđela) za _____ . (Knez Mihjalova ulica)
7 Nada priprema _____ . (večera)
8 Ben daje deci _____ . (čokolada)
9 Moram da kupim _____ . (torba)
10 Ne mogu da vidim _____ . (more)

(b) Write short texts about these people, using the words in the order they are given:

1 On, Ben, Engleska, novinar, pisati, za novine, voleti, čitati knjige
2 Ona, Nada, operska pevačica, Srbija, pevati, u pozorištu, voleti, putovati
3 Oni, Džejms i Meri, studenti, Amerika, studirati, na fakultetu, želeti, učiti, srpski jezik

operska pevačica   opera singer

Language points 2

Accusative plural

Masculine

The accusative plural is formed by removing the final **-i** of the nominative plural and replacing it with **-e**:

Ovde hoteli nisu dobri.	**Ne volim ove hotele.**
The hotels aren't good here.	I don't like these hotels.

Take care with words in which the nominative plural **-i** has caused the final consonant of the stem to be altered, e.g.:

	putnik (n. sing.)	**putnici**
but	**Vidim putnike.**	I see the passengers.

There are similar changes with other consonants, for example **-g+i**: **zi**:

	Ovo je moj kovčeg.	**Ovo su moji kovčezi.**
	This is my suitcase.	These are my suitcases.
but	**Nosim kovčege.**	I am carrying the suitcases.

Note: **kovčeg** is an archaic word, you should use **kofer**.

Neuter

The accusative plural of neuter nouns is the same as the nominative plural:

Nominative	*Accusative*
Ovo su prijatna mala sela.	**Volim ova mala sela.**
These are pleasant little villages.	I like these little villages.

Feminine

The accusative plural of feminine nouns is the same as the nominative plural, whether they end in a consonant or in **-a**:

Nominative	*Accusative*
To su naše stvari.	**Svi nosimo stvari.**
Those are our things.	We are all carrying things.

To su naše torbe.	**Svi nosimo torbe.**
Those are our bags.	We are all carrying bags.

Exercise 2

Form sentences according to the example, putting the nouns in the accusative plural case:

Example: **stvar**:   **Ne vidim naše <u>stvari</u>.**

torba   soba   žena   knjiga   karta

Example: **autobus**:   **Ne vidim naše <u>autobuse</u>.**

hotel   prijatelj   ključ   prozor   pasoš

Language points 3

Sentence building

The accusative case after certain prepositions

The accusative case is used after certain prepositions. These include:

kroz 'through'

> **Pospani putnik gleda *kroz prozor*.**
> The sleepy passenger looks *through the window*.

za 'for'

> **Ovo je pismo za moju majku.**
> This is a letter for my mother.

The accusative case is used after prepositions denoting motion:

u	in, into	**Idemo u grad.**
		We're going into town.
na	on, onto	**Stavljam kafu na sto.**
		I'm putting the coffee on the table.

Broadly speaking, **u** is used of a closed space, and **na** of an open space. Airports, stations and islands are thought of as open spaces, while a park is often thought of as a closed space.

Exercise 3

(a)[†] Use the appropriate preposition to complete the sentences:

1 Džon i Anđela idu _____ grad.
2 Ben i Dejan stižu _____ Kalemegdan.
3 Ovo je čokolada _____ Janka i Anu.
4 _____ prozor se vidi prelepa crkva.
5 On ide _____ aerodrom.
6 Mi dolazimo _____ hotel.
7 Idemo odmah _____ našu sobu.
8 Putujemo _____ Sveti Stefan uskoro.
9 Ovo su karte _____ Džona i Anđelu.
10 Prolazimo _____ stari deo grada.

(b) Form questions according to the example:

Example: **Španija**: **Da li sutra putujete u Španiju?**

Italija   Rusija   Francuska   Norveška   Nemačka   Bugarska

⌒ Reading passage 1 (Audio 1: 20)

Kulturni život u Beogradu (4)

What are Ben and Dejan going to do the next day? Who will they find in the café?

Dok večeraju, Ben i Dejan prave planove za sledeći dan. Slažu se da je dobra ideja da odmah odu u grad – iako Dejan kaže da ima mnogo toga da se vidi i u Zemunu. Dejan predlaže da odu u kafanu na glavnom trgu gde se često nalaze njegovi prijatelji, novinari, pa onda mogu da se dogovaraju i svi zajedno.

Vocabulary

ako	if	**često**	often
dogovarati se	to arrange, agree	**i**	also (here)
iako	although	**kafana**	café
mnogo	much	**najbolje**	best
odmah	immediately	**onda**	then
pa	then, so	**plan**	plan

praviti¹	to make	**predlagati**	to suggest
sledeći	next	(**predlažem**)	
takođe	also	**trg**	square
zajedno	together		

1 From now on, if the first person present can be deduced from the infinitive, it will not be given.

Exercise 4

(a) Ben and Dejan are making plans for tomorrow. Fill in the gaps in the dialogue based on the text above:

BEN: Dejane, šta radimo sutra?
DEJAN: Ja mislim da je dobra ideja _____.
        Iako ima mnogo toga _____.
BEN: Dobro, onda idemo prvo u šetnju po Zemunu.
DEJAN: Možemo prvo da _____
        i da se onda svi zajedno _____.
BEN: Važi.

šetnja   a walk

(b) Answer the following questions on 'Kulturni život u Beogradu' (4):

1 Šta rade Ben i Dejan?
2 Da li idu prvo u grad ili ostaju u Zemunu?
3 Ko se nalazi u kafani u centru?
4 Šta planiraju da rade svi zajedno?

(c) Fill in the gaps in the following dialogue by putting the words in brackets into the appropriate form:

A: Kako da dođemo do Zelenog Venca?
B: Ne znam. Sad smo blizu Slavije. Da li imaš _____ (mapa)?
A: _____ (nemati). A da li ti imaš _____ (vodič kroz Beograd)?
B: _____ (nemati). Šta da _____ (raditi)?
A: Možemo da _____ (pitati) nekoga. Izvinite, kako da _____ (doći) do Zelenog Venca?

mapa   map   **vodič**   guide, guidebook

Language points 4

The genitive case (the possessive case)

Without a preposition, the genitive case is used primarily to denote possession:

Ovo je glavna znamenitost *Beograda.*
This is the main sight *of Belgrade.*

Ovo je slika *moje ćerke.*
This is a picture *of my daughter.*

It is also used after nearly 80 per cent of all prepositions. These generally denote origin, distance or removal from somewhere or something.

iz + gen.: 'out of, from'

Da li ste *iz Beograda?*
Are you from *Belgrade?*

Izvadi pasoše iz *torbe.*
Take the passports out of *the bag.*

blizu + gen.: 'near' (i.e. not distant from)

Hotel je blizu *autobuske stanice.*
The hotel is near *the bus stop.*

Formation of the genitive

Singular

Masculine. Genitive ends in **-a**:

To je torba gospodina Jovanovića.
That's *Mr Jovanović's* bag.

Neuter. Genitive ends in **-a**:

Grad je nedaleko od mora.
The town is not far from *the sea.*

Feminine.

  (i) Nouns ending in **-a** have genitive in **-e**:

Engleske. Mi smo iz Engleske.

(ii) Nouns ending in a consonant have genitive in **-i**:

> **Posle te lepe noći . . .**
> After that beautiful night . . .

Plural

The genitive plural for all genders is **-a**, except for a very small number of feminine nouns ending in **-a** (**sekunda** 'second', **žurka** 'party') and those ending in a consonant, which have genitive plural in **-i**.

Sentence building

Structures using the genitive case

(i)   **nema** 3rd pers. sing. of **nemati** 'there is/are not' or 'he has not':

> **Nema nikoga kod kuće.**
> There is no one at home.
>
> **Nema ni novca ni novčanika.**
> He has neither money nor wallet.

(ii) **Evo** + gen. 'here is/here are' (like French 'voici'):

> **Evo mora!**
> Here is the sea!
>
> **Evo naše adrese!**
> Here is our address!

Exercise 5[†]

Put the words in brackets into the genitive case:

1 Dejan i Nada su iz _____ . (Zemun)

2 Oni žive blizu _____ . (trg)

3 Blizu njihove _____ (kuća) je pošta.

4 Preko puta _____ (pošta) je supermarket.

5 Oni vole svoju ulicu i nemaju _____ . (problemi)

Language points 5

Language in action

Questions and answers

Two drivers are talking in a motel on the motorway near Stuttgart.

A – Одакле долазите?
B – Долазимо из Лондона.
A – Да ли путујете у Аустрију?
B – Не, путујемо у Србију.
A – Сјајно. Познајете ли Србију?
B – Још не, али имамо тамо пријатеље.
A – Да ли планирате да идете на планине?
B – Свакако, идемо на Копаоник.
A – Ах, Копаоник је прекрасан! А да ли познајете црногорско приморје?
B – Не баш, али имамо проспекте. Одакле ви сада долазите?
A – Долазим из Париза. Тамо радим.
B – А да ли идете сада кући?
A – Да, идем у Шумадију, у једно мало село.
B – Мора да је тамо лепо.
A – Да, треба да видите и тај крај!
B – Следећи пут! Да ли сте за неко пиће?
A – Врло радо.
B – Овде близу је један одличан бар!

познавати (познајем)	to know
Црногорско приморје	the Montenegrin coast
проспект	prospectus, brochure
мора да ...	it must be ...
крај	region

Exercise 6†

(a) Put the words in brackets in either the genitive or the accusative case as appropriate:

   Evo _____ (Džon)! On je iz _____
   (Engleska). Njegova žena Anđela je takođe iz

_____ (Engleska), iz _____ (London). Oni su sada u Beogradu. Žele da vide _____ (znamenitost) _____ (Beograd). Imaju _____ (mapa) _____ (grad) i autobuske _____ (karta). Planiraju da prvo odu na _____ (Kalemegdan), a onda i u _____ (Knez Mihajlova ulica).

(b) Choose the appropriate word or phrase from the list below to complete the dialogues:

sledeći put   vrlo rado   nema na čemu
lepo se provedite

1 – Da li želite da vidite naš stan?
   – _____.

2 – Sutra putujemo u Hrvatsku. Idemo na more.
   – Baš lepo. _____.

3 – Hvala puno što nosite moje torbe.
   – _____.

4 – Ne idete sada da vidite Kopaonik!?
   – Ne, nažalost. Možda _____.

Pogled na Beograd

🎧 Reading passage 2 (Audio 1: 21)

Екипа (4)

Dado and Sanja introduce themselves. Where are they from? Where is Jelena from? Is anyone from Belgrade?

– О̲дакле сте, вас двоје? – пита Филип.
– Из Босне смо, из Зенице. А ви, да ли сте сви из Београда?
– Нисмо – одговара Филип. – Ја сам из Новог Сада, а Јелена је Црногорка.
– Тако је – каже Јелена. – Ја сам из По̲дгорице.
– А ја сам из Кру̲шевца – каже Маја.
– Барем сам ја прави Београ̲ђанин! – каже Лука.
– Добро дошли у Београд! – каже Јелена.

Vocabulary

барем	at least	**двоје**	two (mixed gender)
прави	real, true	**тако је**	that's right

5 U Beogradu
In Belgrade

In this unit we will look at:

- the dative case
- the locative case
- the instrumental case

Note: From this unit on, the main dialogues will be in Cyrillic.

Dialogue 1 (Audio 1: 22)

When they get off the bus, the Browns ask a passer-by the way to Knez Mihailova Street. Why do they say they want to go to Kalemegdan? What does the passer-by tell them about Knez Mihailova Street?

Анђела: Опростите, госпођо, да ли нам можете рећи како се иде до Кнез Михаилове улице?

Пролазница: Треба да идете право до поште и да онда скренете лево. Али, идем и ја у том правцу. Можемо заједно.

Џон: Желимо да одемо на Калемегдан, да видимо ушће Саве у Дунав.

Пролазница: То свакако треба да видите. Али идите полако Кнез Михаиловом улицом: тамо има врло занимљивих зграда и радњи.

Анђела: Можемо ли негде успут да попијемо кафу?

Пролазница: Сигурно: има неколико кафана и много кафића у Кнез Михаиловој.

Џон:　　　　На Калемегдану се налази турска тврђава, зар не?
Пролазница: Да, и то вреди да се види. Ево, радим у овој згради.
　　　　　　Ово је почетак Кнез Михаилове.
Анђела:　　Хвала на помоћи!
Пролазница: Нема на чему.

Vocabulary

вреди	it is worth	занимљив	interesting
зграда	building	и ја	I too
лево	left	полако	slowly
помоћ (f.)	help	почетак	beginning
правац	direction	право	straight
радња	shop	са мном	with me
сигурно	surely	скренути	to turn
тај	that	(pf. скренем)	
тврђава	fortress	турски	Turkish
у том правцу	in that direction	успут	on the way
ушће	confluence		

Džezva i šoljica za kafu

Language points 1

The dative case (the indirect object case)

The dative is used without a preposition, mainly to indicate the indirect object of a verb. In English this would generally denoted by the preposition 'to'.

Govorim *čoveku.*
I speak *to the man.*

Dajem *dečaku* **prtljag.**
I give the luggage *to the boy.*

In English, the preposition 'to' may be omitted:

Daje *ženi* **ključ.**
He gives *his wife* the key.

Here 'the key' answers the question 'what does he give?'; 'his wife' answers the question 'to whom?'.

Govorim *policajcu* **istinu.**
I tell *the policeman* the truth.

'Speaking to' and 'giving to' are the most common uses of the dative case, but in Serbian there are several instances of verbs, which express related ideas, but where the need for the dative case may not be so immediately obvious:

pomagati (imp.), **pomoći** (pf.)
to help (to give help to)

> **Deca pomažu** *majci.*
> The children help *(their) mother.*

obećavati (imp.), **obećati** (pf.)
to promise (to give a promise to)

> **Devojčica obećava** *majci* **da nikad neće da puši.**
> The little girl promises *her mother* that she will never smoke.

verovati (imp.), **poverovati** (pf.)
to believe (to give one's trust to)

> **Moraš da veruješ** *dečaku:* **on govori istinu.**
> You must believe *the boy:* he's telling the truth.

Masculine and neuter: the ending for singular nouns is **-u**; for plural nouns is **-ima**.

Feminine: for nouns ending in **-a**, the final **-a** becomes **-i** singular, **-ama** plural; for nouns ending in a consonant, **-i** is added for singular nouns, **-ima** plural.

Exercise 1

(a)[†] Fill in the gaps with the dative form of the nouns:

1 Anđela govori _____ (Džon) da ponese mapu.
2 Recepcionar daje _____ (Anđela) ključ.
3 Ne moraš da veruješ _____ (novine).
4 Treba da pomažemo _____ (roditelji).
5 Nada kaže _____ (deca) da kažu hvala.

poneti (pf. **ponesem**)	to take, carry
verovati (imp. **verujem** + dat.)	to believe
novine	newspaper(s)
pomagati (imp. **pomažem**)	to help
roditelj	parent

(b) Answer the following questions on Dialogue 1:

1 Da li su Anđela i Džon već u Knez Mihajlovoj ulici?
2 Šta žele da vide?
3 Da li oni idu u radnju?
4 Šta se nalazi na Kalemegdanu?

Language points 2

The locative case (1)

You will be relieved to know that the endings of this case are identical to those of the dative. Unlike the dative, however, it is always used with a preposition, which is why it is sometimes called the 'prepositional' case. One of its most frequent uses is to express *location*. This is why it is frequently called the 'locative' case, and this is the term we shall use in this book.

You remember that the accusative case must be used after verbs denoting motion:

Džon i Anđela idu u hotel.

But the locative case must be used to describe static location:

Džon i Anđela su u hotelu.

Compare:

Putujemo u Beograd.
We are travelling to Belgrade.

Ostajemo tri dana u Beogradu.
We are staying three days in Belgrade.

Exercise 2

(a) Supply the prepositional case for the following nouns, making sentences using the verb **biti**, according to the example:

Example: **hotel, ja**:
   Ja sam u hotelu.

**autobus, mi   pošta, oni   Zemun, mi
kafana, ti   Kalemegdan, vi**

Note: **Kalemegdan** is thought of as an open space.

(b) Form questions for the following answers:

1 Treba da idete pravo pa da onda skrenete desno kod hotela *Moskva.*

2 Na Kalemegdanu se nalaze tvrđava, galerija i zoološki vrt.

3 U Knez Mihailovoj ima puno starih zgrada i zanimljivih radnji.

4 Knjižara je na kraju ulice, preko puta pijace.

5 Autobus staje tačno ispred hotela.

(c)[†] Translate the following dialogue into Serbian:

A: Hello, can you tell us where the main square is?
B: The main square? It is not far away. Have you got a map?
A: Yes, we have. Here it is.
B: Do you see this street? You just need to go straight. The main square is at the end of the street, opposite the church.
A: Thank you.
B: You are welcome.

Language points 3

The locative case (2)

The locative of feminine nouns:

Ovo je lepa soba.
This is a nice room.

Džon i Anđela su u *sobi*.
John and Angela are in *the room*.

Sarajevo je u *Bosni*.	Sarajevo is in *Bosnia*.
Ljubljana je u *Sloveniji*.	Ljubljana is in *Slovenia*.
Rim je u *Italiji*.	Rome is in *Italy*.
Pasoš je u *torbi*.	The passport is in *the bag*.
Ivan je u *kafani*.	Ivan is in *the café*.

Note: With the locative singular of feminine nouns ending in **-a**, there are two points to be wary of:

1 Certain consonants are subject to changes when they are followed by **-i** (we have already met this with the masc. pl. of **putnik, putnici**):

k + i	**-ci**	**ruka**	hand	**u ruci**
		banka	bank	**u banci**
g + i	**-zi**	**knjiga**	book	**u knjizi**

See also 'Grammar summary', section 6 (p. 306).

2 The names of certain countries etc. are not in fact nouns, but adjectives: e.g. **Engleska** (**zemlja**) **England** (lit. 'the English land'), and they are declined like adjectives. These words are easily identified, because they end in **-ska**; **-čka** or **-ška**. The prepositional singular ends in **-oj**:

Engleska, u Engleskoj
Hrvatska, u Hrvatskoj
Grčka (Greece), u Grčkoj
Nemačka (Germany), u Nemačkoj
Norveška (Norway), u Norveškoj

Exercise 3

(a) Gde se nalaze ovi gradovi?

Rim   Moskva   Frankfurt   Sofija   Pariz   Edinburgh

Example: **Rim se nalazi u Italiji.**

Italija   Rusija   Bugarska   Francuska   Škotska   Nemačka

(b)[†]Fill in the gaps with the noun in the appropriate case:

1 Ja sam na _____ (more).
2 Oni sutra idu u _____ (Hrvatska).
3 Želim da ostanem u _____ (Beograd).
4 Kalemegdan nije u _____ (Zemun).
5 Ben je kod Dejana u _____ (stan).
6 Ja i moji prijatelji idemo u _____ (banka).
7 Ključevi su u _____ (torba).
8 Mi smo sada na _____ (Trg Republike).
9 Oni su u _____ (autobus) na _____ (put) ka
   _____ (centar).[1]
10 Moja kuća se nalazi na _____ (početak ulice).[1]

k, **ka** + loc.   to, towards

1 Note that **centar** and **početak** lose 'a' in the declension: **u centru**, **na početku**.

🎧 Reading passage 1 (Audio 1: 23)

Kulturni život u Beogradu (5)

How do Dejan and Ben go into the centre? How did Belgrade get its name?

Ben i Dejan idu autobusom u grad. Benu je veoma zanimljivo u autobusu: prvo idu kroz stari centar Zemuna, pa onda prelaze Savu i kreću prema belom gradu na brdu. Dejan objašnjava Benu da je grad dobio ime po tome što se bela boja grada vidi izdaleka. Silaze kod Zelenog venca, gde ima mnogo autobusa i sveta.

Vocabulary

autobusom	by bus	**beo, bela**	white
boja	colour	**centar**	centre

dobiti (dobijem)	to acquire	izdaleka	from a distance
kod	at	kretati (krećem)	to move, set off
kroz	through	po tome što	according to the
prelaziti	to cross		fact that
prema (+ loc.)	towards	silaziti	to get off (down)
stari	old	svet	people
zanimljiv	interesting		(lit. 'world')
Zeleni venac	The Green Wreath		
	(a busy market near		
	Branko's Bridge)		

Knez Mihailova ulica

Exercise 4

Answer the following questions on Dialogue 2:

1 Kako Dejan i Ben idu u grad?
2 Kuda idu prvo?
3 Koju reku prelaze?
4 Šta Dejan objašnjava Benu?
5 Šta ima na Zelenom vencu?

Dialogue 2

Разговор у возу

Conversation in a train

Two passengers travelling by train through Austria discuss their journeys.

А – Да ли смо сада у Словенији?
Б – Јесмо. Остајете ли овде?
А – Не, идемо у Грчку.
Б – Да ли већ познајете Грчку?
А – Још не. Добро познајемо Турску.
Б – Је ли? И ја желим да идем у Турску.
А – Да ли путујете у Београд?
Б – Да, живим у Београду.
А – Да ли познајете цео Балкан?
Б – Не баш цео, али доста путујем по Балкану.
А – У које земље најчешће идете?
Б – Па најчешће идем у Црну Гору, на море. Онда идем у Бугарску, на скијање. Идем понекад у Босну и у Хрватску.
А – А замислите, ја још не познајем Шкотску!
Б – Ма нѐмојте! А Ирску?
А – Мало. А у Велс идем често.
Б – Мора да је веома лепо у Велсу.
А – Да, али има тако много лепих крајева у свету. Човек не може да стигне да све види.
Б – Имате право, а често путујемо више по далеким зѐмљама, него по сѐседним!

Vocabulary

цео, цела	whole, complete
најчешће	most often
замислити	to imagine
немојте!	Don't! You don't say!
све	everything
имати право	to be right
далек	distant, far
суседни	neighbouring

Language points 4

The instrumental case

There is one more case to learn. Its use is quite straightforward and we have already seen it in action. This is the instrumental case, used to express the means by which an action is carried out:

Putujem *vozom.*	I travel *by train.*
Idemo *liftom.*	We go *by lift.*
Pismo ide *avionom.*	The letter goes *by airmail.*

The instrumental is also used after certain prepositions:

s, sa 'with'

Džon dolazi *liftom* **sa** *prtljagom.*
John is coming *by lift* with *the luggage.*

Singular

The instrumental ending is the same for all genders: **-om**:

Putujem sa bratom, sestrom i detetom.
I am travelling with (my) brother, (my) sister and the child.

Plural

The endings are the same as for the dative and prepositional cases:

masculine and neuter: **-ima**

Idem s prijateljima.   I'm going with friends.

feminine ending in a consonant:

Putujem sa stvarima.   I'm travelling with the things.

feminine ending in **-a**: **-ama**

Putujem s devojkama.   I'm travelling with the girls.

Note: The masculine singular instrumental ending **-om** changes to **-em** after a soft consonant:

Razgovaram s prijateljem.
I'm talking with (my) friend.

For exceptions, and a complete list of noun declensions, see 'Grammar summary', section 1 (pp. 298–300).

Notice that **s** and **sa** are used equally frequently. There is no rule for you to learn here: **sa** tends to be used before similar letters **s**, **z** etc. or before groups of consonants, e.g. **sa mnom** 'with me', but it is used in other situations as well.

Exercise 5

(a) Answer the question using the appropriate means of transport:

> *Example*: **Idemo tramvajem.**
> We are going by tram.

1 Kako/čime idete iz Zemuna u centar? (autobus)
2 Kako/čime putujete u Ameriku? (avion)
3 Kako/čime idete do njihovog stana? (lift)
4 Kako/čime idu na more? (voz)
5 Kako/čime idete do fakulteta? (bicikl)

> **čime**   by what means (instr. of **što**)

(b)[†] Answer the following questions:

1 S kim putuješ na more? S _____ (prijatelji)
2 S kim ideš u centar grada? S _____ (muž)
3 S kim ideš na žurku? S _____ (drugarica)
4 S kim putuješ u Ameriku? S _____ (deca)
5 S kim pričaš? S _____ (recepcionar)

> **žurka**   party   **drugarica**   friend (female)   **pričati**   to talk

(c) Select the most appropriate endings to the sentences numbered 1 to 5 from the column lettered (a) to (e):

1 Na Kalemegdanu nema puno kafana,
2 Ne moramo da nosimo mapu
3 Idemo na Kalemegdan
4 Idu prvo autobusom kroz centar
5 Ne možemo da popijemo kafu ovde,
6 Dejan kaže

(a) da je to dobra ideja.

(b) pa onda prelaze most.

(c) ali možemo da kupimo kafu.

(d) negde usput.

(e) jer poznajemo dobro grad.

(f) da vidimo ušće.

(g) ali u Knez Mihajlovoj ima.

(d) Make questions relating to the underlined words, using **s kim** 'with whom', **čime** 'by what means' or **kako** 'how', as appropriate:

> *Example*: **Pričamo sa prijateljicom. S kim pričaš?**

1 Živim sa ćerkom.

2 Idem u bioskop pešice.

3 Pišem pismo olovkom.

4 Pričam sa mužem telefonom.

5 Putujemo u Beograd kolima.

Dialogue 3 (Audio 1: 24)

Екипа (5)

The friends talk at the club. When did Sanja and Dado come to Belgrade? Are their parents still in Bosnia?

Сања седи поред Маје, прекопута Јелене и Луке.

– Лука, послужи наше нове пријатеље вином! – каже Јелена.

Лука сипа Сањи и Дади вина.

– Откад сте у Београду? – пита Маја.
– Од зиме – одговара Дадо.
– Да ли су ваши родитељи још увек у Босни?
– Јесу, али више нису у Зеници. Сада су у Бања Луци, код наше баке.
– Добро дошли и живели! – каже Филип. – За ново пријатељство!
– Живели! – одговарају сви.
– Живјели! – кажу Дадо и Сања.

Vocabulary

бака	grandmother	више	more
живели!	Cheers!	зима	winter
	(lit. 'long live')	наш	our
још увек	still	поред (+ gen.)	beside
откад	since when	пријатељство	friendship
послужити	to serve[1]	сипати	to pour
родитељ	parent		

1 Notice the construction: the people served are in the accusative, the thing with which they are served in the instrumental.

6 Razgovor o stanu

Conversation about a flat

In this unit we will look at:

- adjectives
- the nominative case of adjectives
- vocabulary about flats and furniture

Dialogue 1

Позив на вечеру

The Browns' friends, Ana and Danilo, invite them home to dinner. The telephone rings in the Browns' room. Are they ready to leave? What is their friends' flat like? How many bedrooms are there? Is it is a quiet area?

Џон:	Хало, Џон Браун на телефону.
Данило:	Здраво, Џоне, добро дошао! Овде Данило.
Џон:	Данило! Где си?
Данило:	У хотелу сам, на рецепцији. Извини што долазим овако ненајављено, али Ана и ја желимо да вас позовемо на вечеру. Јесте ли можда спремни да кренете? Ана нас чека код куће.
Џон:	Јесмо, ево, сад силазимо!
	Код Ане и Данила
Анђела:	Какав леп стан, Ана! Простран је, удобан и светао. Задовољни сте, зар не?
Ана:	Јесмо, и ми мислимо да је леп. И довољно је велик за нас, сад кад деца више нису код куће.

Анђела:	Хоћеш ли да ми покажеш стан?
Ана:	Радо. Као што видиш, ово је трособан стан. Ово је дневна соба, ту су две мале спаваће собе, а тамо у оном ходнику су кухиња и купатило.
Анђела:	Имате јако леп намештај. Одлична је та стара фотеља у углу и та модерна лампа поред полице за књиге.
Џон:	А тек стари дрвени сто и столице у трпезарији! Него Ана, да ли је ово миран крај?
Ана:	Не баш, јер је центар јако близу. Али, на срећу, наша улица није толико бучна.
Џон:	Имате и прекрасан балкон, пун цвећа.
Ана:	Да, можемо тамо мало и да поседимо, док нас Данило служи неким домаћим пићем. Изволите!

Vocabulary

балкон	balcony	**бучан**	noisy
две (f.)	two	**дневна соба**	living room
довољан, -љна	sufficient	**домаћи**	local, home-made
дрвени	wooden	**књига**	book

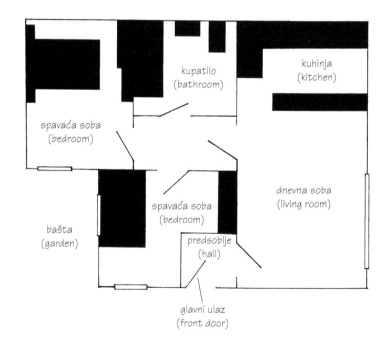

код куће	at home	крај	area, region
кухиња	kitchen	миран (-на)	peaceful
на срећу	luckily	намештај	furniture
неки	some	ненајављен	unannounced
позивати (imp.)	to invite	показати	to show
полица	shelf	(pf. покажем)	
посед̲ети (pf.)	to sit for a while	прекрасан, -сна	beautiful
простран	spacious	пун	full
светао, светла	light, bright	сићи (pf. сиђем)	to go/come down
служити (imp.)	to serve	сматрати (imp.)	to consider
спаваћа соба	bedroom	трособан, -бна	three-room
угао (gen. угла)	corner	удобан -бна	comfortable
фотеља	armchair	ходник	corridor
цвеће (n., coll.)	flowers		

Language points 1

Adjectives 1

Like nouns, adjectives have three genders, singular and plural forms and case endings, which, unfortunately, differ somewhat from those of the nouns. Adjectives must agree in gender, number and case with the nouns they qualify.

Masculine: nominative case

Singular

Most, but not all, masculine singular adjectives have an additional dimension: they may be definite or indefinite. The use of these forms corresponds roughly to the idea of definiteness or indefiniteness conveyed by the English articles.

Imate *lep* stan. (indef.)
You have a *nice* flat.

Taj *lepi* (def.) stan je *udoban*. (indef.)
That *nice* flat is *comfortable*.

Taj *udobni* (def.) stan je *prostran*. (indef.)
That comfortable flat is spacious.

- The *definite* form ends in **-i**. There are certain situations in which it must be used: after demonstrative and possessive pronouns; and, as in English, once the subject has been mentioned.
- The *indefinite* form must be used when the adjective is the complement of **biti**:

> **Taj student je *mlad.***
> That student is young.

> but **Mladi student je *umoran.***
> The young student is tired.

Do not be too alarmed by this additional complication: the definite adjective differs from the indefinite only in the masculine singular nominative, genitive and dative/prepositional cases, and neuter singular genitive and dative/prepositional. What is more, the rule is strictly applied only in situations such as those mentioned here.

The indefinite form ends either in a consonant or in **-o** which is derived from **-l**. This **-l** is present in the other genders and in all cases other than masculine nominative:

Taj čovek je *debeo.*	That man is *fat.*
Moja mačka je *debela.*	My cat is *fat.*
Vi niste *debeli.*	You are not *fat.*

Plural

The masculine plural ends in **-i**. There are no indefinite forms.

Debeli ljudi su često veseli.	Fat people are often cheerful.
Ti putnici su umorni.	Those travellers are tired.

Final -o *of masculine adjectives and 'mobile* a*'*

The final **-o** of masculine adjectives is always preceded by a vowel. If the stem does not otherwise contain a vowel before the **-l** from which the **-o** is derived, something known as 'mobile **a**' is inserted. For a general note on 'mobile **a**' see 'Grammar summary', section 5 (p. 305). Many indefinite masculine adjectives may have 'mobile **a**' inserted between the final two consonants of the nominative singular. The **a**, which is only added for convenience where necessary, disappears in the other cases and other genders.

On je dobar čovek.	He is a good man (person).
Oni su dobri ljudi.	They are good people.
To je dobra riba.	That is a good fish.
Ovo je dobro vino.	This is good wine.

When you learn a new adjective with indefinite masculine nominative ending in **a** + *consonant*, check in a dictionary to see whether this is a mobile **a**. In exercises in this book such adjectives will be marked with an asterisk.

Exercise 1

(a) Which of the following statements are true and which false? Mark them as either **Tačno** (**T**) 'correct' or **Netačno** (**N**) 'incorrect':

1 Džon i Anđela su u parku.	T/N
2 Danilo je na recepciji.	T/N
3 Stan Ane i Danila nije dovoljno velik.	T/N
4 Oni imaju dvosoban stan.	T/N
5 Lampa se nalazi pored fotelje.	T/N
6 Njihova ulica je vrlo bučna.	T/N
7 Ana i gosti žele da posede u dnevnoj sobi.	T/N

(b) John is telling Ana about their hotel room. Here are his answers. What are her questions?

ANA: _____ ?

JOHN: Zadovoljni smo smeštajem u našem hotelu. Jedino što nam smeta je naša bučna ulica, ali sve ostalo je u redu.

ANA: _____ ?

JOHN: Imamo dvokrevetnu sobu. Soba je mala, ali ima sve što nama treba: veliki orman za stvari, udoban krevet, kupatilo sa tuš kabinom.

ANA: _____ ?

JOHN: Da, vrlo je čisto.

smeštaj	accommodation
jedino	only
smetati + dat.	to bother (someone)
tuš kabina	shower unit

(c) Supply the definite form of the following masculine adjectives, as in the example:

    Example: **Taj student je mlad.**   **Mladi student je ovde.**

1 Vaš hotel je velik.   _____ hotel se nalazi preko puta trga.
2 Moj automobil je crn.   _____ automobil je ispred kuće.
3 Naš stan je prostran.   _____ stanovi su skupi.
4 Vaš prijatelj je umoran.   _____ prijatelj je na aerodromu.

(d) Supply the indefinite form, as in the example:

    Example: **Imate prostrani stan.**   **Vaš stan je prostran.**

1 Zadovoljni prijatelj spava.   Prijatelj je _____ .
2 Gledam kroz veliki prozor.   Prozor je _____ .
3 On ima moderni* šešir.   Šešir je _____ .
4 Imate lepi pogled na grad.   Pogled na grad je _____ .
5 Selim se u mirni* kraj grada.   Ovaj kraj grada je _____ .

    šešir hat   **seliti se** to move (house)

(e) Match the nouns with appropriate adjectives. Pay attention to both the meaning and the form:

ulica	prostran
stan	drvena
stolica	udobna
piće	moderna
fotelja	domaće
lampa	bučna

Language points 2

Adjectives 2

Neuter: nominative case

There is an indefinite form, but only of the genitive and dative/prepositional cases.

    Singular: **-o lepo, veliko, dobro**

or after soft consonants: **-e**   **domaće**

Plural: -a **lepa, velika, dobra, domaća**

Jadransko more	**mala šumadijska sela**
the Adriatic sea	small Šumadija villages
Ohridsko jezero	**dobra domaća vina**
Ohrid lake	good local wines

Feminine: nominative case

Singular: -a **lepa, velika, dobra**
Plural: -e **lepe, velike, dobre**

Voda je topla.	**Devojke su umorne.**
The water is warm.	The girls are tired.
Lepa letnja noć.	**Prostrane sobe su udobne.**
A lovely summer night.	The spacious rooms are comfortable.

 Reading passage 1 (Audio 1: 25)

Kulturni život u Beogradu (6)

Dejan takes Ben to visit the National Museum. Where is it? What kind of exhibits does it contain?

Dejan i Ben idu u Narodni muzej. Muzej se nalazi na Trgu Republike, nedaleko od Knez Mihailove ulice. To je velika, stara zgrada sa više spratova. Tu ima eksponata iz različitih oblasti i perioda srpske kulture. Tu su narodne nošnje, seoska rezbarija, umetničke slike i moderne skulpture. Dok gledaju prostrane sale u pratnji direktora Muzeja, Dejan objašnjava neke važne momente iz srpske istorije.

Vocabulary

eksponat	exhibit	**gledati** (imp.)	to look
ima	there is/are	**istorija**	history
moderan	modern	**momenat**	moment, event
narodni	national	**nedaleko od**	not far from
nošnja	costume	**oblast** (f.)	area
pratnja	company,	**različit**	various
	accompaniment	**rezbarija**	carving

sa	with	sala	hall
s<u>e</u>oski	village (adj.)	skulpt<u>u</u>ra	sculpture
slika	painting	sprat	storey, floor
<u>u</u>metnički	artistic	važan	important
velik	large	više	several

Exercise 3

(a) Answer the following questions on Dialogue 2:

1 Gde se nalazi Narodni muzej?
2 Kakva je to zgrada?
3 Šta tamo ima?
4 Da li su Ben i Dejan sami?
5 Šta Dejan objašnjava?

(b) Complete the sentences with the appropriate adjective from the list below. Remember to alter the ending to agree with the noun:

> **domaći lep udoban* svetao* zadovoljan* zanimljiv
> velik narodni moderan* prijatan***

1 Beograd je _____ grad.
2 Njegova soba je _____ .
3 Fotelja je _____ .
4 Prijatelji su _____ vinom.
5 Ljudi ovde su _____ .
6 Šljivovica je _____ piće.
7 Želimo vam _____ boravak.
8 Dejan ima nov i vrlo _____ automobil.
9 _____ nošnja nije više moderna.

Language points 3

Adverbs

As we saw in Unit 2, many adverbs are the neuter nominative singular of adjectives:

Masculine	*Neuter*	*Adverbial use*
dobar	**dobro**	**Dobro došli!**
		Welcome! (lit. 'well come')

lep	lepo	Soba je lepo nameštena. The room is nicely furnished.
mali	malo	On je malo umoran. He's a little tired.
lak	lako	lako možemo da nađemo hotel. We can easily find the hotel.
divan	divno	Večera divno miriše! Dinner smells wonderful!

Vocabulary building

Kuća, stan, nameštaj   house, flat, furniture

Building
jednospratnica 'one-storey house'; **dvospratnica** 'two-storey house'; **zid** 'wall'; **krov** 'roof'; **vrata** 'door'; **prozor** 'window'; **dimnjak** 'chimney' (**dim** 'smoke') **stambena zgrada** 'block of flats, apartment block'; **ulazna vrata** 'front door'

Rooms
predsoblje 'vestibule'; **hodnik** 'hall'; **dnevna soba** 'living room'; **trpezarija** 'dining room'; **kuhinja** 'kitchen'; **spavaća soba** 'bedroom'; **kupatilo** 'bathroom'

Living room
sto 'table'; **stolica** 'chair'; **fotelja** 'armchair'; **tepih** 'carpet'; **slika** 'picture'; **telefon** 'telephone'; **televizor** 'television set'; **zavesa** 'curtain'; **tapete** 'wallpaper'; **polica za knjige** 'bookshelf'

Bedroom
krevet 'bed'; **orman** 'wardrobe'; **ogledalo** 'mirror'; **fioka** 'drawer'; **dušek** 'mattress'; **jorgan** 'duvet'; **posteljina** 'bedclothes'; **ćebe** 'blanket'; **jastuk** 'pillow'

Kitchen
šporet 'cooker'; **rerna** 'oven'; **frižider** 'fridge'; **mašina za pranje veša** 'washing machine'; **mašina za pranje suđa** 'dishwasher'; **lonac** 'pot, pan'; **nož** 'knife'; **viljuška** 'fork'; **kašika** 'spoon'; **tanjir** 'plate'; **šolja** 'cup'; **čaša** 'glass'

Exercise 4

In which of the rooms underlined below would you put the
following items of furniture:

> **krevet   polica za knjige   sto**
> **fotelja   orman   lampa   stolice   šporet**
> **ogledalo   frižider**

spavaća soba   dnevna soba   trpezarija   kuhinja

 Dialogue 2 (Audio 1: 26)

Bill has been lent his friend Duško's flat while he is in Belgrade.
Duško is showing him round.

DUŠKO:	Ovde se pali sv<u>e</u>tlo.
BILL:	Gde se uklj<u>u</u>čuje televizor?
DUŠKO:	Ovde. Nema gr<u>e</u>janja preko leta. Ako ti je hladno, imaš gr<u>e</u>jalicu.
BILL:	Gde se nalazi bojler? Treba li da ga <u>u</u>ključim?
DUŠKO:	Ne, stalno je uključen. Na plin je. Voda je veoma topla.
BILL:	A šporet je na struju, zar ne?
DUŠKO:	Jeste. A pribor za jelo, noževi, viljuške, kašike, ti je u ovoj fioci.

Vocabulary

paliti (imp.)	to light, switch on	**uključiti** (pf.)	to plug in
grejanje	heating	**grejalica**	heater
stalno	constant	**plin**	gas
struja	electricity	**pribor za jelo**	cutlery
	(lit. 'current')	**fioka**	drawer

Exercise 5

(a) Describe your house/flat.

(b)† Translate the following sentences into Serbian:

1 Is your room comfortable?
2 Is your flat modern?
3 Their house is big.
4 They live close to the centre.
5 They go to work by bus.
6 They work a lot but they are not tired.
7 She is a beautiful and very elegant woman.
8 He sees many interesting people.

(c) Look at the advertisement for renting a flat in Sarajevska Street in Belgrade. Mr Popović is calling to find out more about it. Fill in the gaps in the dialogue below with suitable words from the list. Remember you may need to alter the endings.

Sarajevska ulica, centar,
2-sob., 53 m², namešten,
200 evra, 011 762 356

spavaća   dvosoban   oglas   izdajete   kirija   slobodan

A: Dobar dan, ovde inženjer Popović. Zovem zbog vašeg
_____ . Da li vi izdajete stan u Sarajevskoj ulici?
B: Da, izvolite.
A: Stan je _____ ?
B: Da, ima dnevnu i _____ sobu, malu kuhinju i kupatilo.
Sve ukupno 50 kvadrata. _____ je 200 evra mesečno.

A: Od kada je stan slobodan?
B: Već je _____ i možete doći da ga vidite.
A: Da li možete prepodne?
B: Kako da ne. Vidimo se onda sutra.

namešten	furnished	**kvadrat(ni metar)**	square metre
izdavati	to rent	**kirija**	rent
(imp. **izdajem**)		**oglas**	advertisement
mesečno	monthly	**slobodan***	free
već	already	**prepodne**	in the morning
kako da ne	of course	**onda**	then
sutra	tomorrow		

(d) Now you call and enquire about the following flat:
🎧 (Audio 1: 27)

Dorćol, **jednosoban stan,**
centralno grejanje,
prvi sprat, nenamešten,
300 evra

A: Dobro veče.
B: *Say good evening and why you are calling. Ask whether the flat is still available.*
A: Da, stan je slobodan. Kada možete da dodjete da ga vidite?
B: *Say that you can come tomorrow. Ask how many rooms there are and are they spacious. Say that you have many things and that you need space.*
A: Stan ima jednu sobu i trpezariju, kuhinju i kupatilo i veliki hodnik. Dosta je prostran.
B: *Ask if there is a bus stop nearby.*
A: Ne, nema autobuske stanice u blizini. Treba pešačiti oko 5 minuta do stanice.
B: *OK then, see you tomorrow.*

nenamešten	unfurnished
centralno grejanje	central heating
pešačiti	to walk
pet	five

Reading passage 2 (Audio 1: 28)

Екипа (6)

Filip suggests that they go to his place: his mother has made a wonderful cake. What sort of flat does Filip have? How are they all going to get there?

Филип се обраћа пријатељима.

– Имам предлог: идемо сви код мене. Мама је умесила диван колач.
– Филип има прекрасну гарсоњеру у поткровљу једне зграде у Кондиној улици – Јелена објашњава Сањи и Дади. Често се скупљамо тамо.

Лука тражи рачун и плаћа. Остали устају од стола и крећу према вратима.

– Лепо је вече! Идемо пешке – предлаже Јелена.
– Важи, није далеко.
– Ти станујеш у центру? – пита Сања.
– Да, баш имам среће! – одговара Филип уз весели осмех.

Vocabulary

весео (весела)	cheerful	врата (n. pl.)	door
гарсоњера	bachelor flat	далеко	far
код мене	at (to) my place	колач	cake
обраћати се (imp.)	to turn to	осмех	smile
		остали	the others
плаћати (imp.)	to pay	поткровље	attic
предлог	suggestion	рачун	bill, account
скупљати се (imp.)	to gather, meet up	срећа	luck, happiness
		имати среће	to be lucky
становати (imp. станујем)	to live, reside	тражити	to seek, ask for, look for
умесити (pf.)	to bake	устати (pf. устанем)	to get up

7 U pošti

At the post office

In this unit we will look at:

- cardinal numbers 1, 2, 3 etc.
- the use of verbs with numbers
- telephone conversations

Dialogue 1

Where is the post office? How many postcards are the Browns sending? Is it easy to send registered letters? What else do they do in the post office?

Џон и Анђела морају да иду у пошту. Данило им објашњава како да нађу пут. Није далеко: на ћошку је, одмах поред основне школе.

Службеница:	Изволите, шта вам треба?
Анђела:	Требају нам четири марке за ове разгледнице за Велику Британију. Онда, морамо да пошаљемо и ова два писма препоручено. Требају нам и две коверте.
Службеница:	Добро. Ево вам маркице и коверте. Дајте ми писма, а ја вама дајем формулар који треба да попуните.
Џон:	Такође морамо да телефонирамо у Енглеску. Да ли се то може из поште?
Службеница:	Свакако. Да ли видите та врата у ћошку, иза овог шалтера? Прођите кроз њих и тамо су вам кабине. Ви мени напишите број који треба да позовем.

Џон:	Број је девет девет, четири четири. То је позивни број за Велику Британију, зар не? Онда: један осам седам пет, један шест осам три два три.
Службеница:	Изволите у кабину број два.

После разговора са својом децом, Џон и Анђела долазе да питају колико то свеукупно кошта.

Џон:	Колико смо дужни?
Службеница:	Марке за разгледнице и коверте: сто двадесет динара, плус два препоручена писма, плус разговор од седам минута – све заједно вам дође четиристо педесет динара.
Анђела:	Извините, колико кажете да све кошта?
Службеница:	Четиристо педесет динара.
Анђела:	Изволите, ево вам петсто динара.
Службеница:	Вама враћам педесет динара.
Џон:	Најлепше хвала!
Службеница:	Нема на чему!

Vocabulary

број	number	**враћати се**	to return
дужан	in debt, owing	**(враћам се)**	
им	to them	**коверта**	envelope
	(dat. of **они**)	**марка**	postage stamp
написати	to write	**основни**	basic, elementary
(напишем)		**позивни број**	area, country code

попунити	to fill in	послати	to send
препоручено	registered	(пошаљем)	
проводити	to spend (time)	проћи	to pass
(време)		(прођем)	(through)
разгледница	postcard	свеукупно	altogether
тачно	exactly	ћошак	corner
формулар	form	шалтер	counter
школа	school		

Language points 1

Cardinal numbers

Numbers (**broj**, **brojevi**) in Serbian are something of a hurdle, but you will soon become accustomed to them, although they will probably seem quite complicated to start with.

0	**nula**	7	**sedam**	14	**četrnaest**
1	**jedan, jedna, jedno**	8	**osam**	15	**petnaest**
2	**dva, dve**	9	**devet**	16	**šesnaest**
3	**tri**	10	**deset**	17	**sedamnaest**
4	**četiri**	11	**jedanaest**	18	**osamnaest**
5	**pet**	12	**dvanaest**	19	**devetnaest**
6	**šest**	13	**trinaest**	20	**dvadeset**

21 **dvadeset jedan** *or* **dvadeset i jedan**
22 **dvadeset dva, dvadeset i dva** (**dve**) etc.

30	**trideset**	70	**sedamdeset**
40	**četrdeset**	80	**osamdeset**
50	**pedeset**	90	**devedeset**
60	**šezdeset**		

100 **sto** *or* **stotina**
200 **dvesto** *or* **dve stotine**
300 **tristo** *or* **tri stotine**
400 **četiristo**
500 **petsto** etc.

1,000 **hiljada**
3,000 **tri hiljade**

1,000,000 **milion**
5,000,000 **pet miliona**

Number 1: **jedan**. This at least is straightforward; it is an ordinary adjective, declined like **umoran**.

Note: **Jedan** is sometimes used in place of an indefinite article:

jedan čovek	one man, a man
jedna žena	one woman, a woman
jedno selo	one village, a village

There are also plural forms:

jedni ljudi	some people
jedne cipele	one pair of shoes, a pair of shoes
jedna vrata	one door, a door (**vrata**, n. pl.)

Otvaraju se jedna vrata.
A door opens./One door opens.

Exercise 1

Supply the correct form of **jedan**:

1 _____ žena stoji ispred pošte.
2 Idemo u bioskop _____ prijatelj i ja.
3 _____ stvar je jasna: ti ne voliš filmove.
4 _____ prijatelj ne može da dođe.
5 _____ knjiga je na stolu.
6 _____ piće za nas, molim vas.

Language points 2

Numbers 2, 3 and 4 and all compound numbers ending in 2, 3 and 4 (22, 23, 24, 92, 104, 553, 2,084 etc.) are followed by the genitive singular:

> **dva mladića**
> **dvadeset tri putnika**
> **četiri sestre**

The number 2 has both a masculine and a feminine form: **dva stola** but **dve stolice**. There is also a neuter form for mixed gender pairs: **dvoje dece, dvoje zaljubljenih**. There are declensions for 2, 3 and 4 but they are hardly used in the modern language. You will find them in a grammar book if you are interested.

Note: When adjectives are used with the nouns following these
numerals, the same endings are used. You will learn the adjective
declensions in the next units. These examples are included here for
reference.

dva umorna putnika
tri lepe devojke
četiri mala sela

The remaining numerals, i.e. those higher than 5, are followed by
the genitive plural:

5	**pet mladića**	6	**šest devojaka**	7	**sedam sestara**
8	**osam sinova**	9	**devet pisama**	10	**deset maraka**

Exercise 2

(a) Here is a list of prices in the post office. Form questions and
then answer how much the following things cost:

> *Example*: **Koliko košta razglednica?**
> **Jedna razglednica košta ...**

razglednica	25 dinara
koverta	10 dinara
preporučeno pismo za inostranstvo	139 dinara
1 minut razgovora sa inostranstvom	6 dinara
markice za Srbiju	5 dinara

How much have these people paid in the post office:

A	B	C
2 razglednice	3 razglednice	1 koverta 1 markica
1 koverta	2 markice za	2 preporučena pisma
	Srbiju	5 minuta razgovora
		sa inostranstvom

(b)[†]Write out the following numbers in word form and translate
the sentences into English:

1 Moramo rezervisati 2 sobe u hotelu. _____
2 U pošti kupujemo 3 razglednice. _____
3 Treba da pošaljem 5 pisama. _____
4 Moraš pozvati još 2 prijatelja. _____
5 Gde mogu da predam ova 4 formulara? _____
6 Treba da kupimo 1 čokoladu. _____

7 Treba nam još 2 stolice. _____
8 Možete da promenite 100 dolara u banci. _____

(c)† Put the correct case of the nouns in brackets and write out the numerals in word form:

1 U ovom hotelu ima 25 _____ (soba).
2 Marko ima 2 _____ (brat).
3 Molim vas 3 _____ (boca vina).
4 Na putu planiraju da vide 2 _____ (selo).
5 On ima preko hiljadu _____ (knjiga).
6 Ostajemo 7 _____ (dan).
7 Kupujem 4 _____ (rečnik).
8 Kupuju 22 _____ (karta) za pozorište.
9 Večera u restoranu košta 742 _____ (dinara).
10 Ja sam već 15 _____ (dan) na putu.

Postanška markica

(d) Now you are in the post office:

SLUŽBENICA: Izvolite.
VI: *Say you need to buy 3 stamps and an envelope.*
SLUŽBENICA: Izvolite, to je 25 dinara.
VI: *Ask again for the price.*
SLUŽBENICA: 25 dinara.
VI: *Ask if you could make a telephone call from the post office.*

SLUŽBENICA:	Da, kabina 4 je slobodna.
VI:	*Where is that booth?*
SLUŽBENIĊA:	Odmah pored šaltera 8.
VI:	*Do I pay now?*
SLUŽBENICA:	Ne, posle razgovora možete platiti sve zajedno.
VI:	*Thank you and see you in 5 minutes.*

Dialogue 2 (Audio 1: 30)

Mary has been invited to dinner with her friend Mirjana's parents. She needs to have her hair done.

MARY:	Kosa mi je očajna! Moram da se ošišam!
MIRJANA:	Odvešću te kod mog frizera.
MARY:	Molim vas, želim da malo skratim kosu.
FRIZER:	Dobro, gospođice. Hoćete li da vam napravimo trajnu?
MARY:	Hvala ne, samo malo skratite.
FRIZER:	Da vam malo ofarbamo kosu?
MARY:	Hvala lepo, ne. Zadovoljna sam bojom, jedino mi dužina smeta!

Vocabulary

kosa	hair	**očajan**	desperate, terrible
ošišati se (pf.)	to have one's hair cut	**odvesti** (pf.)	to take (someone somewhere)
frizer	hairdresser	**skratiti** (pf.)	to shorten
trajna	permanent wave, perm	**ofarbati** (pf.)	to colour, dye
		dužina	length

Language points 3

Use of adjectives and verbs with numbers

Numbers 2 to 4

The adjective endings are the same as those of the noun. The verb is plural:

Dva zgodna mladića se voze biciklom.
Two good-looking young men are riding bicycles.

Tri umorne žene čekaju autobus.
Three tired women are waiting for the bus.

Numbers 5 to 20 etc.

The verb is usually singular:

Dvadeset šest putnika čeka autobus.
Twenty-six travellers are waiting for the bus.

Exercise 3†

Complete these sentences with the correct form of the adjective
and noun:

1 (*umoran* putnik*)
Na stanici čekaju dva _____ .

2 (*crvena vaza*)
Na polici stoje tri _____ .

3 (*ozbiljan* student*)
U biblioteci sede dva _____ .

4 (*crni kofer*)
U hodniku stoje četiri _____ .

5 (*prostrana soba*)
Na park gledaju četiri _____ .

6 (*udoban* stan*)
U zgradi se prodaju dva_____ .

7 (*ukusno jelo*)
Na stolu čekaju tri _____ .

8 (*važno pismo*)
Dva _____ za oca su ovde.

9 (*telefonski razgovor*)
Četiri _____ dugo traju.

10 (*ljut gost*)
Tri _____ čekaju ispred hotela.

crven red   **ukusan** delicious   **ljut** angry

🎧 Dialogue 3 (Audio 1: 31)

Telefonski razgovor

A tourist in Belgrade is looking for a telephone box to make an urgent call.

А: Молим вас, где се налази најближа телефонска говорница?
Б: Иза угла, десно.
А: Та је говорница у квару. Да ли ви можда имате мобилни телефон? Могу ли да се послужим?
Б: Ако је хитно, изволите.
А: Хвала лепо. Хитно је. Касним на сопствени рођендан, а немам мобилни телефон код себе. Да ли знате позивни за Нови Сад?
Б: Не знам, али назовите информације [988].
А: Добар дан, треба ми позивни број за Нови Сад.
В: Позивни за Нови Сад је 021.
А: Хвала. . . . Хм, прво је заузето, а онда се нико не јавља.
Б: Да не зовете погрешан број?
А: Не, али очигледно данас није мој дан.

Vocabulary

телефонска говорница	call box	у квару	broken
хитно	urgent	послужити се	to use
		каснити	to be late

1. Podignite slušalicu i sačekajte da čujete zvuk koji Vam omogućava biranje željenog broja.

2. Ubacite karticu. Na ekranu ćete videti preostali iznos na Vašoj kartici.

3. Izaberite željeni broj. Tokom razgovora na ekranu je prikazan preostali iznos na Vašoj kartici.

4. Na kraju razgovora vratite telefonsku slušalicu na mesto i izvucite karticu iz aparata, ali tek pošto je na ekranu ispisano uputstvo da to uradite. Na taj način izbegavate dodatno zaduživanje Vaše kartice.

Halo KARTICA
200 din
100.000 / 11. 2002.
Važi do/Exp. date: 11. 2004.
0202206254

KROZ SRBIJU / Milosav Jovanović, Veče
iz zbirke Muzeja naivne umetnosti, Jagodina

Telekom Srbija

Telefonska kartica

сопсвтен	own	назвати	to call
заузет	busy, occupied	(назовем)	
нико	no one	јављати се	to answer (here)
погрешан*	wrong	очигледан*	evident

Exercise 4

Put the sentences in the right order to form a complete telephone conversation, taking sentences from those numbered 1 to 5 and those lettered A to G alternately:

1 Хало, добар дан.
2 Да ли је то стан Марковић?
3 Да ли је Ивона код куће?
4 Ћао, Ивона, овде Јасна.
5 У принципу добро, али зовем те да ти јавим да не могу да дођем на рођендан.
6 Е то је супер. Сигирно долазим онда. Да ли имаш број мог мобилног?
7 Фино. Дакле, све најбоље за рођендан и видимо се касније.

A Хвала, видимо се.
B Добар дан.
C Ћао, Јасна. Како си?
D Моменат . . . Ивона, телефон за тебе.
E Баш штета. Али не брини, планирамо нешто друго за следећу недељу.
F Јесте, изволите.
G Имам га у мом телефонском именику.

не брини don't worry   **именик** address book

🎧 Reading passage 1 (Audio 1: 32)

Kulturni život u Beogradu (7)

In the afternoon Dejan takes Ben to the Fresco Gallery. He explains the importance of the frescoes in the Orthodox churches and monasteries for Serbian culture. Are the frescoes in the gallery originals? How does Ben respond to them?

Dejan vodi Bena u Galeriju fresaka i objašnjava važnu ulogu pravoslavnih crkvi i manastira u srpskoj kulturi. Freske u muzeju su kopije fresaka na zidovima crkvi, ali su veoma verne i u muzeju je moguće detaljno ih razgledati. Ben je duboko impresioniran lepotom, bojama i živahnošću slika. Imaju sreće što Dejan poznaje kustosa muzeja: on može da im objasni sve što Bena zanima. Obilazak galerije traje 2 sata. Nakon toga, umorni i puni utisaka, Ben i Dejan odlaze u jedan obližnji kafić da popiju kafu. Galerija fresaka se nalazi na Dorćolskoj padini. Ovo je vrlo popularan kraj Beograda prepun šarmantnih starih kuća, modernih kafića i malih, nezavisnih galerija. Dorćol je mesto gde se na jedinstven način ukrštaju staro i moderno.

Vocabulary

detaljno	in detail	**duboko**	deeply
freska	fresco	**impresioniran**	impressed
jedinstven	unique	**kopija**	copy
kustos	curator	**im** (dat. of **oni**)	to them
lepota	beauty	**manastir**	monastery
moguće	possible	**nezavisan***	independent
obilazak	visit (lit. 'going	**obližnji**	nearby
	round')	**padina**	slope
poznavati (imp.	to know	**pravoslavan***	Orthodox
poznajem)	(a person)	**prepun**	very full
razgledati (imp)	to look over	**sve**	everything
trajati	to last	**ukrštati**	to cross, merge
(imp. **trajem**)		**uloga**	role
utisak	impression	**veran***	faithful
zanimati (imp.)	to interest[1]	**zid**	wall
živahnost	liveliness		

1 The thing that is interesting is the subject and the person interested is the direct object.

Exercise 5

(a)† Supply questions for these answers:

1 Ona ima 25 godina.
2 Kirija je 200 evra mesečno.
3 Stan na Dorćolu je vrlo skup.
4 On se preziva Popović.
5 Taksi do centra košta 300 dinara.
6 Oni odsedaju u hotelu *Moskva*.

7 Ostajemo 2 meseca u Srbiji.
8 Ne možemo da dođemo jer smo zauzeti.
9 Ja sam profesor.
10 Na posao idem autobusom.

mesečno monthly **odsedati** (imp.) to stay

(b) Dejan has phoned his friend Saša who works in the gallery. He is not at home and Dejan is talking to his wife. Rearrange the words of the dialogue to make sense:

DEJAN:	stan da je Halo, li to Markov?
SAŠINA ŽENA:	izvolite Da.
DEJAN:	govorim Dejan. mogu Ovde Da li da sa Sašom?
SAŠINA ŽENA:	kod Saša nije kuće.
DEJAN:	njegovog li imate Da broj mobilnog?
SAŠINA ŽENA:	njegov je 063 223 343 Da, broj.

○ Dialogue 4 (Audio 1: 33)

Екипа (7)

Are there enough chairs for everyone? Does Filip offer them anything to eat? What does Jelena make?

Notice that Sanja and Dado speak the Bosnian Ijekavian dialect, using 'j' and 'ije' where Belgrade speech has 'e'.

– Жао ми је што немам више удобних столица – каже Филип.
– Нема проблема, ја волим да сједим на поду – одговара Сања.
– И ја – слаже се Маја – дођи и ти, Лука, седи поред мене на овај прекрасни тепих!
– Чиме могу да вас послужим? Имам црно и бело вино, наравно. Има свежег хлеба, тврдог сира и нешто воћа, ако је неко за то – нуди им Филип.
– Дај да ти помогнем – каже Јелена. – Да ли неко жели да проба моју сјајну кафу?
– Свакако – каже Лука. – Шта имаш од музике, Филипе?
– Можеш да погледаш: тамо су ти ЦДови и касете.
– Баш је лијепо овдје код тебе! – каже Сања.

Vocabulary

воће	fruit	нешто воћа	some fruit
дај (imp. of дати)	give	доћи (imp. of доћи)	come
жао ми је	I'm sorry	изванредно	exceptionally
касета	cassette	музика	music
наравно	of course	немати (neg. of имати)	not to have
нешто	something		
нудити	to offer	под	floor
помоћи (pf. помогнем)	to help (+ dat. of person helped)	пробати (imp.)	to try
		провод	entertainment, fun, 'good time'
свеж	fresh	сир	cheese
сјајан*	brilliant	тврд	hard
ти (dat. of ти)	for you (idiomatic use)	уживати (imp.)	to enjoy (+ у + loc.)
хлеб	bread		

8 U restoranu

In the restaurant

In this unit we will look at:

- ordering meals
- the genitive case of adjectives
- the accusative case of adjectives
- vocabulary building: food and drink

 ## Dialogue 1 (Audio 1: 34)

Браунови иду у ресторан

The Browns' friends, Ana and Danilo, have invited them to spend the day with them in Novi Sad. After looking round the city, they go to a restaurant beside the Danube. Are the Browns hungry? What does Danilo suggest they eat? What are they going to drink?

Ана:	Нама се много свиђа овај мали ресторан. Има пријатан ентеријер, услуга је одлична и није тако скупо.
Данило:	Ево јеловника. Јесте ли гладни?
Џон:	Ја јесам!
Анђела:	И ја! Шта нам препоручујете?
Ана:	За предјело предлажем или рибљу чорбу, која је одлична, или пршут.
Џон:	Ја желим да пробам чорбу. Да ли служе и неке домаће специјалитете?
Данило:	Како да не, ако сте баш гладни можемо да узмемо или рибу или мешано месо на жару и разне салате.
Анђела:	Може риба на жару као главно јело. Уз то добро иде кромпир салата.

Данило:	У праву си. А шта више волите да пијете: црно или бело вино?
Анђела:	Уз рибу можда бело, али како ви желите, мени је свеједно: ја волим и једно и друго.
Ана:	Колико се сећам, овде има одличних црногорских вина. Замоли да донесу винску карту, Данило. Желите ли нешто слатко на крају? Топло вам препоручујем палачинке с орасима за дезерт.
Данило:	Може, а затим кафа и неки укусни ликер уз кафу.

* * *

| Келнер: | Ево аперитива. Кућа части. А ево и чорбе. Пазите јако је врућа. Предлажем да сачекате да се мало охлади. Пријатно! Остала јела стижу касније. |
| Данило: | Хвала. Јако сте љубазни. |

Vocabulary

винска карта	wine list	врућ	hot
донети	to bring	ентеријер	decor
(pf. донесем)		замолити	to ask,
затим	then		request
и једно и друго	both	јело	dish (food)
јеловник	menu	како да не	of course
касније	later	колико	how much,
крај	end		how many
ликер	liqueur	мени (dat. of ја)	to me
месо	meat	мешан	mixed
може (3rd. pers. sing. of моћи)	all right	на жару	grilled (on the grill)
нама (dat. of ми)	to us	орах (pl. ораси)	walnut
охладити се (pf.)	to get cool	палачинка	pancake
предјело	starter	пријатно!	Enjoy! Bon appétit!
пршут	prosciutto, smoked ham	разни	various
		салата	salad
свеједно	all the same	свиђа нам се	we like
свиђати се (imp.)	to appeal to	сећати се (imp.)	to remember (+ gen. of thing remembered)
сладак, слатка	sweet		
топао, топла	warm		
услуга	service	уз (+ acc.)	together with
узети (pf. узмем)	to take	укусан, -сна	tasty, delicious

Language points 1

Adjectives: genitive case

Masculine and neuter

There are two forms, definite and indefinite, but the definite form is far more common and therefore the one you should use most. The ending for this is: **-og(a)** or, if the final consonant of the stem is soft, **-eg(a)**:

To je sin *starog* profesora.
That is the *old* professor's son.

Ovo je slika *lepšeg* pejzaža.
This is the picture of a *more beautiful* landscape.

Ne volim kraj *tog novog* filma.
I don't like the end of *that new* film.

The optional **-a** is added for stylistic purposes in certain circumstances, for example when the adjective occurs at the end of a sentence:

Ne poznajem *starijeg* brata, samo *mlađega*.
I don't know the older brother, only the younger one.

For a note on the use of the longer forms in the genitive, dative and prepositional cases, see 'Grammar summary', section 2 (p. 301).

The indefinite ending, for your information, is **-a**:

Vidim visoka mladića.
I see a tall young man.

Feminine

You will be glad to know that the ending is the same as the genitive of nouns ending in **-a**, namely **-e**:

Restoran je blizu *velike* pošte.
The restaurant is near the *big* post office.

To je muž *mlade* glumice.
That is the husband of the *young* actress.

Prozori *ove lepe prostrane* sobe gledaju na park.
The windows of *this nice spacious* room look onto the park.

Plural

The genitive plural of all genders is **-ih**:

Terase *ovakvih starih* restorana su prijatne.
The terraces of *old* restaurants *like these* are pleasant.

Sviđaju mi se friz̲u̲re *ovih mladih* de̲vojaka.
I like *these young* girls' hairdos.

Miris *ovih domaćih* jela je veoma pri̲vlačan.
The smell of *these national* dishes is most attractive.

Exercise 1

(a)† Put the adjective and noun in brackets into the genitive case:

1 Evo adrese _____ .
(moj dobar prijatelj)

2 Da li znaš ime _____?
(neki novosadski hotel)

3 Danilo je dao Džonu flašu _____ .
(domaće vino)

4 U ovom restoranu služe mnogo _____ .
(narodni specijaliteti)

5 Sviđa mi se terasa _____ .
(ovaj mali restoran)

6 Možemo da jedemo ribu na žaru posle _____ .
(riblja čorba)

7 Kod vas uvek ima _____ .
(odlične palačinke)

8 Nema ničeg boljeg od _____ .
(sveža, domaća hrana)

9 Ova kafana je omiljeno mesto za izlazak _____ .
(moji roditelji)

10 Ovde služe samo čorbu od _____ .
(sveža riba)

(b) Form sentences from the words listed below:

1 mi/morati/zamoliti/doneti/jelovnik i čist escajg
2 ti/moći/uzeti/sveža riba i krompir salata
3 ona/mi/morati/preporučiti/neko domaće jelo
4 ja/želeti/naručiti/nešto za dezert
5 trebati/jesti/brzo/pileća supa/da se ne ohladi

> **escajg** a colloquial alternative to **pribor za jelo**
> **pileći** chicken (adj.)

Language points 2

The partitive genitive

This use of the genitive case of nouns shows that you are referring to a part or portion of a whole; it is often the equivalent of 'some' or 'any' in English.

Da li imate *hleba*?
Have you any bread?

As always, adjectives agree with the nouns:

Da li imate *svežeg hleba*?
Do you have any *fresh bread*?

Da li imaju *dobrog crnog vina*?
Do they have any *good red wine*?

Da li imaju *narodnih specijaliteta*?
Do they have any *national dishes*?

Vocabulary building: meals

obrok	meal	**doručak**	breakfast
ručak	lunch	**večera**	dinner
užina	snack		
	(usually mid-morning		
	or late evening)		

Exercise 2

(a) Make questions as shown in the example, using **ima** and the partitive genitive:

> *Example*: **Hleb**:   **Ima li hleba?**   Is there any bread?
>
> **kafa** coffee   **šećer** sugar   **sir** cheese   **mleko** milk
> **čaj** tea   **džem** jam

(b) Šta sve ima na meniju restorana 'Balkan'?

РЕСТОРАН «БАЛКАН»

РЕСТОРАН «БАЛКАН»

ХЛАДНА ПРЕДЈЕЛА

Сир, шунка јаја.............155
Проја 55
Пршута......................300

ТОПЛА ПРЕДЈЕЛА

Похвани сир....................155
Поховане печурке............170

СУПЕ
Пилећа супа.........................90
Телећа чорба.....................140

ЈЕЛА СА РОШТИЉА

Димљена вешалица..........320
Ћевапи (10)......................200
Пљескавица......................190
Кобасица...........................170

ЈЕЛА ПО ПОРУЏБИНИ
Карађорђева шницла.......300
Бечка шницла...................270

САЛАТЕ

Купус салата......................45
Парадајз салата................70
Мешана салата..................70
Зелена салата....................38

ДЕЗЕРТ

Палачинке...........................75
Торта.................................55
Сладолед.(кугла)...............10
Воћна салата......................55

ПИЋА

Ракија.................................40
Вино (црно, бело)...............50
Пиво....................................45
Шприцер.............................35
Сок......................................35
Минерална вода (1 дл).......60

ТОПЛИ НАПИЦИ

Турска кафа........................25
Нес кафа.............................22
Топла чоколада...................20
Чај......................................20

Dialogue 2A

You may find it useful to memorize some of these sentences.

A tourist is eating alone in a Belgrade restaurant.

Гост:	Молим јеловник.
Келнер:	Изволите.
Гост:	Имате ли неких народних специјалитета?
Келнер:	Свакако, има разних укусних народних јела.
Гост:	Да ли можете да ми препоручите неко домаће јело?
Келнер:	Као предјело вам препоручујем похровани сир или пуњене паприке.
Гост:	Да ли имате супу?
Келнер:	Имамо пилећу супу, телећу чорбу, супу од поврћа и врло добру рибљу чорбу.

Vocabulary

похровани сир	fried cheese	**пуњене паприке**	stuffed peppers
пилећи	chicken (adj.)	**телећи**	veal (adj.)
поврће	vegetables (coll.)		

Language points 3

Adjectives: accusative case

Masculine

The accusative ending of masculine adjectives varies, as it does with nouns, according to whether the noun referred to is inanimate or animate.

inanimate: the accusative ending is the same as the nominative;
animate: the accusative ending is the same as the genitive.

Vidim *stari* autobus.
I see the *old* bus.

Vidim *starog* putnika.
I see the *old* passenger.

Neuter

As with nouns, the accusative ending of all neuter adjectives is the same as the nominative.

Vidim *malo* selo.   I see the *small* village.

Feminine

The accusative ending of feminine adjectives is **-u**, the same as for feminine nouns ending in **-a**.

Vidim *mladu* devojku.
I see the *young* girl.

Volim *ovu lepu* noć.
I love *this beautiful* night.

Plural

In all genders, the accusative plural ending is the same as that of the nouns; there is no distinction between animate and inanimate nouns.

Vidim *nove* autobuse.
I see *new* buses.

Vidim *visoke* mladiće.
I see *tall* young men.

Da li vidiš *ta mala* sela?
Do you see *those small* villages?

Da li volite *nove male* kuće?
Do you like the *new small* houses?

Mladi vole *ove lepe* noći.
The young like *these beautiful* nights.

Exercise 3

(a)[†] Fill in the gaps in the dialogue, putting the adjective and noun in brackets into the accusative case:

Келнер: Изволите, шта желите?
Анђела: За мене, молим вас, _____ _____ .
        (воћни сок)

Џон: А ја желим _____ _____ и _____
         _____ . (бело вино, кисела вода)
Келнер: Да ли желите још нешто? Можда _____ .
         (колачи)
Анђела: То је добра идеја! Ја хоћу _____ _____
         (пита од јабука) и _____ . (сладолед)
Џон: Видим, имате и _____ _____ .
         (палачинке са џемом)
Келнер: Нажалост, сада не служимо палачинке. Само у
         време ручка.
Џон: Добро, а да ли можда имате _____
         _____ ? (нека чоколадна торта)
Келнер: Имамо.

воћни сок fruit juice   сладолед ice cream
    пита pie   торта cake

(b) Link sentences 1 to 5 with appropriate responses from (a)–(f)
    to make a complete dialogue:

U kafani

1 MUŠTERIJA: Konobar!
2 MUŠTERIJA: Konooooobar!
3 MUŠTERIJA: Jednu kaficu i lozu, molim.
4 MUŠTERIJA: Gorku, molim! A da li može šljivovica umesto
                loze?
5 MUŠTERIJA: Ne, to je sve. Ustvari, i jednu čašu obične vode,
                ako može . . .

(a) KONOBAR: Izvolite šta želite?
(b) KONOBAR: (razgovara sa kolegom i ignoriše gosta)
(c) KONOBAR: U redu. Hvala.
(d) KONOBAR: Nemamo lozu, nestalo nam je juče. Kakvu kafu
                želite? Slatku, gorku, srednju?
(e) KONOBAR: Može, to imamo! Još nešto?

ustvari actually   ignorisati (imp. ignorišem) to ignore
    nestati (pf. nestanem)   to disappear, run out

Dialogue 2B

Гост:	Желим неко месо. Шта имате на јеловнику?
Келнер:	Има телеће печење или бечка шницла; свињско печење; говеђи одрезак или бифтек; има и похована пилетина; па још и ћурка са резанцима. Наравно служимо и ћевапе и пљескавице.
Гост:	Може бечка шницла.
Келнер:	А ви, госпођо?
Гошћа:	Дајте ми кајгану или можда омлет.
Келнер:	Имамо омлет са шунком, сиром или печуркама.
Гошћа:	Може обична кајгана.
Гост:	Ипак не желим месо. А шта имате од рибе?
Келнер:	Имамо шарана, пастрмку и смуђа; затим, скушу и мурину.
Гост:	А има ли свежег поврћа?
Келнер:	Како да не. Имамо кромпира, купуса, грашка и бораније.
Гошћа:	Какве салате имате?
Келнер:	Имамо зелену салату, салату од парадајза, од краставаца, од цвекле или мешану салату.
Гост:	Где су уље и сирће, со и бибер?
Келнер:	Тамо, на суседном столу. Изволите.

Vocabulary

суседни   next, neighbouring

Language points 4

Vocabulary building: food

месо:

телетина 'veal'; **телеће печење** 'roast veal'; **бечка шницла** 'Wiener schnitzel'; **свињетина** 'pork'; **свињско печење** 'roast pork'; **шницла** 'cutlet'; **говедина** 'beef'; **говеђи одрезак** 'beef cutlet'; **бифтек** 'steak'; **патка** 'duck'; **ћурка** 'turkey' (**резанци** 'noodles'); **ћевап** 'kebab' (**ћевапчићи** 'meat balls'); **пљескавица** 'hamburger'

jaje 'egg':
кајгана 'scrambled egg'; омлет (шунка 'ham'; печурке 'mushroom')

риба:
(речна) шаран 'carp'; пастрмка 'trout'; смуђ 'perch'; (морска) скуша 'mackerel'; зубатац 'dentex'; мурина 'Moray eel'; лигње 'squid'; шкампе 'scampi'

поврће 'vegetables':
кромпир 'potatoes'; шаргарепа 'carrot'; купус 'cabbage'; грашак 'peas'; бораније 'beans'

салата:
зелена 'green'; парадајз 'tomato'; краставац 'cucumber'; цвекла 'beetroot'

зачин:
уље 'oil'; сирће 'vinegar'; со (gen. соли) 'salt'; бибер 'pepper'

воће:
јабука 'apple'; крушка 'pear'; кајсија 'apricot'; бресква 'peach'; шљива 'plum'; смоква 'fig'; трешња 'cherry'; вишња 'Morello cherry'; грожђе 'grapes'; диња 'melon'; лубеница 'water melon'

Exercise 4

(a) Identify the odd one out:

1 шницла, ћевап, печурка
2 смуђ, пастрмка, омлет
3 грашак, ораси, боранија
4 кромпир, парадајз, краставац
5 кафа, вино, чај

(b)† Translate the following passage into Serbian:

I don't see my good friend Ivan very often because he lives in Novi Sad. But I like travelling to Novi Sad when I have time. When I am there we always go out for dinner together. There is an excellent restaurant close to Ivan's flat. It has a small terrace with a beautiful view over the Danube. The restaurant serves traditional dishes and my favourites are veal soup, grilled meat and potatoes, mixed salad and

Restoran na Dunavu

pancakes at the end. Ivan prefers fish. He always has grilled carp and potato salad. But he also likes pancakes. I never leave Novi Sad hungry!

Dialogue 2C

Гост:	Имате ли нечег слатког?
Келнер:	Имамо питу од јабука и питу од трешања. Имамо и палачинке са џемом, чоколадом или орасима.
Гост:	Шта имате од воћа?
Келнер:	Имамо смокве и грожђе.
Гост:	Дајте ми питу од јабука. И донесите ми једну турску кафу, молим вас.
Келнер:	Да ли желите слађу кафу?
Гост:	Не, горчу. Да платим, молим.
Келнер:	Изволите рачун.

Vocabulary

пита	pie	**слађи**	sweet(er)
горчи	(more) bitter	**платити**	to pay

Exercise 5

(a) Make lists of the following items under the appropriate heading on the menu:

ПРЕДЈЕЛО   ГЛАВНО ЈЕЛО   ДЕЗЕРТ

пилећа супа, бечка шницла, палачинке, рибља чорба, похована сир, воћна салата, свињско печење, пита од јабука, похована пилетина

(b) Complete the dialogue:

Келнер:	Добар дан. Изволите.
Гост:	Добар дан. _____ .
Келнер:	Ево изволите. Шта желите да попијете?
Гост:	За сада само киселу воду. _____ данас?
Келнер:	Имамо пуњене паприке и јела са роштиља.
Гост:	_____ .
Келнер:	Да ли желите нешто за _____ .
Гост:	Може пита од јабука.
Келнер:	_____ ?
Гост:	Да, то је све. Колико морам да платим?
Келнер:	_____ .

🎧 Reading passage 1 (Audio 1: 35)

Kulturni život u Beogradu (8)

Dejan takes Ben to the Museum of Modern Art. Where is the Museum of Modern Art? What do people do on the bank of the Danube? Does Ben like the museum building?

Sledeći dan, posle obilnog ručka, Dejan vodi Bena u Muzej moderne umetnosti, koji sa nalazi na obali Save, preko puta starog Beograda, blizu Brankovog mosta i ušća. Lep je dan pa se od centra Zemuna do Muzeja šetaju pored Dunava: tu, uz reku, je lepo šetalište gde se ljudi šetaju, vode pse i voze bicikle. Muzej je lepa, moderna zgrada sa puno zanimljivih i neobičnih dela savremenih srpskih slikara i vajara. Bena posebno zanimaju slike najmlađe generacije slikara i impresioniran je samom zgradom koja ima divan položaj, i okružena je parkom.

Vocabulary

delo	work	**ljudi**	people (plural
najmlađi	youngest		of **čovek**)
neobičan, -čna	unusual	**obala**	shore, bank
obilan, -lna	abundant, large	**okružen**	surrounded
pas (pl. **psi**)	dog	**položaj**	position
posebno	especially	**puno**	a lot of, much,
sam	itself		many
savremen	contemporary	**slikar**	painter
šetalište	place to walk	**šetati se** (imp.)	to walk, go for
uz (+ acc.)	alongside		a walk
vajar	sculptor		

Exercise 6

(a) Mark the following statements with **tačno** (**T**) or **netačno** (**N**):

1 Dejan vodi Bena u Narodni muzej.   T/N
2 Do muzeja idu autobusom.   T/N
3 Muzej se nalazi blizu Brankovog mosta.   T/N
4 Muzej je okružen parkom.   T/N
5 Ben je impresioniran muzejem.   T/N

(b)[†] Fill in the gaps with the appropriate word:

1 U _____ piše da supa košta 100 dinara.
   (a) imeniku   (b) jelovniku   (c) knjizi   (d) fioci

2 Da li ste spremni da _____ dezert?
   (a) kupite   (b) vratite   (c) naručite   (d) ponesete

3 Ti dobro poznaješ ovaj restoran. Šta nam _____?
   (a) preporučuješ (b) pošalješ   (c) govoriš   (d) prelaziš

4 _____ sam dužna?
   (a) kako   (b) šta   (c) gde   (d) koliko

5 Crno vino ide odlično ___ ovo meso.
   (a) sa   (b) na   (c) uz   (d) od

6 Ovo je predivno mesto. Ja sam _____!
   (a) zadovoljan   (b) tužan   (c) impresioniran   (d) sit

   tužan   sad   **sit**   full, sated

Reading passage 2 (Audio 1: 36)

Екипа (8)

Време је да се иде кући

It's time to go home. What does Filip suggest to Sanja? Why does he say he wants to accompany the girls? How does Jelena look at Filip?

Филип пита Сању где станују.

– Дозволи да вас отпратим кући – каже Сањи.
– Хвала, Филипе, али није далеко – одговара Сања.
– Знам, али свеједно, може да се деси да се изгубите, а то никако не желим јер је касно.
– Нема смисла да ти сада излазиш, Филипе – каже Маја. – Могу да иду с нама до трга, а онда можемо да им објаснимо како да наставе пут.
– Нема проблема, Мајо, хвала ти, али баш желим да будем мало на ваздуху.
– Добро, ако инсистираш – каже Маја.

Јелена пажљиво гледа Филипа: познаје га веома добро и он обично не инсистира на овакав начин.

Vocabulary

ваздух	air	вас (acc. of ви)	you (object)
да будем	to be (pf. present of бити)	десити се (pf.)	to happen
изаћи (pf. изађем)	to go out	дозволи (imp. дозволити)	allow
јер	because	изгубити се (pf.)	to get lost
касно	late	кући	(to) home
наставити (pf.)	to continue	начин	way
нема смисла	there's no point	никако	no way, not at all
објаснити (pf.)	to explain		
овакав	this kind of	отпратити (pf.)	to accompany, see home
пажљиво	carefully		
с нама (instr. of ми)	with us	свеједно	all the same

9 U turističkoj agenciji

At the tourist agent's

In **this** unit we will look at:

- street directions
- adjectives: dative and instrumental
- prepositions
- the use of reflexive verbs

 ## Dialogue 1 (Audio 1: 37)

Браунови иду на излет

The Browns are going on a trip

John and Angela want to visit some places outside Belgrade. Is it easy for them to find the tourist agent's? Where do they want to go? What do they decide is the best way to get there?

(A) На улици

In the street

Џон: Опростите, молим вас, да ли знате где се налази
           туристичка агенеција?

Пролазник: Није далеко: идите узбрдо још 100 метара па
           скрените лево код семафора, и агенција се налази
           на другој страни те улице, преко пута продавнице
           ципела, а поред хотела Сплендид.

Анђела: Значи да идемо улицом Кнеза Милоша, па да
           скренемо у Српских владара?

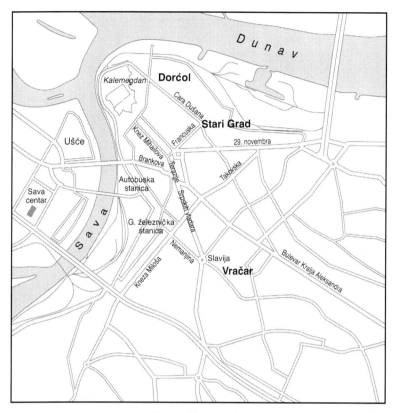

Centar Beograda

Пролазник: Управо тако. Не можете да промашите.
Анђела: Најлепше хвала.
Пролазник: Нема на чему. Довиђења.

(B) У агенцији

In the agency

Анђела: Желимо да идемо у село Сирогојно. Да ли можете да нам кажете како се иде тамо?
Агент: Свакако. Можете да идете директно, удобним аутобусом, или брзим возом до Ужица, а онда локалним аутобусом до села.

Џон:	Ужице је велики град, зар не? Шта ако се изгуб-имо? Можда је путовање возом ипак сувише компликовано.
Агент:	Мислим да сте у праву: веома је једноставно кад се путује аутобусом.
Анђела:	А одакле полази аутобус, молим вас?
Агент:	Са аутобуске станице, која се налази одмах до главне железничке станице. Карте се купују на станици.
Џон:	Хвала вам на помоћи. До виђења.

Vocabulary

биоскоп	cinema	**брз**	fast
до виђења	goodbye	**други**	other
железнички	railway	**једноставно**	simply
како се иде	how does one get (to ...)	**карта**	ticket
		компликован	complicated
куповати (imp. **купујем**)	to buy	**најлепше хвала**	thank you very much
семафор	traffic lights	**скрените** (imp.	turn
страна	side	of **скренути**)	
сувише	too	**те** (gen. fem. of **тај**)	that

Language points 1

The dative/locative case of adjectives

Masculine

There is an indefinite form of the adjective, which is the same as that of the noun:

Došla je u *staru* kaputu.
She came in an old coat.

As with the genitive, however, you will need only to be able to recognize this. The definite form ends in **-om**:

Govorim *ljubaznom* kelneru.
I am speaking to *the kind* waiter.

Sobe u *ovom starom* hotelu su udobne.
The rooms in *this old* hotel are comfortable.

Neuter

The ending is the same as that of the masculine:

Ima lepa crkva u *ovom malom* selu.
There is a nice church in *this little* village.

Dajem bonbone *dobrom* detetu.
I am giving sweets to *the good* child.

Feminine

The ending is **-oj**:

Mladić daje cveće *ljutoj* devojci.
The young man is giving flowers to *the angry* girl.

U *ovoj maloj* crkvi ima divnih ikona.
There are some wonderful icons in *this little* church.

Note: This ending will be familiar to you from those names of countries which are in fact adjectives: **Engleska** – **u Engleskoj**; **Grčka** – **u Grčkoj**. Remember that all names of countries ending in **-ska**, **-ška** or **-čka** are *adjectives*.

Exercise 1

(a) Answer the following questions:

1 Gde su Anđela i Džon?
2 Gde žele da idu?
3 Kako se može putovati tamo gde oni žele da idu?
4 Zašto je putovanje vozom komplikovano?
5 Gde se mogu kupiti karte?

(b)[†] Translate the following conversations into Serbian:

A: Can you tell me where the train station is?
B: Go straight to the end of Srpskih vladara Street and turn right there. Go straight on again for another 100 metres and either turn right and go down Nemanjina Street straight to the station or take a tram from there.

A: Which tram?
B: Every tram that stops there goes to the station.
A: Thank you very much.
B: You're welcome.

(c)[†] Fill in the gaps with the appropriate form of the adjective and noun in the brackets:

(i)

1 Želim pokazati grad _____ (stari profesor).
2 Dajem _____ (Ana) još jednu šansu.
3 Govorim _____ (vaša deca) da su dobra.
4 Objašnjava _____ (grupa turista) gde se nalazi turistička agencija.
5 Moramo da napišemo pismo _____ (dobar prijatelj) u Srbiji.

(ii)

1 U _____ ima puno lepih malih galerija (ovaj grad).
2 On studira na _____ (jedan stari univerzitet).
3 Ona radi u _____ (jedno popularno pozorište).
4 Ko je kompozitor poznatog valcera 'Na _____, (lepi plavi Dunav)?
5 U _____ (naša kuća) uvek ima gostiju.

Language points 2

The dative/locative plural of adjectives

This is very simple, since the ending is the same for all genders: **-im(a)**. See 'Grammary summary', section 2 (p. 301) for the note on usage of the longer form.

Dajemo knjige *dobrim* studentima.
We give books to *good* students.

Nema mesta u *kotorskim* hotelima.
There's no room in the *Kotor* hotels.

U *primorskim* selima možeš da kupiš dobrog vina.
You can buy good wine in the *coastal* villages.

Ona tiho čita *umornim* devojkama.
She is reading quietly to the *tired* girls.

Volim da sedim po *malim beogradskim* kafanama.
I like sitting in *small Belgrade* cafés.

You will probably be relieved to know that this ending is also that of the instrumental plural of adjectives, again for all genders.

Exercise 2†

Read the following text. Identify all the nouns and adjectives and their cases. Be sure that you understand the use of each case before proceeding. Then answer the questions on the text. The translation is in the 'Key to exercises'.

⋒ Reading passage 1 (Audio 1: 38)

Belgrade

Милош Т., возач трамваја:

Зар се Београд уопште може не волети? Од првих дечачких дана, од када датирају моја сећања на црвене трамваје и тролејбусе, Дунав и калемегдански зоолошки врт, траје моја заљубљеност у овај град. Сећам се и легендарне књижаре у Југословенском драмском позоришту, радио емисија Душка Радовића и концерата у Дому омладине.

Али наравно да ово нису једине ствари које волим у Београду. Овај град има много лица и константно се мења. Немогуће је не споменути како су лепи Калемегдан у јесен, Кошутњак зими, а Ботаничка башта и Ташмајдан у пролеће.

Волим Београд и због његове отворености, због парадоксалних контраста које стварају старо и ново: стари Београд и Нови Београд, Народно позориште и Стакленац, тролејбуси и аутобуси. Моје омиљено место у граду је кафић у Културном центру града на Тргу Републике. Неко га зове Трг Републике, а неко Трг Слободе. Ту се налази све што највише волим у овом граду. Ту је Народно позориште. Поред позоришта са десне стране је тржни центар Стакленац, а преко пута позоришта је Народни музеј. На тргу се налази споменик Кнезу Михајлу. Преко пута споменика су дечије позориште Бошко Буха и кафана 'Код коња'. У близини трга су и Скадарлија и Бајлонијева пијаца.

1 Од када траје Милошева заљубљеност у Београд?
2 Које боје су трамваји и тролејбуси у Београду?
3 Чије радио емисије Милош памти?
4 Који делови града су посебно лепи зими, а који у пролеће?
5 Које је Милошево омиљено место у граду?
6 Где се налазе Стакленац и народни музеј?
7 Шта се налази преко пута споменика?

Language points 3

The instrumental case of adjectives

Masculine and neuter singular, **-im**:

> **Idem na more s *dobrim* prijateljem.**
> I'm going to the sea with a *good* friend (male).

> **Avion leti nad *mirnim* morem.**
> The plane is flying over a *calm* sea.

Feminine singular, **-om**:

> **Idem na more s *dobrom* prijateljicom.**
> I'm going to the sea with a *good* friend (female).

> **Idem sa *celom* porodicom.**
> I'm going with the *whole* family.

Plural, all genders, **-im**:

> **Idem na more s *dobrim* prijateljima.**
> I'm going to the sea with (some) *good* friends.

Note: See 'Grammar summary', section 2 (p. 300) for a complete table of the adjective declensions.

Prepositions followed by the locative case

k (or **ka** if followed by a consonant cluster or word beginning with **k**) 'towards, to':

> **Idemo ka autobuskoj stanici.**
> We go/are going towards the bus station.

prema 'towards, according to':

> **Voz ide prema granici.**
> The train is going towards the border.

> **Prema profesorovom objašnjenju, tako je.**
> That's right, according to the teacher's explanation.

pri 'by, near':

> **Nemam knjigu pri ruci.**
> I haven't got the book to hand.

o 'about':

> **Znaš li nešto o novom susedu?**
> Do you know anything about the new neighbour?

u[1] 'in':

> **Ima mnogo lepih zgrada u Novom Sadu.**
> There are many fine buildings in Novi Sad.

na[1] 'on':

> **Soba je na drugom spratu.**
> The room is on the second floor.

1 With these prepositions, as with many others, a clear distinction must be made between their use to express static *location*, when the locative is used, and the expression of *motion*, when the accusative is used:

> **Stanujem u Beogradu.**
> *but* **Putujem u Beograd.**

> **Kafa je na stolu.**
> *but* **Stavljam kafu na sto.**

Prepositions followed by the instrumental case

među 'among':

> **Crkva se vidi među kućama.**
> The church can be seen among the houses.

nad 'above':

> **Avion leti nad gradom.**
> The plane is flying above the town.

pod 'below':

> **Grad se vidi pod avionom.**
> The town can be seen below the plane.

za 'behind, after':

> **Trčim za autobusom.**
> I'm running for the bus.

pred 'in front of':

> **Čekam prijatelja pred kućom.**
> I'm waiting for a friend in front of the house.

Note: All of these prepositions can also take accusative if they are used to convey motion towards a position:

> **Stavljam kofer pod krevet.**
> I'm placing the suitcase under the bed

za + acc.: 'for':

> **Ovo je poklon za Dubravku.**
> This is a gift for Dubravka.

In practice, speakers are far more likely to use alternative prepositions, followed by the genitive case: **između**, **iznad**, **ispod**, **iza**, **ispred**. These are the forms you should learn and use yourself.

Exercise 3

(a)[†] Complete the sentences with the appropriate preposition from the list:

> **blizu   na   u   pre   pored   pod**
> **o   od   sa   ka   kroz**

1 Hotel nije daleko _____ glavne pošte.
2 Prijatelji pričaju _____ prekrasnom odmoru _____ moru.

3 Kad prođete ＿＿＿ kafane, apoteka je odmah tu ＿＿＿ desne strane.
4 Tvoj pasoš je ＿＿＿ stolu, ＿＿＿ kreveta.
5 Sada idemo ＿＿＿ hramu Svetog Save.
6 Pozorište i muzej su ＿＿＿ Trgu Republike.
7 Putujem ＿＿＿ Sirogojno ＿＿＿ starim prijateljem.
8 Kofer je ＿＿＿ krevetom.
9 Volim da gledam ＿＿＿ prozor.
10 Moj posao se nalazi ＿＿＿ moje kuće.

(b)[†]Translate the following sentences into Serbian using the prepositions indicated:

1 There's a nice little park in front of the church. (pred)
2 I am taking a friend to Kalemegdan. (na)
3 There's a beautiful church in that village. (u)
4 They are going towards the station by this road. (prema)
5 Beneath the hill there is a river. (pod)

(c) Give the opposites of the following adverbs and prepositions:

**uzbrdo odatle ovde gore blizu ispred
levo jednostavno**

∩ Dialogue 2 (Audio 1: 39)

Two acquaintances meet in a Belgrade street.

A: Da li idete prema Trgu Republike?
B: Da. Idem kod prijatelja.
A: I ja idem u tom smeru. Gde je mala?
B: Još je u školi, a sutra ide na
   more.
A: Blago njoj! Zar ne možete i vi da idete?
B: Za sada ne mogu. Imam posla u novoj bolnici.
A: Za arhitekte uvek ima posla!
B: Da, ali ne volim što sada radim u bolnici.
A: Ipak, ta bolnica se nalazi na jako lepom mestu. Preko puta hrama Svetog Save.

B: Tako je. A pred bolnicom
    ima zgodan parkić.
A: Divno. Evo, tu smo na Trgu.
B: Navratite do nas kad imate
    vremena!
A: Hvala vam, hoću, vrlo rado.
    Do viđenja!

Vocabulary

smer	direction	**blago njoj!**	lucky her!
bolnica	hospital	**navratiti**	to call in
nazad	back	**napred**	forward

Language points 4

Use of reflexive forms (impersonal construction) to express general statements

Look at these sentences:

Kako se ide u selo Sirogojno?
How does one get to the village of Sirogojno?

Ide se autobusom ili vozom.
One goes by bus or train.

Many verbs can be made reflexive in this way in order to express
a general statement:

Ovde se ulazi u pozorište.
One enters the theatre here.

Exercise 4

Have a look at the map. You are in front of the Turkish Embassy
in Kneza Miloša Street. Ask a passer-by how to get to the JAT
tourist agency. Write up the whole dialogue.

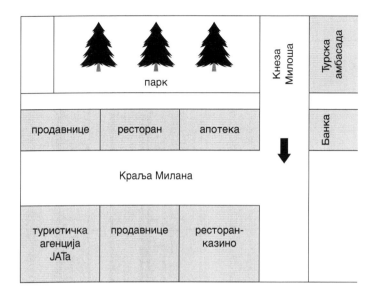

Reading passage 2 (Audio 1: 40)

Kulturni život u Beogradu (9)

That evening Ben and Dejan go to the Yugoslav Drama Theatre in Belgrade. When did the theatre burn down? What is the new building made of? Does Ben understand everything the actors say?

Uveče Dejan i Ben idu, sa Nadom, u pozorište. Dejan objašnjava da je Jugoslovensko dramsko pozorište izgorelo pre nekoliko godina i sada je ponovo izgrađeno. Nova zgrada izgleda impresivno: sva je od stakla i metala.

Gledaju predstavu "Bure baruta" po tekstu Dejana Dukovskog, a u režiji Slobodana Unkovskog. Predstava je živahna, sa realističnim dekorom i odličnim glumcima. Ben nije siguran da razume sve što glumci govore, ali se trudi. Nada je oduševljena predstavom i priča o pojedinim scenama i režiji na način koji je Benu veoma zanimljiv. Svi su vrlo zadovoljni predstavom.

Vocabulary

barut	gunpowder	**bure**	barrel
dekor	decor	**glumac**	actor

izgoreti	to burn down	**izgrađen**	built
(pf. **izgorim**)	(this is the	**konačno**	finally
	past tense)	**kostim**	costume
oduševljen	delighted,	**pojedini**	individual
	enthusiastic	**ponovo**	again
pre nekoliko	a few years ago	**predstava**	performance
godina		**pričati** (imp.)	to talk
režija	direction	**staklo**	glass
truditi se (imp.)	to try, make	**uveče**	in the evening
	an effort	**živahan**	lively

Exercise 5†

Fill in the gap with appropriate words:

'BITI ILI NE BITI' – pitanje je sada.

Juče sam bio u pozorištu i gledao sam _____
'Hamlet' u _____ jednog mladog nepoznatog režisera.
_____ su bili odlični, vrlo ekspresivni i uverljivi. Išao
sam u _____ sa prijateljem koji je bio oduševljen
_____ . Šekspir je uvek moderan!

      ekspresivan expressive   **uverljiv** convincing

 ## Dialogue 3 (Audio 1: 41)

Екипа (9)

У суботу се другови опет налазе у клубу. Филип седне поред
Сање, а Јелена покушава да уведе Даду у разговор.

*On Saturday the friends meet at the club again. Filip sits down beside
Sanja, and Jelena tries to engage Dado in conversation. How does
Dado like to spend his spare time? What does Filip ask Sanja?Why
doesn't she have much time for getting to know Belgrade?*

– Како проводиш време у Београду? – пита Јелена.
– Мало учим, мало гледам телевизију – одговара Дадо.
– Да ли се бавиш неким спортом? – пита Јелена.
– Много волим фудбал, али овдје не познајем људе.
– То можемо да поправимо! – каже весело Јелена, али Дадо
 ћути.

Са друге стране стола, Филип води жив разговор са Сањом.

– Имаш ли времена да упознаш Београд? – пита.
– Не баш много. Сада више није хладно, али сада морам да студирам и немам много времена за разгледање града – одговара Сања.
– То можемо да променимо! – каже Филип. – Има лепих и занимљивих места у овом великом граду. Да ли желиш да их упознаш?
– Свакако – одговара Сања. – И Дадо такође мора више да излази.
– Договорено, дакле! – каже Филип.

Vocabulary

бавити се (imp.)	to occupy oneself with		
водити разговор	to carry on a conversation		
време (gen. **времена**)	time		
дакле	therefore	**договорено**	agreed
други	other	**жив**	lively
опет	again	**покушавати**	to try
поправити (pf.)	to put right	(imp.)	
проводити	to spend (time)	**променити** (pf.)	to change
(imp.)		**разговор**	conversation
сести	to sit down	**страна**	side
(pf. **седнем**)		**субота**	Saturday
ћутати	to be silent	**увести**	to bring into
(imp. **ћутим**)		(pf. **уведем**)	
фудбал	football	**хладан**	cold

10 Putovanje autobusom

Bus journey

In this unit we will look at:

- the past tense
- word order
- past tense questions
- negative past tense
- the emphatic use of pronouns
- use of past tense with numbers

Dialogue 1

У аутобусу

John and Angela have heard about the village of Sirogojno as a centre of village tourism, where they hope to learn about living in the Serbian countryside. On the bus they start talking to the passenger next to Angela, who comes from Sirogojno. How did the Browns hear about Sirogojno? What are they particularly interested in? What was Marija doing in Belgrade?

Анђела:	Да ли је ово аутобус за Сирогојно?
Возач:	Јесте. Полазимо за 10 минута. Ваше карте молим.
Анђела:	Изволите.

* * *

Анђела:	Да ли је ово седиште број 20?
Марија:	Не, није. Ово до прозора је седиште 20. Изволите прођите.

* * *

Марија:	Извините што питам, али чујем да имате другачији нагласак, да ли сте ви странци?
Анђела:	Да. Ми смо из Енглеске.
Марија:	Кад сте дошли у Србију и како сте чули за Сирогојно?
Анђела:	У Србију смо дошли пре недељу дана. А за Сирогојно смо чули тако што смо читали брошуре о Србији и Црној Гори. И сазнали смо да је сеоски туризам организован у том крају. Нас занима живот на селу.
Џон:	Да, посебно нас интересује очување природе и традиције као и обичаји.
Марија:	Стари обичаји су и даље присутни код нас. Поготову неке традиционалне сеоске активности као што је плетење, на пример.
Анђела:	Да ли сте зато били у Београду?
Марија:	Да, како сте погодили: протекле две недеље сам продавала неке вунене ствари које су наше сељанке плеле преко зиме.
Џон:	Надам се да сте успешно прошли.

U autobusu

Марија: Јесам, хвала, прекјуче сам продала све што сам
          однела. Сад морамо одмах да почнемо поново да
          радимо!
Анђела: Честитам на успеху!
Марија: Хвала! Ево нас, стигли смо! Добро дошли у
          Сирогојно!

Vocabulary

активност	activity	**брошура**	brochure
вунени	woollen	**доста**	enough, quite
доћи (pf., **дођем**)	to come	**другачији**	different
ево нас!	here we are!	**зато**	for that reason
интересовати	to interest	**на пример**	for example
(imp. **интересујем**)		**нагласак**	accent
надати се	to hope	**наш**	our
о (+ loc.)	about	**обичај**	custom
организован	organized	**очување**	conservation
питање	question	**плести**	to knit
плетење	knitting	(imp. **плетем**)	
повезан	connected	**погодити** (pf.)	to guess
поготово	particularly	**почети**	to start
пре недељу	a week ago	(pf. **почнем**)	
дана		**прекјуче**	the day before
преко (+ gen.)	through, across		yesterday
природа	nature	**присутан, -тна**	present
продавати	to sell	**производ**	product
(imp. **продајем**;		**протекао, -кла**	past
продати)		**развијен**	developed
сазнати (pf.)	to get to know	**сељак** (m.),	villager
странац	foreigner,	**сељанка** (f.)	
	stranger	**успех**	success
читати (imp.)	to read	**чути**	to hear
што	that	(imp. **чујем**)	

Language points 1

Formation of the past (perfect) tense

You will be glad to know that you only need to be able to use
three tenses yourself: simple present, perfect and future. There are

one or two others you need to be able to recognize, but for all practical purposes these three are sufficient. The perfect tense is very easily formed. It is a compound tense, consisting of the present tense of the auxiliary **biti** and the active past participle.

The active past participle

(1) Verbs with infinitive ending in **-ti**.

The majority of Serbian verbs are in this category. Take the infinitive, e.g. **spavati**, remove final **-ti** and add the following endings:

	Masculine	*Feminine*	*Neuter*
Singular	**-o**	**-la**	**-lo**
Plural	**-li**	**-le**	**-la**

spavao, spavala, spavalo; spavali, spavale, spavala

Past tense

ja sam spavao / ja sam spavala   **mi smo spavali**
ti si spavao / ti si spavala   **vi ste spavali**
on je spavao   **dečaci su spavali**
ona je spavala   **devojke su spavale**
dete je spavalo   **sela su spavala**

Regular verbs with infinitive in -ti

Infinitive	*Infinitive stem*	*Active past participle*		
imati	**ima-**	**imao** (m.)	**imala** (f.)	**imalo** (n.)
piti	**pi-**	**pio**	**pila**	**pilo**
putovati	**putova-**	**putovao**	**putovala**	**putovalo**
raditi	**radi-**	**radio**	**radila**	**radilo**
odmoriti	**odmori-**	**odmorio**	**odmorila**	**odmorilo**
hodati	**hoda-**	**hodao**	**hodala**	**hodalo**

(2) Verbs with infinitive ending in **-ći** or **-sti**.

These form the active past participle slightly differently. For the time being, it is simplest to learn the participle of each new verb of this kind as you come to it. You will soon find that you are able to predict most of them.

Infinitive ending in **-sti: s** is dropped:

	Masculine	Feminine	Neuter
jesti	**jeo**	**jela**	**jelo**
pasti	**pao**	**pala**	**palo**
sesti	**seo**	**sela**	**selo**

Infinitive ending in **-ći**:

Infinitive	Infinitive stem	Active past participle		
stići	**stig-**	**stigao**	**stigla**	**stiglo**
moći	**mog-**	**mogao**	**mogla**	**moglo**
reći	**rek-**	**rekao**	**rekla**	**reklo**

All the compounds of **ići** form the participle in the same way:

ići	**išao, išla, išlo, išli**
doći	**došao, došla, došlo, došli**
ući	**ušao, ušla, ušlo, ušli**

(3) The active past participle of **biti** is quite regular:

Ja sam bio.	**Dete je bilo.**
Ona je bila.	**Mi smo bili.**

Word order 1

Note: Because the short forms of **biti** are, as you know, enclitics, they must be placed immediately after the *first* stressed word in the sentence. Thus, if the pronoun or other subject is used: **Ja sam došla. Mladić je stigao.** However, if the pronoun is not used, the enclitic is placed *after* the participle: **Došli smo. Videla si.**

Exercise 1

(a)[†] Supply the past tense of the verbs in the following sentences:

1 (čuti)   Kako _____ za Sirogojno? (vi)
2 (čitati) Mi _____ u jednoj brošuri o ovom selu.
3 (saznati) Oni _____ da je ovde razvijen seoski turizam.
4 (biti)   Gde _____ tvoja žena juče?

5 (prodavati)   Ona _____ džempere u Beogradu.
6 (proći)   Prijatelji _____ pored naše kuće, a nisu svratili.
7 (imati)   On _____ problema da nađe našu adresu.
8 (doći)   Vi _____ u Beograd pre dve nedelje.
9 (reći)   Majka _____ da je umorna.
10 (jesti)   Marko je rekao da _____ pre dva sata.

> **svratiti** to call on   **pre dve nedelje** two weeks ago
> **pre dva sata** two hours ago

(b) Supply the missing words:

Razgovor u vozu:

A: Izvinite, čujem po _____ da niste odavde. _____ ste?
B: Ja sam _____ Engleske. _____ ?
A: Ja sam _____ . Živim u Užicu, ali _____ na službenom putu u Beogradu.
B: Šta ste po _____ ?
A: Po zanimanju sam ekonimista. Radim kao menadžer jedne velike užičke firme. _____ ?
B: Ja sam po zanimanju lekar, ali se ne bavim više time. _____ kao profesor engleskog sada.

> **službeni put** business trip   **lekar** doctor

Language points 2

Word order 2

The consequence of the rule mentioned above – that enclitics must be placed immediately after the first stressed word (or phrase) in a sentence or clause – is that in a complex sentence, the auxiliary can sometimes be quite far removed from the participle:

Putnik *je* često tokom putovanja *izlazio* da popuši cigaretu.
The passenger *went out* often in the course of his journey to smoke a cigarette.

Kažem da *sam se* posle prvih lepih dana u Beogradu *osećala* kao da oduvek živim ovde.
I say that after the first lovely days in Belgrade *I felt* as though I had always lived here.

Jako mi je drago što *je* tvoj sin, koga nisam još upoznala, konačno *uspeo* da dođe ovamo.
I'm very glad that your son, whom I have not yet met, *has* at last *succeeded* in coming here.

Past tense questions

Remember that there are two basic ways of introducing a question:

(1) Verb + **li**

Imate li kartu?
Have you got a ticket?

Remember that when the verb is **biti**, the long form must be used:

Jesi li umorna?
Are you tired?

In exactly the same way, in questions formed on this model with the past tense the long form of the auxiliary must be used:

Jesi li bila umorna?   **Jeste li spavali?**
Were you tired?   Did you sleep?

Jesam li (ja) zvao?
Je li (ona) zvala?
Jeste li (vi) zvali?

(2) **Da li** + verb

Da li imate kartu?

The short form of the auxiliary is placed after **da li**:

Da li ste spavali?
Da li sam (ja) uspeo?
Da li je (ona) uspela?
Da li ste (vi) uspeli?

Exercise 2†

(a)† Translate the following sentences into Serbian and then make
      questions as in the example:

> *Example*: She has reserved a seat in the train.
>   **Rezervisala je mesto u vozu. Da li je rezervisala
>   mesto u vozu?**

1 You arrived in Novi Sad yesterday.
2 He ordered fish and potatoes.
3 They saw the church and the theatre.
4 She has gone to visit friends.
5 They drank red wine and ate cakes.
6 You have been walking the whole day.
7 I came to Belgrade a week ago.
8 We read about this place in a tourist guide.

(b) Form sentences from the words given below:

1 on   bio   ovde   je   juče
2 išli   svi   u   smo   zajedno   Užice
3 je   što   mogli   da   ste   drago   dođete   mi
4 na   rekao   selu   da   prijateljima   je   je   bio   sa
5 si   video   gde   da   sam   ostavila   li   mobilni telefon?

Language points 3

Negative of past tense

This is very straightforward: use the negative form of the auxiliary (**nisam** etc.) + the active past participle. As the negative forms of **biti** are not enclitics, the rules about word order do not apply. The negative auxiliary normally precedes the participle:

Nisam zvao.	I did not call.
Zar niste išli?	Didn't you go?
Rekao je da nije uspeo.	He said he didn't succeed.

Exercise 3

Answer these questions with a negative sentence and add a positive statement, as in the example.

> *Example*: **Jeste li probali domaće vino?**
> **Nisam pio domaće vino, pio sam pivo.**

1 Jeste li bili u bioskopu?
2 Da li ste putovali autobusom?
3 Jeste li već bili u Sirogojnu?
4 Da li su bili u Narodnom pozorištu?

5 Jeste li rezervisali mesto u restoranu?
6 Da li si kupio karte za predstavu?
7 Jesi li razmišljao o odlasku na more?
8 Da li si saznao nešto o tom gradu?
9 Da li idemo kod prijatelja večeras?
10 Jesi li video Kalemegdansku tvrđavu?

Language points 4

Emphatic use of personal pronouns

Note the use of the long form of the personal pronoun where it is emphasized (personal pronouns are treated in Unit 11).

Meni daj tu lozovaču.
Give that brandy *to me*.

I *meni*, molim te.
And *to me*, please.

⌒ Dialogue 2 (Audio 1: 42)

Two friends are talking over a drink.

A: Nisam gledao novi američki film, a ti?
B: Nisam ni ja. A jeste li ti i Vesna bili u novoj kafani pored Dunava?
A: Ne, nismo. Nismo bili nigde. Jesu li deca došla kod vas?
B: Nisu. Nisu želela da budu u gradu.

Exercise 4

(a) Translate Dialogue 2 into English.

(b) Match the following statements and questions (from 1 to 8) with the appropriate responses (from A to H).

1 Srećan rođendan!
2 Gde se nalazi pošta?
3 Kako ste saznali za ovo selo?
4 Da li želite kafu posle ručka?
5 Da li možeš ti da organizuješ putovanje po Srbiji?

6 Nisam bio u bioskopu sto godina.
7 Oni vole da putuju.
8 Da li je ovo sedište broj 16?

A Ovo nije, ali ono do prozora jeste.
B Čuli smo od prijatelja.
C Nisam ni ja.
D Evo tu iza ugla, nije daleko.
E Pogotovu na selu.
F Svakako.
G Nema problema, vrlo rado.
H Hvala lepo.

       sto godina   for ages (lit. 'one hundred years')

Language points 5

Present tense to express English present perfect

Note the use of the present tense:

U Beogradu sam već tri nedelje.
I have been in Belgrade for three weeks already.

Koliko dugo uči jezik?
How long has he been studying the language?

Use of past tense with numbers

Numbers 2 to 4

The past participle has the same ending as the adjective:

Došla su tri visoka mladića.
Three tall young men came.

Za stolom su sedele dve zgodne devojke.
Two good-looking girls were sitting at the table.

Numbers 5 to 20 etc.

As in the present tense, the verb is usually singular:

Deset izvrsnih plivačica je skočilo u more.
Ten excellent (female) swimmers dived into the sea.

 Reading passage 1 (Audio 1: 43)

Kulturni život u Beogradu (10)

*Dejan introduces Ben to the theatre scene in Serbia. How often is
the BITEF festival held? Who takes part in it? Is theatre popular in
Belgrade?*

Sledećeg dana Dejan je odveo Bena da ga upozna sa nekim svojim
prijateljima u pozorištu 'Atelje 212'. Razgovarali su o jednom
poznatom festivalu internacionalnog pozorišta, BITEFu, koji se
održava svake godine u Beogradu. Festival promoviše nove
pozorišne tendencije i na njemu učestvuju trupe iz celog sveta.
   Ben prati pozorišni život u Britaniji i zainteresovan je da dovede
neku britansku pozorišnu trupu u Beograd. Međutim, Ben se čudi
kako to da ima toliko pozorišta u Beogradu. I kako to da su ljudi
toliko zainteresovani za pozorište. Objasnili su mu da je pozorište
veoma važna i popularna kulturna institucija u Srbiji: neverovatno,
ali ni tokom teških godina srpske istorije, pozorišta nisu prestajala
da rade.

Vocabulary

čuditi se (imp.)	to be surprised	**dovesti**	to bring
godina	year	(pf. **dovedem**)	
i	even	**istorija**	history
međutim	however	**neverovatno**	incredible
održavati se	to be held	**popularan**	popular
(imp.)		**poznat**	well-known,
pratiti (imp.)	to follow		famous
prestajati	to stop	**promovisati**	to promote
(imp. **prestajem**)		(imp. **promovišem**)	
svaki	each	**svetski**	international

svoj   one's own   **težak** (f. **teška**)   difficult
u̲čestvovati   to participate
(imp. **u̲čestvujem**)

Exercise 5

Read 'Kulturni život u Beogradu' (10) again and try to fill in the
gaps in the dialogue:

DEJAN: Marko, ovo je moj prijatelj Ben.
MARKO: Marko, _____ .
BEN: Ben, _____ . Vi ste direktor pozorišta,
         zar ne?
MARKO: Da, ja sam direktor pozorišta i ponekad i režiser. Evo
         upravo režiram _____ za BITEF.
BEN: Šta je to BITEF?
MARKO: BITEF je _____ .
         _____ svake godine. Na njemu
         _____ trupe iz _____ .
BEN: To je baš zanimljivo. Ja pratim_____
         u Velikoj Britaniji. I _____ da
         dovedem neku britansku trupu u Beograd.
MARKO: To zvuči sjajno!
BEN: A kako to da u Beogradu ima _____ ?
         I kako to da su ljudi toliko _____ ?
MARKO: Pozorište je _____ kulturna institucija
         u Beogradu. Neverovatno, ali ni za vreme teške krize
         pozorišta _____ .

🎧 Dialogue 3 (Audio 1: 44)

Екипа (10)

Пријатељи разговарају о породици

The friends discuss families. Do Sanja and Dado come from a large
family? Do their relatives all live in Bosnia? What does Luka want?

– Да ли имате в̲елику ф̲амилију? – Маја пита Сању и Даду.
– Наша фамилија је пр̲илично велика – одговара Сања. – Али
  су сада сви р̲азбацани по свиј̲ету. Једна тетка са мужем и

Svadbeni kolač

синовима је сада у Канади, друга је у Француској, док нам је ујак на Новом Зеланду.

– Имамо неког далеког рођака овдје, у Београду – каже Дадо.
– Да, мало је компликовано – додаје Сања. – Он је зет наше мајке, иако није више ожењен њеном сестром. Они су од прије двије године разведени, нажалост. Али га сви и даље јако волимо, а он је веома добар према нама.
– Нема своје дјеце, па је нас на неки начин усвојио – каже Дадо.
– Лепо од њега! Попијмо по чашу вина у част родбине! – предлаже увек расположени Лука, док узима Мају за руку. – Желим да ми Маја једног дана буде жена и да нам сви дођете на свадбу!

Vocabulary

додавати (imp. **додајем**)	to add	**зет**	son-in-law, brother-in-law
компликовано	complicated	**мајка**	mother
на неки начин	in a way	**ожењен**	married (of man)
помало	a bit	**попити** (pf. **попијем**)	to have a drink, drink up

поцрв<u>е</u>нети	to blush	пр<u>и</u>лично	fairly
р<u>а</u>збацан	scattered	разв<u>е</u>ден	divorced
расп<u>о</u>ложен	in a good mood	ро̄ак	relative
рука	hand	сестра	sister
син (pl. синови)	son	тетка	aunt
<u>у</u>зимати	to take	ујак	uncle (mother's
усв<u>о</u>јити	to adopt		brother)
част	honour		

11 Porodični odnosi

Family relationships

In this unit we will look at:

* personal pronoun declensions
* family relationships
* word order (3)
* usage of pronouns

 ## Dialogue 1 (Audio 1: 45)

Razgovor o rodbini

Conversation about relatives. What is Marija's house like? Who is the baby in the photograph? Who lives in the house behind the trees?

Џон и Анђела су имали врло испуњен дан. Разгледали су село, а увече их је Марија позвала код себе на вечеру.

Марија:	Добро дошли, дозволите да вас упознам: ово је мој муж, Милош, а ово нам је ћерка, Мирјана.
Анђела:	Драго ми је. Баш је лепо што сте нас позвали код вас!
Милош:	Чуо сам да вас занима сеоски живот, па сада имате прилику да видите праву сеоску кућу!
Џон:	Веома је симпатична и изгледа врло аутентично. Да ли је ово ваша породична кућа?
Милош:	Јесте. Моји отац и деда су овде одрасли.
Анђела:	А ко је ова преслатка беба на слици?
Марија:	То ми је унук: син наше друге ћерке. Моји су родитељи одушевљени што су постали прабаба и прадеда!

Милош: А да ли видите ту кућу иза дрвећа?
Џон: Са терасом?
Милош: Да. Ту станују мој брат и моја снаја, стриц и стрина наше Мирјане. Они имају сина и ћерку.
Анђела: То значи да су ваше ћерке одрасле уз браћу и сестре од стрица?
Марија: Тако је. То је био стари обичај у нашим селима: породице су често градиле куће око заједничког дворишта.

Vocabulary

беба	baby	**брат/сестра од стрица**	cousin
браћа (coll.)	brothers		
градити (imp.)	to build	**двориште**	yard, garden
деда	grandfather	**дрвеће** (coll.)	trees
заједнички	common, shared	**значити** (imp.)	to mean
испуњен	full, filled	**иза** (+ gen.)	behind
изгледати (imp.)	to look, seem	**одрасти** (pf. **одрастем**)	to grow up
око (+ gen.)	around	**отац** (gen. **оца** pl. **очеви**)	father
породични	family (adj.)		
постати (pf. **постанем**)	to become	**прабаба**	great-grandmother
		прадеда	great-grandfather
пресладак, -тка	very sweet	**прилика**	opportunity
саградити (pf.)	to build	**симпатичан, -чна**	charming, nice

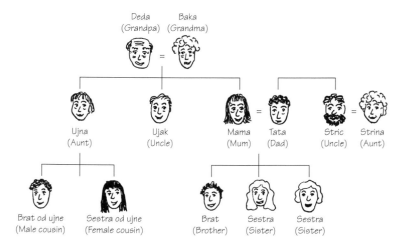

снаја	daughter-in-law	**стриц**	uncle
стрина	aunt	**ћерка**	daughter
унук	grandson		
	(granddaughter **унука**)		

Note: The most usual word for 'aunt' is **tetka**, sister of a father or a mother. Her husband is **teča**.

Language points 1

You should by now be feeling quite comfortable with Cyrillic, so from now on it will be used to introduce some of the main language points. Please note that there is no need for you to write in Cyrillic unless you want to: you need to familiarize yourself with reading it, but there are plenty of Serbs who do not themselves use it when they write. You might use it for exercises which are presented in Cyrillic, just for practice.

Declension of personal pronouns

The first thing to remember is that personal pronouns are not used in the nominative except for emphasis. Compare:

Зашто си дошао?	Why have you come?
Дошао сам да видим мајку.	I've come to see my mother.

and

Ко је? Јеси ли ти, душо?	Who is it? Is it *you*, dear?
Ja **sam, majko.**	It is *I*, mother.

The other cases of the pronouns are used as required by the sentence structure: they behave like any other kind of noun.

The second main point is that there are two forms of some of the cases (genitive/accusative and dative) – a neutral short form and an emphatic long form. Like the short forms of **бити**, the short forms of pronouns are enclitic, i.e. they cannot carry stress and cannot therefore be placed in a position where they would be stressed. Compare:

Зашто си дошао?
Why have you come?

Дошао сам да <u>те</u> видим. (short form)
I've come to see you.

Јеси ли дошао да видиш Ану?
Have you come to see Ana?

Нисам, него да видим <u>тебе</u>. (long form)
No, I've come to see *you*.

Remember that the long forms must be used when pronouns follow a preposition:

Седи поред мене и причај ми о њему.
Sit *beside me* and tell me *about him*.

Declension of personal pronoun 'I': ja

Genitive/accusative

The genitive and accusative of all personal pronouns are the same and can therefore be taken together:

	Short form: **ме**	*Long form*: **мене**
(gen.)	**Он ме се не сећа.**	**Далеко је од мене.**
	He doesn't remember me.	He is far from me.
(acc.)	**Видела ме је.**	**Је ли то поклон за мене?**
	She saw me.	Is that a present for me?

Dative

Short form: **ми**   *Long form*: **мени**

Рекао ми је истину.   ***Мени* није ништа рекао.**
He told *me* the truth.   He didn't tell *me* anything.

Locative

The locative case has the same form, but since it is used only with prepositions, it is always long:

Кола су возила према мени.
The car was driving towards me.

Шта су говорили о мени.
What did they say about me?

Instrumental

мном (or **мноме** if the word requires greater emphasis):

Дођи са мном, ако желиш.
Come with me, if you want.

Exercise 1

(a) Mark the following statements **Tačno** (**T**) or **Netačno** (**N**):

1 Braunovi su imali vrlo dosadan dan.   (T/N)
2 Uveče su otišli na večeru.   (T/N)
3 Marija i Miloš imaju dve ćerke.   (T/N)
4 Miloš živi sa svojim ocem i svojim dedom.   (T/N)
5 Njegove ćerke su odrasle uz braću i sestre
  od strica.   (T/N)

(b) Supply the missing words in the following four groups of family
members:

mama	_____	_____	tetka
_____	stric	ujak	_____
sin	brat od strica	_____	_____
_____	_____	sestra od ujaka	_____

(c) Look at the family tree and try to answer the questions on
family relations in Miloš's family:

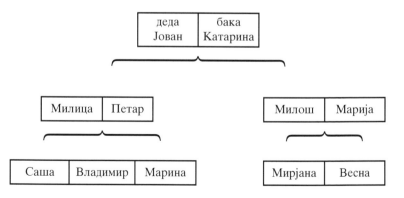

Example: **Шта је Јован Марини?**
               Јован је Марини деда.

1 Шта је Милица Петру?
2 Шта је Мирјана Весни?
3 Шта су Саша и Весна?
4 Шта је Владимиру Марија?
5 Шта је Весна Катарини?
6 Шта је Петар Мирјани?
7 Шта је Саша Јовану?
8 Шта су Петар и Милош?

(d)[†] Complete the sentences with the correct form of **ja**:

1 Они су одрасли са _____ .
2 -Ово је Мирјана. -Драго _____ је, Петар.
3 Да ли су ови колачи за _____ ?
4 Рекао _____ је да путује сутра.
5 Они стоје иза _____ .
6 _____ се чини да је он већ отишао.
7 Он _____ је брат.
8 Моји родитељи увек причају са пријатељима о _____ .
9 Хајде са _____ у биоскоп.
10 Волим када је пуно људи око _____ .
11 Могу да пијем и чај и кафу. Свеједно _____ је.

Language points 2

'you' ти; *reflexive pronoun* се, себе

These follow the same pattern:

Genitive

Он те се добро сећа.	**То сам добила од тебе.**
He remembers you well.	I got that from you.

Dative

Шта сам ти рекао?	**Теби дајем ову књигу.**
What did I tell you?	I'm giving you this book.

Locative

О теби су говорили само добро.
They said only good things about you.

Instrumental

Желим да будем с тобом.
I want to be with you.

The reflexive pronoun (**ce**) has no nominative form. In reflexive verbs it is used to denote the 'object' of the action. It can only refer to the subject of a verb, and cannot itself be the subject. In all reflexive verbs it is the genitive/accusative form which is used:

Ја сам се почешљала.
I combed my hair.

Ти си се лепо обукла.
You've dressed nicely.

Он се купа. Она се спрема.
He is bathing. She is getting ready.

Ми смо се упознали.
We have met.

Ви се нисте одавно видели.
You haven't seen each other for a long time.

Они се врло добро познају.
They know each other very well.

The long form of the genitive/accusative is used for all persons – for emphasis or after a preposition:

Genitive/accusative себе

Чувај себе, не брини о нама.
Look after yourself, don't worry about us.

Откад знам за себе, волим море.
As long as I can remember I've loved the sea.
(lit. 'Since I have known of myself . . .')

Нису купили поклоне за себе.
They didn't buy gifts for themselves.

Dative себи

Говорио је сам себи ...
He was saying to himself ...

Locative себи

Она говори стално о себи.
She's always talking about herself.

Instrumental собом

Донели су пртљаг са собом.
They brought their luggage with them.

Dialogue 2

Two friends meet. One is driving a new car:

A: Jesu li ti to nova kola?
B: Jesu. Kako ti se sviđaju?
A: Mnogo mi se sviđaju! Hoćeš li da me voziš negde?
B: Rado! Odmah dolazim po tebe. Idem samo po benzin!

benzin petrol

Bioskop 'Jadran'

Language points 3

Declension он, она, оно *'he, she, it'*

он/оно

The accusative and the genitive are the same:

Short form: **га** | *Long form*: **њега**

Одавно га нисам видела. | **Шта ће да буде од њега?**
I haven't seen him for a | What will become of him?
  long time.

Ево ти писма, ја сам га већ прочитала.
Here's the letter, I've already read it.

Dative

му | **њему**
Дала сам му књигу. | **Ниси то ваљда рекао њему?**
I gave him the book. | You presumably didn't tell *him*?

Locative

Чули смо много о њему.
We've heard a lot about him.

Instrumental

њим (**њиме**)

Она иде с њим у позориште.
She's going to the theatre with him.

Поклањам ти ово налив перо, њиме сам написао ове песме.
I'm giving you this fountain pen, I wrote these poems with it.

Она

Genitive

Short form: **је** | *Long form*: **ње**

Радо смо је се сећали. | **Отишао је далеко од ње.**
We remembered her with | He went far away from her.
  pleasure.

The accusative short form is the same as the genitive, but the long form is: **њу**

Видели смо је тамо.
We saw her there.

Видели смо тебе, а њу нисмо видели.
We saw you, but we didn't see her.

However, if the accusative of **она** (**je**) occurs in the same sentence as the short form of the third person singular of **бити**, an alternative form of accusative of **она** may be used: **jу**.

Да ли је видео Ану? Видео jу је.
Did he see Ana? He saw her.

Dative

joj, њоj

Дajeм joj књигу.
I'm giving her the book.

Instrumental

њом (њоме)

Виђамо се често с њом.
We often see her.

Plurals

The declensions of **ми** 'we' and **ви** 'you' are similar:

Accusative/genitive:	**нас**	**вас**
Dative:	**нам (нама)**	**вам (вама)**
Locative:	**нама**	**вама**
Instrumental:	**нама**	**вама**

они, оне, она 'they'

Accusative/genitive:	**их**	**њих** (long form)
Dative:	**им**	**њим** (long form)
Locative:	**њима**	
Instrumental:	**њима**	

Exercise 2

(a)† Use the correct form of **sebe, se**:

1 Naručila sam _____ kolače, a tebi tortu.
2 Vidimo _____ uskoro.
3 Ona samo priča o _____ .
4 Kupili su kuću za _____ i za svoju decu.
5 Nikad nemaš novca kod _____ .

(b) Complete the anwers to the following questions using pronouns:

> *Example*: **Da li si sinu kupila poklon?**
> **Ne, nisam mu još kupila poklon.**

1 Jesi li upoznala Borisa? Da, upoznala sam _____ juče.
2 Jesi li videla novu knjigu? Ne, još _____ nisam videla.
3 Viđaš li se s Brankom? Da, često idem s _____ u bioskop.
4 Jesi li upoznala studente? Ne, nisam se još uvek upoznao s _____ .
5 Da li ona zna put do naše kuće? Da, dala sam _____ adresu.

(c)† Substitute pronouns for the nouns in italics:

1 Gledam *filmove* svako veče.
2 Čitam *turističke brošure* jer putujem uskoro.
3 Viđam *Ivanu* svaki dan.
4 Mislim na *moju sestru* svaki dan.
5 Razmišljam o *Milanu i Ani* svaki put kad odem u taj restoran.
6 Razgovaram sa *roditeljima* telefonom svakog vikenda.
7 Želim da vidim *strica i strinu* što pre.
8 Putujem sa *bratom* na more ovog leta.
9 Pokazali su nam *kuću*.
10 Sagradili su *bioskop* blizu moje kuće.

Language points 4

Word order with pronouns

Pronouns must be placed in a strict order.

Dative precedes accusative/genitive:

> **Ovo je poklon**, **dajem** *ti ga.*
> This is a gift; I'm giving *it to you.*

Where short forms of pronouns occur in the same sentence as short forms of verbs (**biti** and two other auxiliaries we have yet to meet), the verbal forms precede the pronouns:

> **Dao** *sam ti ga.*   I gave *it to you.*

The reflexive pronoun **se** follows these:

> **Rado** *smo je se* **sećali.**   We remembered her with
>   pleasure.

There is one exception: the third person singular of **biti** – **je** – is placed after all the other enclitics:

> **Da** *li ih se je* **setio?**   Did *he* remember *them*?

This is the formula you should learn:

> **li** (interrog. part.); **ve** (verbal); dative accusative/genitive
> (of pronouns); **se**; **je**

This seems a great deal to remember all at once, but it will become instinctive gradually. For the time being, try to observe all clusters of enclitics as you come to them, write some typical ones down for reference and remember the formula when you need to compose a sentence yourself.

Exercise 3

(a) Form sentences using the words below:

    1 sam video je
    2 knjigu sam kupio mu
    3 njom mi sa pričamo
    4 li sećaš njega da se
    5 da bio rekao je im u je Sirogojnu

(b)[†] Translate the following sentences into Serbian:

1 They were sitting behind you.
2 Did he see me?
3 I gave you the keys.
4 She is my sister.
5 She's going to the theatre with him.
6 We remember her with pleasure.
7 I met them the day before yesterday.
8 We talked about him on the bus.
9 What did I tell you?

🎧 Reading passage 1 (Audio 1: 46)

Kulturni život u Beogradu (11)

Dejan is going to introduce Ben to the film world. Where will they go the next day? Who is the well-known director Dejan mentions?

Na putu kući, Dejan je Benu rekao da sledećeg dana mora da ga upozna sa svojim prijateljima koji rade na filmu. Prvo treba da odu u studio jedne filmske škole gde se snimaju uglavnom kratki filmovi i dokumentarci da vide kako se filmovi prave. U poslednjih par godina u Beogradu je otvoreno nekoliko filmskih škola. Ljubitelji filma i entuzijasti dosta rade na popularizaciji filma pa od 90-ih u Beogradu postoji čak nekoliko festivala amaterskog filma.

Dejan se nada da Ben ovako može da čuje nešto i o istoriji igranog filma u bivšoj Jugoslaviji i novonastalim zemljama. Od režisera sa ovih prostora čuo je samo za Kusturicu i Makavejeva. Pošto su se u bioskopima davali samo američki filmovi, Dejan je planirao da mu kod kuće pusti neke klasike domaćeg filma koje ima na video kasetama. Prvi film koji mu pada na pamet, je 'Ko to tamo peva', režisera Slobodana Šijana, a on obično sve obara s nogu. Radi se o komediji u kojoj je humor vrlo specifičan i teško prevodiv. Dejan nije bio siguran da li Ben može da razume film, ali on može da se potrudi da mu objasni neke stvari tokom filma. Nema veze, imaju celo veče pred sobom!

Vocabulary

bivši	former	**ceo, cela**	whole
čak	even	**dokumentarac**	documentary
igrani film	feature film	**kratak (kratka)**	short
ljubitelj	lover, fan	**nastao, -ala**	emerged (**nastati**,
nema veze	never mind!		pf. 'to come into
obarati s nogu	to bowl over		being')
(imp.)		**obično**	usually
padati na	to occur to	**par godina**	couple of years
pamet	(one)	**postojati** (imp.	to exist
		postojim)	
potruditi se	to try,	**pred** (+ instr.)	before, in front of
(pf.)	endeavour	**prevodiv**	translatable
pustiti (imp.)	to let go (here	**radi se o**	it's a question of
	'to show')	**snimati** (imp.)	to record, shoot
tokom (+ gen.)	during, in the		(of film)
	course of	**trenutno**	at the moment
uglavnom	on the whole	**zemlja**	country

Exercise 4[†]

(a) Supply the correct word from the list below and put it in the correct form:

> **glavna uloga   premijera   igrani   karta   snima**

1 Ne volim dokumentarne filmove, volim samo _____ filmove.
2 – Ko igra _____ u filmu *Otac na službenom putu?*
  – Miki Manojlović, zar ne znaš?
3 Jesi li čuo da Kusturica _____ novi film?
4 Kad je _____ njegovog novog filma?
5 Ne verujem da na dan premijere možemo da nađemo _____ za bioskop.

(b) Translate the following dialogue into Serbian:

A: I have just seen an excellent documentary in the cinema! I really liked it.
B: Really? What film?
A: It's called *Super 8.*
B: I've never heard of it. Who's the director?

A: Emir Kusturica.
B: Ah, I remember it now. I read a lot about it in the news-
    papers. I don't agree that it's a good film.
A: How can you say that when you haven't seen it?

Language points 5

Language in action

Here are some examples of pronouns and other short forms in
context. See whether you can translate them.

Izgubila sam kartu za bioskop. Da li si je videla?
Ne, nisam je videla. Možda ju je Ivan video.
U pravu si, dala sam mu je juče.
Potraži je, dakle, kod njega.

Da li poznaješ Mirinog brata?
Da, upoznali smo se na filmskom festivalu na Paliću letos.
Sećam se, vratili ste se zajedno sa festivala.
Da li si ga pitala da li me se seća?

Ko im je to rekao?
Ne znam, ja to nisam rekao njima, samo tebi.
A njoj je to rekao on, je li?
Možda, nisam ga čuo, sedeo sam iza vas.

| **potražiti** | to look for | **letos** | last summer |
| **vratiti se** | to return | | |

Dative of pronouns to express possession

In the text of this unit note the use of the dative of pronouns to
convey possession:

On mi je brat.
He is my brother.

There are two examples of this usage in Dialogue 1.

See Grammar summary, section 3 (p. 302) for complete table of
pronoun declensions.

🎧 Dialogue 3 (Audio 1: 47)

Екипа (11)

Why does Jelena invite Dado to the cinema? Does he agree to go with her? Why does he always think of Sanja?

Јелена је Филипова најбоља пријатељица. Она види да га Сања привлачи на њему нов начин, па жели да му помогне. Одлучује да позове Даду у биоскоп.

– Шта радиш идућег петка, Дадо? – пита Јелена.
– Ништа нарочито, колико знам – одговара.
– У биоскопима се даје нови домаћи филм. Критике су одличне. Сви га хвале.
– Лијепо. Волим биоскоп. Не знам шта раде остали . . .
– Не знам ни ја, али имам пријатеља који може да нам да две бесплатне карте.
– Имаш добре везе, дакле! Па не знам, морам да видим са Сањом.
– Мислим да Филип планира да је позове негде. Ајде, Дадо, не мораш баш стално да си уз њу!
– Знам да не морам, али, толико смо заједно ових посљедњих мјесеци, навикао сам да увијек мислим на њу.
– То је лепо од тебе. Али једног дана мораш и да се одвојиш! Ајде, овај филм је стварно занимљив!

Јелени је било јасно да се Дадо збунио, али се ипак надала да ће се на крају одлучити да јој прави друштво.

Vocabulary

ајде, хајде	come on!	**бесплатан**	free
веза	connection	**збунити се** (pf.)	to be confused,
идући	next, coming		embarrassed
ипак	nevertheless	**јасан, јасна**	clear
критика	review	**месец (мјесец)**	month
навикао	accustomed	**најбољи**	best
одвојити се (pf.)	to separate from	**одлучивати се** (imp. **одлучујем**;	to decide
петак	Friday	**одлучити се**)	

по̀следњи	last	пра̀вити	to keep
привла́чити	to attract	(нѐкоме)	(someone)
(imp.)		друштво	company
ствар̀но	really	увијек/увек	always
хва́лити (imp.)	to praise		

12 Seoski život

Village life

 Dialogue 1 (Audio 2: 1)

Where are the Browns staying? Where are they sitting? How far is it to Zlatibor? How long are the Browns intending to stay? What animals do Petar and Milica have? What are the Browns going to do tomorrow?

Џон и Анђела су тренутно код Милошевог брата Петра и његове жене Милице. Вечерас ће да преспавају код њих. Петар и Милица су их дочекали традиционалном добродошлицом. Послужили су погачу и со, а затим и слатко, кафу и ракију. Сада седе испред куће у хладовини и разговарају.

Анђела:	Колико је Сирогојно удаљено од Златибора?
Петар:	Није далеко. Око 10 км. Ја ћу ићи сутра до пашњака на обронцима Златибора да обиђем своје стадо оваца. Можете поћи са мном, ако хоћете. Видећете језеро и златиборске шуме. Поред тога, моћи ћете да уживате у чистом планинском ваздуху и здравој изворској води.
Џон:	Што да не! Ионако смо планирали дужи обилазак овог краја. Остаћемо овде још недељу дана и надам се да ћемо стићи да видимо цео крај. Него Петре, какве су ово куће овде?

Петар:	Ово је кућа коју је саградио мој деда. То поред је млекара, а оно доле, низбрдо што видите је штала у којој држимо краве.
Анђела:	Млекара?
Милица:	Да, ту држимо сир и кајмак које правим сваки дан. Сутра ћу устати рано и пробудићу вас да видите како ја то радим. А онда ћемо да правимо проју за доручак. Пробаћете и домаћу димљену пршуту и свеж парадајз из моје баште.
Анђела:	Једва чекам. Ваљда ћемо успети да се пробудимо тако рано!

Vocabulary

ваљда	presumably	**димљен**	smoked
добродошлица	welcome	**здрав**	healthy
извор	spring, source	**једва**	hardly
језеро	lake	**кајмак**	soft cheese
крава	cow		(similar to
млекара	dairy		crème fraîche)
него	but	**низбрдо**	downhill

Seoska koliba

обићи	to visit, go round	обронак	slope
(pf. обиђем)		овца	sheep
пашњак	pasture, grazing	планина	mountain
погача	round loaf	поље	field
преспавати	to spend the	проја	maize bread
(pf.)	night	слатко	sweet fruit jam
со (gen. соли)	salt	стадо	flock, herd
удаљен	distant	успети (pf.)	to succeed
хладовина	shade	штала	barn, stable
шума	forest, wood		

Language points 1

The future tense

This is another compound tense and it is formed very simply. It consists of the infinitive *or* да + present tense and a new auxiliary: хтети 'to want'. Like **бити, хтети** has two forms: a short form which is the norm, and a long form which must be used in certain circumstances, i.e. when placed in a position which carries stress.

	Short form	Long	Interrogative	Negative
(ja)	ћу	хоћу	да ли ћу?	нећу
(ти)	ћеш	хоћеш	да ли ћеш?	нећеш
(он, она, оно)	ће	хоће	да ли ће?	неће
(ми)	ћемо	хоћемо	да ли ћемо?	нећемо
(ви)	ћете	хоћете	да ли ћете?	нећете
(они, оне, она)	ће	хоће	да ли ће?	неће

Examples:

Ja ћу спавати.	**Да ли ћеш доћи?**	**Нећете успети.**
Ja ћу да спавам.	**Да ли ћеш да дођеш?**	**Нећете да успете.**
I shall sleep.	Will you come?	You won't succeed.

Use of the long form of the auxiliary

We have already observed that in Serbian it is more common to answer questions with a verb than to use да or не.

Да ли си уморан?   Јесам./Нисам.

Хтети is used in just the same way:

Хоћеш ли доћи? *or*
Хоћеш ли да дођеш?   **Хоћу./Нећу.**

To ask and answer such questions, then, the long form of **хтети** must be used. In all other circumstances, unless particular emphasis is required, the short form is used.

Examples of emphatic sentences:

Ниси ваљда уморан? Ја *јесам* **уморан, али ћу ипак да помогнем.**
You surely can't be tired? I am tired, but I'll still help.

Нећете ваљда да дођете сада? Ја *хоћу,* **али Мира неће.**
You're presumably not coming now? *I shall come,* but Mira won't.

Note: Because Serbian favours the construction **да** + verb, rather than the infinitive, this is also the preferred construction with future sentences.

Vocabulary building

Životinje 'animals'

pas 'dog', **mačka** 'cat', **konj** 'horse', **magarac** 'donkey', **tele** 'calf', **koza** 'goat', **svinja** 'pig', **vo** 'ox', **kokoška** 'hen', **pile** 'chick', **guska** 'goose', **vuk** 'wolf', **lav** 'lion', **tigar** 'tiger'

The following expressions involve animals: see whether you can work out what they mean.

Umoran kao pas.
Gladan kao vuk.
Tvrdoglav kao magarac.
Prljav kao svinja.
Glup kao vo.
Glupa kao guska.

        tvrdoglav stubborn   **prljav** dirty
                glup stupid

Language in action

Word order

As was the case with the past tense, the future auxiliary may precede or follow the main verb, depending on whether the pronoun is used or not.

ja ћу доћи, ja ћу да дођем

but

доћи ћу

With verbs ending in **-ти**, the final **и** is removed and the infinitive and auxiliary are run together. The future is then written:

ja ћу бити, ja ћу да будем	*but*	**биħу**
ти ħеш спавати, ти ħеш да спаваш		**спаваħеш**
ми ħемо видети, ми ħемо да видимо		**видеħемо**

Note: The enclitic follows the infinitive only if the infinitive is the *first* word in the sentence or clause. This is because the enclitic continues to obey the rule, which places it as near the beginning of the sentence as possible, even if it may be run into the infinitive.

Путоваħемо касније.

but

Мислим да ħемо путовати касније.

Exercise 1

(a) Answer the following questions:

1 Ko su Petar i Milica?
2 Kako su Braunovi bili posluženi kad su stigli kod Petra i Milice?
3 Gde su sedeli i razgovarali sa domaćinima?
4 Šta će Petar raditi sutra?
5 Šta će Braunovi moći da rade ako pođu sa njim?
6 Šta je to 'mlekara'?
7 Šta će Milica da radi ujutro?
8 Da li se Milica i Petar odmaraju leti?

(b) Add the missing verbs:

    Example: _____ **kafu i slatko. poslužiti**

1 _____ u čistom planinskom vazduhu i lepoti pejzaža.
2 _____ kuću.
3 _____ proju.
4 _____ stado.
5 _____ pršutu.

(c) Arrange in order of size:

    krava, ovca, pas, kokoška, svinja, tele, pile, mačka

(d) Put the following sentences into the future tense:

  1 Ja sam rezervisala autobuske karte.
  2 Mi ostajemo 10 dana ovde.
  3 Vraćamo se u Beograd u subotu.
  4 Sutra idemo u obilazak Zlatibora.
  5 Budimo se rano.
  6 Milica pravi sir i kajmak.
  7 Petar sprema proju.
  8 Kupio sam novi ruksak za planinarenje.
  9 Hodali smo ceo dan.
10 Ja sam pozvala prijatelje da dođu kod nas.

    ruksak rucksack   **planinarenje** hiking, climbing

Language points 2

Vocabulary building

Points of the compass

istok	east	**zapad**	west
sever	north	**jug**	south

Dialogue 2 (Audio 2: 2)

TURISTA:	Čuo sam puno o seoskom turizmu u Srbiji. Da li možete da mi preporučite nešto?
AGENT:	Zavisi gde hoćete da idete: istočna Srbija, zapadna Srbija, jug ili Vojvodina?
TURISTA:	Zanima me zapadna Srbija jer ću posle ići u Bosnu.
AGENT:	Onda vam mogu preporučiti sela na planinama Zlatiboru i Tari.
TURISTA:	Čuo sam za Sirogojno i čuvene Sirogojno džempere.
AGENT:	Da, Sirogojno je odlično mesto. Tu ćete naći primerke tradicionalne srpske seoske arhitekture, tradicionalne veštine, poput pletenja, i naravno odličnu hranu. Organizujemo i izlete do obližnjih sela, vrhova Zlatibora i do Užica.
TURISTA:	Gde mogu da odsednem?
AGENT:	Moći ćete da odsednete ili u hotelu ili u tradicionalnom domaćinstvu. Šta više volite?
TURISTA:	Definitivno želim da budem u nekoj porodici.
AGENT:	Dobro, evo vam autobuska karta i rezervacija smeštaja. Javite se našem agentu na Zlatiboru kada stignete tamo.
TURISTA:	Hvala.
AGENT:	Nema na čemu. Srećan put.

Vocabulary

primerak	example	**veština**	skill
poput (+ gen.)	like	**pletenje**	weaving
obližnji	neighbouring	**vrh**	peak
odsednuti	to stay	**domaćinstvo**	household
smeštaj	accommodation		

Exercise 2

(a)[†] Look at the map of Serbia and Montenegro in Unit 15 (p. 211) and try to supply the correct word:

    (i)   Use one of the following:

        na istoku, na zapadu, na jugu, na severu, na jugozapadu, na jugoistoku, na severozapadu, na severoistoku

Example: **Niš se nalazi na istoku Srbije.**

1 Subotica se nalazi _____ Srbije.
2 Kotor se nalazi _____ Crne Gore.
3 Užice se nalazi _____ Srbije.
4 Nikšić se nalazi _____ Crne Gore.
5 Leskovac se nalazi _____ Srbije.

(ii) Use one of the following:

južno od, severno od, zapadno od, istočno od

1 _____ Beograda su Pančevo i Novi Sad.
2 _____ Podgorice su Petrovac i Budva.
3 _____ Subotice se nalazi Zrenjanin.
4 _____ od Prištine je Peć.

(b) Complete the following dialogue:

Vı: _____.
AGENT: Kako želite da putujete u Kotor?

Vı: _____.
AGENT: Put avionom ne traje tako dugo, ali, sa druge strane, morate da presedate na autobus na aerodromu.

Vı: _____?
AGENT: Direktno jedino možete da putujete autobusom.

Vı: _____?
AGENT: Autobuska karta košta 2000 dinara.

Vı: _____?
AGENT: Možete da odsednete u hotelu ili u privatnom smeštaju.

Vı: _____.
AGENT: Kada putujete i koliko dugo ćete da ostanete?

Vı: _____.
AGENT: Imate autobusku rezervaciju za sutra popodne. Na koje ime da rezervišem smeštaj?

Vı: _____.
AGENT: Rezervisao sam jednokrevetnu sobu.

Vı: _____.

presedati (imp.)   to change (method of transport)

Language points 3

Examples of structures using the future tense

Affirmative

	With pronoun or other 'prop'		Without preceding word
	Aux.	*Infinitive*	
(ja)	ћу	доћи са вама у биоскоп	Доћи ћу ...
(ти)	ћеш	спавати до подне	Спаваћеш ...
(она)	ће	бацити писмо на пошту	Бациће ...
(ми)	ћемо	попити по чашицу	Попићемо ...
(ви)	ћете	мирно читати новине	Читаћете ...
(они)	ће	гледати телевизију	Гледаће ...

Interrogative

Aux.	*Interr. part.*	*Emph. pron.*		*Qu. marker*	*Aux.*	*Emph. pron.*	
Хоће	ли	(оне)	бити цео дан ту?	Да ли	ће	(оне)	бити ...?
Хоћете	"	(ви)	помоћи око ручка?	"	ћете	(ви)	помоћи ...?
Хоће	"	(он)	носити тај шешир?	"	ће	(он)	носити ...?
Хоћемо	"	(ми)	купити карте?	"	ћемо	(ми)	купити ...?
Хоћеш	"	(ти)	сачекати код улаза?	"	ћеш	(ти)	сачекати?

Negative

Aux.	*Emph. pron.*	*Conj.*	*Refl. part.*	
Неће	(они)	да	се	дуго задрже
Нећемо	(ми)	"		стигнемо на време
Нећеш	(ти)	"		седиш на сунцу
Неће	(он)	"	се	ускоро врати
Нећу	(ja)	"		пушим више

Negative interrogative

Aux.	Interr. part.	Emph. pron.	Conj.		Neg. qu. mkr	Emph. pron.		Aux.	Conj.
Нећете	ли	(ви)	да	седнете до нас?	Зар	(ви)	нећете	да	седнете ...?
Нећу	″	(ја)	″	пођем с њима?	″	(ја)	нећу	″	пођем ...?
Неће	″	(она)	″	прочита писмо?	″	(она)	неће	″	прочита ...?
Нећеш	″	(ти)	″	платиш такси?	″	(ти)	нећеш	″	платиш ...?
Нећемо	″	(ми)	″	пробамо печурке?	″	(ми)	нећемо	″	пробамо ...?
Неће	″	(оне)	″	наместе кревет?	″	(оне)	неће	″	наместе ...?

печурка mushroom　　　**наместити кревет** to make a bed

Exercise 3

(a) Answer the following questions in the affirmative:

1 Хоће ли путник путовати на Златибор?
2 Да ли ће се Марија и Петар одморити на зиму?
3 Хоће ли Марија сутра да прави пројy?
4 Да ли ће Џон да иде у обилазак?
5 Да ли ће они остати у Сирогојну целе недеље?

(b) Answer the questions in the negative:

1 Хоће ли Марија устати касно?
2 Да ли ће се Петар одмарати сутра?
3 Нећеш ваљда одсести у хотелу?
4 Хоћеш ли имати проблема око смештаја?
5 Да ли ћемо путовати возом?

(c) Using Angela and John's plans for the next week and the future tense, complete Angela's letter to her friend:

понедељак: планинарење по Златибору
уторак: обилазак локалних манастира
среда: одлазак у Ужице

четвртак:	прављење традиционалног ручка
петак:	помагање око радова у пољу
субота:	идемо на пецање
недеља:	повратак у Београд

Драги Ана и Данило,

Ми смо у Сирогојну. Јако нам је лепо овде. Имамо добре домаћине и већ смо испланирали са њима шта ћемо радити током целе недеље. У понедељак _____ . У уторак _____ . А онда _____ у среду. једва чекам, јер тамо још нисмо били. У четвртак _____ . У петак _____ . Имају толико посла да осећамо да морамо да помогнемо. А у суботу, релаксација! _____ . У недељу _____ . Онда се видимо.

Топли поздрави од
Анђеле и Џона

🎧 Reading passage 1 (Audio 2: 3)

Kulturni život u Beogradu (12)

Why do Dejan and Ben decide to have a rest today? What is Dejan going to try to do during the day? What will Ben be doing? Who is he going to try to telephone?

Dejan i Ben su rešili da se danas malo odmore. Imali su previše intenzivan program ovih dana i pravo je vreme da malo srede utiske. Uveče će samo da odu u Kinoteku da pogledaju film *Maratonci trče počasni krug* o legendarnoj porodici Topalović.

Tokom dana Dejan će da pokuša da organizuje putovanje na Frušku goru. Zvaće svoje prijatelje koji imaju kuću tamo. Mora da proveri da li će oni biti tamo u vreme kad oni žele da im dođu u posetu. Ben će da piše mejlove prijateljima i svojoj redakciji. Moraće da pročita sve što je zapisao do sada i da napiše prvi članak o kulturnom životu u Beogradu. Takođe će pokušati da pozove svoje roditelje telefonom ako stigne. Nije im se javio baš dugo. Sigurno će ih zanimati da čuju kako se Ben snalazi u Srbiji.

Vocabulary

kinoteka	cinema¹
odmoriti se (pf.)	to rest
počasni krug	lap of honour
poseta	visit
previše	too, excessively
proveriti (pf.)	to check
redakcija	editorial office, board
rešiti (pf.)	to decide
srediti (pf.)	arrange, sort out
trčati (imp. **trčim**)	to run

1 Archive, usually showing old or minority interest films.

Exercise 4

(a) There are a few odd things in Dejan's email to his friend. Pick out the wrong words and try to rewrite the letter:

Dragi Nikola,
U poseti mi je jedan prijatelj iz Nemačke. Zove se Ben i po zanimanju je kelner. Želim da ga povedem na Frušku goru i nadam se da ćemo moći da ostanemo kod vas nekoliko dana. Mog prijatelja ne zanima ništa što mu ja pokazujem ovde u Beogradu. Umetnost ne voli, kultura mu je dosadna. Samo hoće da ga vodim u kafanu da pije pivo. Jako mu se sviđa domaće pivo. Zato želim da ga izvedem iz grada u prirodu na čist vazduh. Možda će to da mu se dopadne.
Kako ste vi? Kako su ti žena i deca?
Nada i ja smo dobro, mada jedva čekamo da se ovaj moj prijatelj vrati svojoj kući.

Pozdrav, tvoj Dejan

dopasti (pf. **dopadnem**; **dopadati**)   to please, appeal to
(cf. **sviđati**, **svideti**)

(b)†Translate into Serbian:

I must make plans for the holiday. I want to travel to Serbia at the beginning of June. I shall visit friends in Belgrade. I'll stay a few days with them. Then I'll go to the mountains, to Tara, to visit my aunt. I think I'll travel by train to Užice. And then I'll take a bus. I like travelling by train because you can see a lot through the window. On Tara I'll enjoy good food, fresh air and the hospitality of people. Tara is a beautiful mountain and I go there every year. This year I'll stay only one week. Then I'll go to Kotor. I'll reserve a private room beside the sea. My friends will already be there.

to visit   **posetiti**   to enjoy   **uživati u** + loc.

🎧 Dialogue 3 (Audio 2: 4)

Екипа (12)

Where does Filip take Sanja? Are there a lot of people? Do Filip and Sanja play musical instruments themselves?

Филип је позвао Сању на концерт своје омиљене групе. Када су се приближили Сава центру испред је била страшна гужва.

– Мислим да ће бити најбоље да се држимо за руку. Не желим да те изгубим у овој гужви – рекао је Филип.
– Важи. Мало се бојим: никада нисам видјела толико много свијета – рекла је Сања.
– Не бој се, само ме чврсто држи! Група је веома популарна и млад свет у Београду је жељан добре свирке, разоноде и уживања!
– Разумијем. Слично је и у Босни. Одмах послије рата су сви почели да свирају музику из Србије због њене необичне енергије.
– Музика је ипак неки универзални језик, без обзира на политику, зар не?
– Слажем се. Али смо још увијек јако поносни и на своје домаће групе! Да ли ти свираш?
– Свирам гитару, али не баш бриљантно! Био сам у групи у средњој школи. А ти?
– Свирам клавир и то веома волим. Нажалост нема клавира код нашег рођака.
– Наћи ћемо начин да поново свираш. Мислим да има један клавир код Маје. Али, сада, улазимо у салу, чврсто ме држи!

Vocabulary

без обзира на (+ acc.)	without regard to, regardless of	бо̲јати се (imp. бо̲јим се)	to be afraid
група	group (musical)	гужва	crowd
држати (imp. др̲жим)	to hold	жељан	eager for
		за ру̲ку	by the hand
ја̲ко	very	кла̲вир	piano
млад	young	не бо̲ј се	don't be afraid
никад(а)	never	о̲миљен	favourite
по̲носан	proud	приближити	to approach,
ра̲зонода	entertainment	се (pf.)	draw near
рат	war	само	only
свирати (imp.)	to play (music)	свирка	playing, music
слично	like, similarly	сре̲дња шко̲ла	secondary school
стра̲шан	terrible	ужи̲вање	enjoyment
у̲ћи (pf. у̲ђем)	to enter	чврсто	firmly
Сава центар	a large building for concerts, conferences etc. in Belgrade		

13 Muzika
Music

In this unit we will look at:

- ordinal numbers: first, second etc.
- periods of time
- dates
- days of the week
- vocabulary building: time

Dialogue 1

What kind of music did the Browns hear with Marija and Miloš?
*What is a **gusle**? What is Šumadija tea?Which Serbian musicians are*
particularly popular abroad?

Увече тога дана, после напорног рада, Марија и Милош су
одвели Џона и Анђелу на сеоско посело. Њихови гости су
уживали у приредби народне и традиционалне музике.

Марија:	Људи у овим крајевима јако воле музику и врло су талентовани. Постоји огроман број народних песама: прву групу чине песме, које су певале углавном жене док су радиле у пољима и у кући.
Милош:	Да, а као што знате, култура Балкана је позната у свету по другој групи народних песама: по епским песмама, које су певали певачи уз гусле.
Анђела:	Шта су то гусле?
Милош:	Занимљив старински инструмент са једном жицом. Мелодија није толико важна: битна је прича.
Марија:	Затим постоји и прекрасна црквена музика, коју сада обнављају разне групе и хорови.

Анђела:	Чули смо и за популарну народну музику, такозване "народњаке".
Милош:	Да тога има доста, може се видети на телевизији или чути на радију. Али поново се јавило интересовање за стару и традиционалну музику. Нарочито је позната шумадијска музика и трубачки сабор у Гучи.
Џон:	Да, трубачи су постали популарни у целом свету, нарочито после Кустуричиних филмова.
Милош:	Е, а да не заборавимо старе градске песме. То је омиљена музика мог зета из Војводине.
Марија:	Да, староградске песме су повезане углавном са Београдом и Војводином. Певале су се нарочито почетком двадесетог века, али и дан данас их по старим кафанама певају и свирају тамбураши оркестри. Али, довољно смо причали, морате да слушате док имате прилику.
Џон:	У праву си!

Tamburaški orkestar

Vocabulary

битан, -тна	essential	богат	rich
градски	urban, town	гусле	single-stringed lute
догађај	event, happening	епски	epic
женски	women's	жица	string, wire
заборавити (imp.)	to forget	лети	in summer
напоран, -рна	arduous	можда	perhaps
обнављати (imp.)	to renew	народњак	modern 'folk-style' song
певати (imp.)	to sing	огроман	enormous
песма	song, poem	певач	singer
посело	gathering (village)	плодан	fertile
приредба	performance	прилика	opportunity
сабор	assembly	прича	story
тамбурица	traditional mandolin	старински	ancient, old-fashioned
хор	choir	труба	trumpet
		црквени	church (adj.)

Language points 1

Ordinal numbers

These are very straightforward as all are regular definite adjectives. Most ordinal numbers are formed by adding **-i** (m.), **-a** (f.), **-o** (n.) to the cardinal, while a few forms need to be learned:

1st	**prvi, prva, prvo**
2nd	**drugi, druga, drugo**
3rd	**treći, treća, treće**
4th	**četvrti, četvrta, četvrto**
5th	**peti, peta, peto**
11th	**jedanaesti, jedanaesta, jedanaesto**
20th	**dvadeseti, dvadeseta, dvadeseto**
21st	**dvadeset prvi, prva, prvo**
99th	**devedeset deveti, deveta, deveto**
100th	**stoti, stota, stoto**
200th	**dvestoti, dvestota, dvestoto**
999th	**devetsto devedeset deveti, deveta, deveto**

Note: In compound numbers only the last element is declined:

Stigli smo na more dvadeset petog avgusta.
We arrived at the coast on the twenty fifth of August.

Dialogue 2 (Audio 2: 5)

Two tourists meet in a travel agent's in Podgorica.

A: Да ли сте први пут у Подгорици?
B: Јесам, а ви?
A: Далеко од тога! Ово ми је пети пут!
B: Већ трећи пут сам у Црној Гори, али раније нисам била у Подгорици.
A: А ја долазим сваке године. Мора да ми је ово десети пут да сам у Црној Гори!

Exercise 1

(a) Mark the following statements with **ТАЧНО** (**Т**) or **НЕТАЧНО** (**Н**):

1 Марија и Милош су одвели Џона и Анђелу на концерт.   Т/Н
2 Култура Балкана је позната у свету по епским песмама.   Т/Н
3 Гусларска музика се може чути на Косову.   Т/Н
4 Народњаци се могу често чути на радију.   Т/Н
5 Анђела и Џон сигурно иду на сабор у Гучи.   Т/Н
6 Домаћи трубачи су постали популарни широм света након Кустуричиних филмова.   Т/Н
7 Староградске песме су омиљена музика Милоша и Марије.   Т/Н
8 Староградске песме свирају по кафанама тамбурашки оркестри.   Т/Н

(b)†Check how much you have remembered of Dialogue 1. Complete the following sentences with the correct verb:

1 Марија и Милош су _____ напорно цео дан.
2 Упркос умору, они су _____ Џона и Анђелу на сеоско посело.

3 Људи у Србији _____ музику и врло су талентовани.

4 У нашој народној традицији _____ огроман број народних песама.

5 Код гусларске музике оно што је _____ је прича.

6 Можда ћете _____ прилику да слушате гусларе у Црној Гори.

7 Црквену музику сада _____ разне групе и хорови.

8 _____ смо и за популарну народну музику, такозване "народњаке".

9 Сабор у Гучи не смете да _____ !

10 Сабор се _____ увек крајем августа и непоновљив је догађај.

11 Ту музику _____ и _____ тамбурашки оркестри.

упркос + loc.   in spite of

(c)[†] Translate the following sentences into Serbian:

1 The room is on the second floor.
2 The post office is round the first corner on the left.
3 This is his[1] fifth book.
4 The bathroom is the third door on the right.
5 Is this your[1] first dinner in the 'Dalmatia' restaurant?

1 Use dative of pronoun

(d) Arrange the following in order of size:

gitara, gusle, klavir, violina, bubanj 'drum', **tamburica, truba**

Language points 2

Vocabulary building

Time 1

Periods of time: **дан** 'day'; **сат** 'hour' (irreg. gen. pl. **сати**); **недеља** 'week'; **месец** 'month' (irreg. gen. pl. **месеци**); **година** 'year'.

Један дан има двадесет четири сата, једна недеља има седам
дана, један месец има четири недеље, једна година има дванаест
месеци или триста шесдесет пет дана.

Dates

Note: The names of the days of the week and months are not
capitalized.

Days of the week (Sunday is counted as the first day):

неде̲ља	Sunday	**четв̲ртак**	Thursday
поне̲дељак	Monday	**петак**	Friday
у̲торак	Tuesday	**су̲бота**	Saturday
среда	Wednesday		

Months:

**ја̲нуар фе̲бруар март април мај јуни,
јули а̲вгуст се̲птембар о̲ктобар но̲вембар де̲цембар**

Који је данас датум?
What is the date today?

Данас је понедељак први јануар.
Today is Monday, 1 January.

Seasons:

Про̲леће spring   **лето** summer   **јесен** autumn   **зима** winter

Expressions of time

'On Monday' etc. is expressed by **у** + accusative: **у понедељак,
у среду**. Other dates on which an event occurs are expressed by
the genitive:

Стигли смо че̲твртог августа.
We arrived on 4th August.

Мојој ћерки је рођендан другог септембра.
My daughter's birthday is 2nd September.

Other expressions of time follow a similar pattern:

Следећег дана су устали врло рано.
They got up very early (on) the next day.

Тог месеца сам заиста заузет.
I'm really busy that month.

Те године ће бити велика прослава.
There will be a great celebration that year.

Duration of time is generally expressed by the accusative:

Покушавам да те добијем телефоном цео дан.
I've been trying to get you on the phone all day.

Провешћемо месец дана у Београду.
We shall spend a month in Belgrade.

Они су становали годину дана у улици до наше, а нисмо их упознали.
They lived in the next street to ours for a year, but we didn't meet them.

Habitual events, occurring on specific days of the week, are expressed by the instrumental:

Суботом увек некуда идемо у шетњу.
We always go somewhere for a walk on Saturdays.

Обично иду у клуб уторком.
They usually go to the club on Tuesdays.

Exercise 2

(a) Write out the dates in full in words:

1 Ići ćemo u Australiju 8.1.2005.
2 On je rođen 5.12.1973.
3 Putujemo 3.6.
4 Novosadski festival *Exit* počinje 1.7.
5 Bio sam na tom koncertu 1988. godine.

(b)[†] Put the nouns in brackets into the correct form. Add the preposition 'у' where appropriate:

1 Идем на часове клавира _____ . (петак)
2 Путујемо у Котор _____ . (петак)
3 Били смо на концерту _____ . (прошли петак)
4 Заборавио сам да дођем _____ . (среда)
5 Обично свирамо заједно _____ . (среда)
6 Видимо се _____ . (следећа среда)

(c)† Translate the following sentences into Serbian:

1 I don't go to work on Sundays.
2 What are you doing this weekend?
3 My father plays the trumpet every Wednesday.
4 The concert is on Monday evening.
5 He has been watching TV all day.

(d) Below is part of the programme of the popular EXIT Music
Festival which takes place every year in Novi Sad. Look at the
table which gives details of musicians/bands playing on the
Balkan Fusion Stage and answer the questions:

EXIT 01–04 jul 2004	ČETVRTAK 01 JUL 2004	PETAK 02 JUL 2004	SUBOTA 03 JUL 2004

Balkan
Fusion
Stage
	• Zvonko
	  Bogdan
		• Vlatko
		  Stefanovski
		  (Makedonija)
			• Lajko Felix

	• Društvo
	  skrivenih
	  talenata
		• Amajlija	• Rambo
			  Amadeus

	• Urban
	  (Hrvatska)
		• Orthodox Celts	• Kanda Kodža
			  i Nebojša

1 Kada će svirati Zvonko Bogdan?
2 Odakle je grupa koja se zove Urban?
3 Kada svira Vlatko Stefanovski?
4 Kada nastupaju Kanda Kodža i Nebojša?
5 Ko nastupa pre njih?

nastupati   perform, come on stage

🎧 Reading passage 1 (Audio 2: 6)

Kulturni život u Beogradu (13)

Why does Dejan telephone Ben? Where will the concert take place?
How long has Ben been in Belgrade? How much longer can he stay?

Ben je u šetnji gradom. Dejan mu se javio telefonom da ga obavesti da će petnaestog jula biti jedan lep kamerni koncert. Koncert će se održati u izložbenim prostorijama Srpske Akademije nauka i umetnosti i počeće u pola osam. Ben je morao da potvrdi da to znači sedam i trideset, za svaki slučaj, i odgovorio da će vrlo rado da dođe. Čuo je da se moderno opremljena, svetla izložbena sala nalazi na ćošku Knez Mihailove i ulice Vuka Karadžića. U tim prostorijama se redovno održavaju izložbe. Taj se koncert daje u utorak, dok će u subotu da svira jedna izuzetno talentovana mlada violinistkinja iz Japana. Ben počinje da razmišlja koliko još može da vidi i čuje: u Beogradu je već desetak dana, ima još pet dana na raspolaganju, a želi da provede i par dana na Fruškoj gori. Njegov kalendar je već prilično popunjen.

Vocabulary

desetak	roughly ten	**Fruška gora**	hilly region near
izložba	exhibition		Novi Sad
izložbeni	exhibition (adj.)	**kalendar**	diary
kamerni	chamber	**na raspolaganju**	at one's disposal
obavestiti (pf.)	to inform	**održavati** (imp.)	to be held, put
opremljen	equipped		on (**održati** pf.)
počinjati	to begin	**potvrditi** (pf.)	to confirm
(imp.)	(**početi** pf.)	**provesti**	to spend (time)
razmišljati	to reflect,	(**provedem** pf.)	
(imp.)	consider		

Srpska akademija nauka i umetnosti (SANU)
Serbian Academy of Sciences and Arts

Exercise 3

(a)[†] Fill the gaps in the following dialogue with the appropriate expression of time:

3 sata, 15. jula, za mesec dana, 100 godina, pre dve nedelje

A: Zdravo. Nismo se videli _____ . Šta radiš u ovom kilometarskom redu?
B: Hoću da kupim karte za koncert Zvonka Bogdana. Čekam u redu već _____ .
A: A kad je koncert?
B: _____ . Znači tek _____ . Ali vidiš, veliko je interesovanje. Bojim se da će sve karte biti rasprodate dok ja dođem na red.

A: Mislim da je jedan moj prijatelj karte za isti koncert kupio
    preko interneta _____ .
B: Stvarno!? Nisam znao da je to m<u>og</u>uće.
A: U slučaju da ne nađeš karte, javi mi se, čini mi se da on
    ima kartu viška.

U ovom kilometarskom redu		in this kilometre-long queue	
tek	only, just	**r<u>a</u>sprodat**	sold out
doći na red	to be someone's turn	**karta viška**	an extra ticket

(b) Now you want to buy tickets for a concert, as a present for a friend:
   🎧 **(Audio 2: 7)**

   Bilet servis na Trgu Republike

PRODAVAC: Dobro jutro.
VI: *I want to buy tickets for the concert at Kolarac on 21
           May.*
PRODAVAC: Koncert Simfonijskog orkestra RTSa?
VI: *Yes. Are the tickets sold out?*
PRODAVAC: Ne, još nisu, ali interesovanje je zaista veliko. Prodali
           smo skoro sve karte preko interneta. Koliko karata
           želite?
VI: *Two tickets. I have a question. I want to give these
           tickets as a present. In case my friends have already
           bought them, can I return them?*
PRODAVAC: Da, vratite ih pre koncerta i dobićete novac nazad.
VI: *Thank you. How much are the tickets?*
PRODAVAC: Ostale su nam samo karte od 400 dinara. Jeftine karte
           su rasprodate. Dakle, 800 dinara.
VI: *I'll take them. Here you are and thank you.*

Language points 3

Vocabulary building

Time 2

јутро,	morning	**подне**	noon
пре подне		**после подне**	afternoon
вече	evening	**ноћ**	night
поноћ	midnight		

There is also a useful series of adverbs:

јутрос	this morning	**ноћас**	tonight
вечерас	this evening	**синоћ**	last night

Колико је сати?	What time is it?
Сада је један сат.	It's now one o'clock.
два сата	two o'clock
пет сати (gen. pl.)	five o'clock

девет сати и пет минута
five past nine
десет и петнаест
quarter past ten

**једанаест и тридесет/
    пола дванаест**[1]
half past eleven

1 Care must be taken by those accustomed to English 'half twelve': translated into Serbian this would mean 11.30.

Колико је тачно сати?
Have you got the right time?

У колико сати стиже воз?
What time does the train arrive?

Тачно у четири.
At exactly four o'clock.

двадесет пет до један	25 to 1 (12:35)
петнаест до два	quarter to 2 (13:45)
десет до три	10 to 3 (14:50)

Exercise 4

(a) Write out the times in the following passage in full.

Radnim danom Bojan ustaje jako rano: u 5.30. Na brzinu se umiva i brije. Oblači se. U 6 doručkuje. Malo jede i izlazi iz kuće u 6.20. Ima tačno 13 minuta hoda do autobuske stanice. Autobus polazi u 6.35. Vožnja traje oko 17 minuta, zavisno od gužve na putevima. Ako se žuri i ni s kim usput ne razgovara, Bojan stiže na posao u 6.58. Vozi se liftom do kancelarije na 4-om spratu, veša kaput iza vrata i u 7.03 već sedi za radnim stolom. Radi do 16.00 i onda se vraća kući. Kod kuće je negde oko 16.30.

radni dan	working day	**na brzinu**	in haste
umivati se	to wash	**brijati se**	to shave
oblačiti se	to dress	**doručkovati**	to have breakfast
hod	walk	**zavisno od**	depending on
gužva	crowd	**žuriti se**	to hurry
usput	on the way	**kancelarija**	office
vešati	to hang	**kaput**	coat
radni sto	desk		

(b) Look at these answers and write questions about Bojan's day:

1 U koliko _____ ?
  U 5:30.

2 Kada _____ ?
  U 6:20.

3 Koliko _____ ?
  13 minuta.

4 U koliko _____ ?
  U 6:58.

5 Na kom spratu _____ ?
  Na četvrtom spratu.

6 Do kada _____ ?
  Do 16:00.

(c) Translate the text about Bojan's day into English.

(d) Write an account of your own daily routine.

◯ Dialogue 3 (Audio 2: 8)

Екипа (13)

What time is it when Filip and Sanja come out of the concert? What time does Filip say Sanja will be home? How long have Sanja and Dado been in Belgrade? Where did they live before that? What is happening at Maja's flat the next evening?

После концерта, Филип предлаже да оду негде на пиће.

– Не знам, рекла је Сања. – Већ је прилично касно.
– Тек је пола једанаест – рекао је Филип. – Нећемо се дуго задржавати. Знам једно супер место недалеко од твоје куће.
– Важи, али заиста кратко.
– Не брини, вратићеш се кући до поноћи. Петком се сме мало дуже остати. Мораш да упознаш Београд и по ноћи!
– Хвала ти, али нема потребе да се много трудиш око мене. Ништа ми не фали.
– Осим клавира. Добро, нећу да претерујем, али кад кажем да ће ми бити задовољство да ти покажем свој град, то озбиљно мислим. Ваљда ти је јасно да ми се много свиђаш?
– Хвала ти на пажњи, Филипе. Али не знам да ли сам спремна за везу.
– Полако, само сам хтео да кажем да ми је лепо са тобом и желим да те поново видим. Сутра ће бити журка код Маје и волео бих да пођеш са мном. Можеш тамо да погледаш клавир и да се договориш са Мајом.
– Хвала. Морам да видим шта ради Дадо.
– Добро, разумем да мораш да водиш рачуна и о њему, али треба мало да мислиш и на себе!
– У реду, мислићу! Али сада заиста морам да идем.

Vocabulary

бринути (imp. **бринем**)	to worry		
водити рачуна о некоме/ нечему (imp.)	to take account of someone /something		
вратити се (pf.)	to return	**договорити се** (pf.)	to make an arrangement
дуже	longer		
журка	party	**задржавати се** (imp.)	to stay, be held up
однос	relationship	**озбиљно**	seriously
пажња	attention, care	**петком**	on Fridays
поноћ (f.)	midnight	**потреба**	need
предложити (pf.)	to propose, suggest	**претеривати** (imp. **претерујем**)	to exaggerate
смети (imp.)	to dare, to be allowed	**тек**	only
		фалити (imp.)	to be lacking

14 Pakovanje

Packing

In this unit we will look at:

- the comparative of adjectives
- the comparative of adverbs
- structures with the comparative
- the superlative
- vocabulary building: clothes, colours

Dialogue 1

Шта нам треба за пут?

What do we need for the journey?

What does Angela want to see on the way to Podgorica? Why does Nemanja say there is no need to pack jeans? Is Angela going to wear trousers for the journey? What is John going to wear on his feet?

Следећег дана се Маријин нећак Немања понудио да вози Џона и Анђелу даље својим колима.

Немања: Ионако морам да будем у Подгорици за три дана. Можемо да свратимо негде успут. Шта желите да видите?

Анђела: Много бих волела да видим један од старих манастира.

Немања: Договорено! Идемо после подне у Нови Пазар, одатле ћемо лако моћи да одемо до Сопоћана. То је најближи, а уједно и један од најлепших наших манастира.

Џон:	Ако си заиста сигуран да имаш времена, брзо ћемо се спаковати.
Анђела:	Панталоне су згодне за пут, али ја ћу ипак да носим своју тегет сукњу од тексаса која се не гужва, и уз њу плаву мајицу.
Џон:	Што да не! Она ти баш лепо стоји. А ја ћу да обучем сиве кратке панталоне и белу кошуљу на црвене штрафте.
Немања:	То се добро слаже. Али, шорц није баш препоручено за посету манастиру, из учтивости. А ни у граду где је становништво претежно муслиманско, као што је то случај у Новом Пазару.
Џон:	Видиш, о томе уопште нисам размишљао. У праву си.
Анђела:	Које ћеш ципеле да обујеш, Џоне? Ја ћу сандале: оне су најудобније.
Џон:	И ја ћу носити сандале. Шта мислиш, Немања, хоће ли да буде свежије увече?
Немања:	Може да буде свежије у ово доба године, па је паметно да имате при руци џемпере, за сваки случај.
Анђела:	Док смо у Новом Пазару, свратићу до апотеке: треба нам неколико стварчица – паста за зубе, крема за сунчање, и евентуално нека средства против главобоље.
Немања:	Нема проблема. Враћам се по вас у два сата.
Анђела:	Важи.

Vocabulary

главобоља	headache	гужвати се (imp.)	to crush
даље (comparative)	further	евентуално	possibly
за сваки случај	just in case	заправо	in fact
зуб	tooth	ионако	anyway
кошуља	shirt	мајица	T-shirt
муслимански	Muslim	најближи	nearest
нећак	nephew	обути (pf. обујем)	to put on/
обући	to put on		wear shoes
(pf. обучем)	clothes	паковати се	to pack
паметан, -тна	clever, sensible	(imp. пакујем се,	
панталоне	trousers, slacks	спаковати се)	
паста за зубе	toothpaste	плав	blue

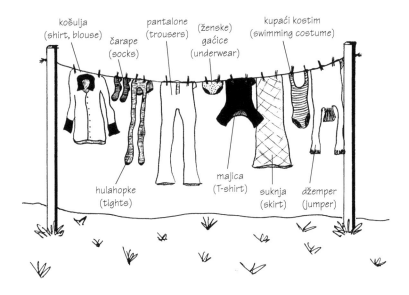

košulja
(shirt, blouse)
čarape
(socks)
pantalone
(trousers)
(ženske)
gaćice
(underwear)
kupaći kostim
(swimming costume)

hulahopke
(tights)
majica
(T-shirt)
suknja
(skirt)
džemper
(jumper)

по̀нудити се (pf.)	to offer oneself	при руци	to hand
производити (imp.)	to produce	приличан	considerable
		против (+ gen.)	against
сив	grey	свратити (pf.)	to visit, call in
средство	means (here 'medicine')	случај	case
		становништво	population
		стварчица	little thing
сукња	skirt	сунчање	sunbathing
тегет	navy blue	тексас	denim
у сваком случају	in any case	уједно	at the same time
уопште	in general (with neg. verb 'at all')	учтивост	politeness
		ципеле	shoes
џемпер	jumper	шорц	shorts

Language points 1

Comparative adjectives

Most comparatives are formed by the addition of the endings **-iji**, **-ija**, **-ije** etc. to the indefinite adjective:

star	st**a**riji, starija, starije
poznat	pozn**a**tiji, poznatija, poznatije
gladan	gl**a**dniji, gladnija, gladnije

Adjectives ending in **-o** derived from **-l** have these endings added to the **-l** (which we have seen returns in oblique cases):

mio 'dear'	m**i**liji, milija, milije
veseo	ves**e**liji, veselija, veselije

Other adjectives have the suffix **-ji**, although this is not always obvious: the exact form depends on the final consonant of the indefinite masculine – as we know, certain combinations of letters result in regular consonant changes. Do not be too alarmed, you will soon learn those comparatives which are in frequent use.

Note: For a complete list of consonant changes, see 'Grammar summary', section 6 (p. 306).

jak	'strong'	**k + j**:	**ć**:	jaći
drag	'dear'	**g + j**:	**ž**:	draži
tih	'quiet'	**h + j**:	**š**:	tiši
ljut	'angry'	**t + j**:	**ć**:	ljući
tvrd	'hard'	**d + j**:	**đ**:	tvrđi

If the adjective stem ends in **p**, **b** or **v**, an **l** is often inserted after this consonant:

skup	'expensive'	skuplji
grub	'coarse'	grublji

But:

lep	lepši

Comparative adjectives are declined like regular definite adjectives.

Here are some examples:

Ko je stariji – Ivan ili Nikola?
Who is older – Ivan or Nikola?

Nikola je stariji, iako je Ivan viši.
Nikola is older, although Ivan is taller.

Da li je vaša nova kuća no**vija?**
Is your new house newer?

Nije, ali je udobnija i bliža poslu.
No, but it's more comfortable and closer to work.

I mi sada stanujemo u mirnijoj ulici. Više volim manja mesta.
We live in a quieter street now as well. I prefer smaller towns.

Da li imate vesti od svog mlađeg brata? Imam, izgleda da mu je bolje: na planini je vazduh sv<u>e</u>žiji i č<u>i</u>stiji nego u ravn<u>i</u>ci.
Have you any news of your younger brother? Yes, he seems to be better: the air in the mountains is fresher and cleaner than in the plain.

Dajte mi flašu tog slađeg vina; skuplje je, ali mi se čini ukusnije. Svakako ima lepšu boju!
Give me a bottle of that sweeter wine; it's more expensive, but it seems tastier. lt's certainly a nicer colour!

Exercise 1

(a) Answer the following questions:

1 Шта је Немања понудио Брауновима и зашто?
2 Шта Анђела жели да види?
3 Шта ће Анђела да обуче?
4 Шта Џон планира да обуче и зашто на крају мења план?
5 Шта треба да имају при руци и зашто?
6 Које ципеле ће Анђела да обуче? А Џон?
7 Где ће Анђела да сврати у Новом Пазару?
8 Кад ће Немања да дође по њих?

(b)[†] Supply the correct form of the comparative:

1 Више волим да носим _____(дуг) сукње.
2 Она увек купује _____(скуп) ствари.
3 Ово је једна од _____(познат) робних кућа у Београду.
4 Ове панталоне су мало _____(стар) и нису више у моди.
5 Та бела мајица је лепа, али је ова црна _____(леп) и _____(нов).
6 Зашто не носиш мало _____(весео) боје?
7 Победили су јер су били _____(паметан).
8 Ово вино има добар укус, али чини ми се да је ово _____(укусан)
9 Шта ради твоја _____(млад) сестра?

(c)[†]Use one of the expressions below to complete the sentences:

нема потребе   није преоручљиво ('advisable')
у међувремену   имати на уму
имати при руци ('to have to hand')

1 Када је јако вруће _____ ићи без креме за сунчање.
2 _____ да се облачите топлије, напољу је баш
  вруће.
3 Ви се одморите, а ја ћу _____ да спремим ручак.
4 Овде у планинама зна да буде свежије и зато увек
  треба _____ џемпер.
5 Треба _____ да имамо доста ствари и да зато треба
  да спакујемо мање одеће, а више хране.

Language points 2

Comparison of adjectives ending in
-ак, -ек, -ок

Most adjectives with these endings drop the final syllable and form
the comparative by the addition of **-ји** to the resulting stem:

близак	'near'	**ближи**
кратак	'short'	**краћи**
далек	'far'	**даљи**
дубок	'deep'	**дубљи**
редак	'rare'	**ређи**
висок	'tall, high'	**виши**

Exercise 2[†]

Supply the correct form of the comparative:

1 Они су ми _____ (блиски) пријатељи. Али их
  _____ (ретко) виђам, нажалост.
2 То су моји _____ (далек) рођаци.
3 Мој и његов отац раде заједно, али је његов отац на
  _____ (висок) позицији у компанији.
4 Не можеш очекивати пуно само на основу _____
  (кратко) познанства.
5 Она жели _____ (дубок) пријатељство са неким.

na osnovu + gen.   'on the basis of'

Language points 3

Comparison of adverbs

Where the neuter singular of an adjective is used as the adverb, the neuter singular of the comparative is similarly used:

(jako)	jaче	more strongly
(лако)	лакше	more easily
(близу)	ближе	more closely
(драго)	драже	more dearly
(скупо)	скупље	more expensively
(тешко)	теже	with more difficulty
(радо)	радије	more gladly

Irregular comparatives

Several common adjectives and adverbs have quite irregular comparative forms:

добар	бољи
зао, лош 'bad'	гори
велик	већи
мален	мањи
много	више
мало	мање

| Jесте ли научили све нове речи? | Мање више. |
| Have you learned all the new words? | More or less. |

Superlative

The superlative is formed by the addition of the prefix **нaj-** to the comparative:

најстарији, најближи, најбоље, највише, најмање etc.

Exercise 3[†]

(a) Fill in the gaps with the appropriate adverb from the list below:

лакше ближе боље скупље радије теже

1 Сада немам никаквих проблема на послу. Било ми је много _____ у старој фирми.
2 И мада сви мисле да је овде јефтино, овде је ипак _____ него на мору.
3 _____ ћу да понесем и џемпер него да ми после буде хладно.
4 Мој нови стан се налази _____ послу.
5 Зар ти није _____ да одеш у продавницу сада, а не после?
6 Ова кошуља иде _____ уз те панталоне.

(b) Supply the comparative or superlative as appropriate:

1 Он је _____ (висок) човек на свету.
2 Те панталоне су ти много _____ (леп).
3 Та књига је занимљива, али је ова много _____ (занимљива).
4 Она је моја _____ (добар) пријатељица.
5 Ове ципеле су _____ (удобне) које имам.

Dialogue 2 (Audio 2: 9)

Two sisters are arguing about what to take on holiday.

A: Nećeš valjda vući sve ovo sa sobom!
B: Što? Ko mi brani?
A: Previše je! A osim toga, sve je samo crno ili belo!
B: A ti ćeš sada da sudiš o mom ukusu, je li?
A: Smiri se! Samo kažem, da je malo tužno bez ijedne druge boje!
B: Hvala na brizi. Ti gledaj svoja posla. Nosi sve dugine boje, ako ti je volja. A mene pusti na miru!

Vocabulary

vući (pf. **vučem**)	to drag	**braniti** (imp.)	to forbid
previše	too much	**osim toga**	besides
suditi (imp)	to judge	**ukus**	taste
smiriti se (pf.)	to calm down	**tužno**	sad
ijedan	a single (one)	**briga**	concern
gledati svoja	to mind one's	**duga**	rainbow
posla	own business	**ako ti je volja**	if you wish
pustiti na miru	to leave alone		

Language points 4

Vocabulary building

Colours

Crn black (also used for red wine), **beo, bela** white, **siv** grey, **smeđ** brown, **žut** yellow, **zelen** green, **svetlo plav** light blue, **modar** deep blue, **teget** navy blue, **ljubičast** mauve, **crven** red, **roza** pink, **ružičast** pinkish, **žućkast** yellowish, **sivkast** greyish.

Exercise 4†

Prevedite na srpski. 'Translate into Serbian.'

We are going on holiday on Saturday, the day after tomorrow! We don't want to carry much, so we'll take only the most essential[1] things. I have one small suitcase and one large bag. I shall take trousers and a jumper, because it is sometimes cool in the evening, three dresses, a skirt, two T-shirts, two blouses, shoes, stockings and underwear. My husband will take trousers, five shirts, three T-shirts, shorts and two jumpers. He can carry the swimming costumes and towels in his suitcase.

1 For 'essential', use 'necessary' **potreban, -bna**.

kofer	suitcase	**haljina**	dress
bluza	blouse	**čarape**	stockings
donje rublje	underwear	**kupaći kostim**	swimming costume
peškir	towel		

Language points 5

Comparison to an object or phrase

When two objects are compared the preposition **od** + genitive is generally used:

Moj brat je stariji od tebe.
My brother is older than you.

Avion je skuplji od voza.
The plane is more expensive than the train.

Tvoj sin je viši od tvog muža, zar ne?
Your son is taller than your husband, isn't he?

But when the comparison involves a whole phrase the conjunction
nego must be used:

Kasnije je nego što sam mislila.
It's later than I thought (it was).

Avionom se putuje brže nego vozom.
It's quicker to travel by plane than (it is to travel) by train.

Note: **nego** may also be used instead of **od** + genitive:

On je stariji nego ti.
Tvoj sin je viši nego tvoj muž.

Language in action

Structures with the comparative

Note the following structures:

sve + comparative 'more and more, increasingly':

Svakim danom *sve bolje* vladate našim jezikom.
You speak our language *better and better* with each day.

Moram da priznam da *sve ređe* pišem pisma.
I must confess that I write letters *increasingly rarely*.

Vreme *sve brže* prolazi!
Time passes *increasingly quickly*!

što + comparative 'as ... as possible':

Dođite nam opet *što pre!*
Come again *as soon as you can*!

Sedi *što bliže meni!*
Sit *as near me as possible*!

Rekao je da će da piše *što češće*.
He said that he would write *as often as possible*.

Reading passage 1 (Audio 2: 10)

Kulturni život u Beogradu (14)

Had Ben read any Serbian writers before his trip? Do people in Serbia read a lot? Why is Ben surprised? Does one style of writing predominate?

Dejan je pozvao Bena u Društvo književnika na ukusan ručak i na razgovor sa nekim od najpoznatijih savremenih pisaca. Benu je ovo bilo izvanredno zanimljivo: on je strastven čitalac i pre puta je pročitao sve što je mogao da pronađe od savremenih srpskih pisaca u prevodu. Iznenadio se kada je tokom razgovora sa piscima čuo da ima veliki broj malih privatnih izdavača u Srbiji, i da se knjige kupuju i čitaju u prilično velikim brojevima, s obzirom na uglavnom skromne plate i priličan broj nezaposlenih. Stekao je utisak da je čitanje ozbiljnih književnih dela popularnija aktivnost u Srbiji i Crnoj Gori nego u Velikoj Britaniji, iako su ga pisci upozorili da su tiraži obično mnogo manji. Svejedno, bilo je očigledno da su ovi pisci poznati i uglavnom ugledni članovi društva, dok su neki od njih prave medijske zvezde! Što se tiče stilova i ukusa, bilo je tu svega i svačega na tapetu: od tradicionalnijih pristupa do najavangardnijih, pogotovo kod najmlađih.

Vocabulary

čitalac	reader	**član**	member
društvo	society	**izdavač**	publisher
iznenaditi se (pf.)	to be surprised	**književnik**	author
na tapetu	on the agenda	**nezaposlen**	unemployed
pisac	writer	**plata**	pay
pre (+ gen.)	before	**prevod**	translation
pristup	approach	**pronaći**	to find
s obzirom na	with regard to, given	(pf. **pronađem**)	
		steći	to achieve,
stil	style	(pf. **steknem**)	acquire
strastven	passionate	**svega i svačega**	all sorts
što se tiče	as far as . . . is concerned	**tiraž**	print-run, edition
		ugledan	respected
upozoriti (pf.)	to warn, to point out	**zvezda**	star

Exercise 5

(a) Before going to the Writers' Club, Ben and Dejan are talking about what to wear for the occasion. Fill the gaps with the appropriate verbs.

BEN: Šta ćeš da _____ večeras?
DEJAN: Još uvek ne znam tačno. Treba da se _____ malo svečanije, a ja to ne volim.
BEN: Ja ću _____ odelo i kravatu.
DEJAN: Pa verovatno ću i ja nositi isto.
BEN: A koje cipele ćeš da _____?
DEJAN: Verovatno one braon cipele. One mi lepo _____, a i _____ dobro uz moje smeđe letnje odelo.

> **obući** (pf. **obučem**; imp. **oblačiti**) to dress, put on clothes
> **svečan** formal

(b)[†] Use the words listed below to write complete sentences:

> **omot** 'dust jacket, wrapping'; **biblioteka** 'library'; **naslov** 'title'; **knjižara**; **pisac** (gen. **pisca**) 'writer'; **bestseler** 'bestseller'; **poglavlje** 'chapter'

1 Ako želite da pročitate knjigu, možete ili da je kupite u _____ ili da je pozajmite iz _____.

2 Knjige koje se dobro prodaju zovu se _____.

3 Na _____ knjige možete videti njen _____ i ime _____. Knjiga je podeljena na delove koji se zovu _____.

(c) Match the questions with the answers:

Izvolite, šta želite?	A	41
Koji broj džempera nosite?	B	Crvene
Koliko košta ova suknja?	C	Kabina je tu iza ćoška
Koje boje su te čarape?	D	54
Koliko koštaju te majice?	E	Ne, one su od sintetike
Koji broj cipela nosite?	F	Cipele .
Gde može da se proba?	G	Ona košta 300 dinara
Da li su ove pantalone od teksasa?	H	Jedna košta 200 dinara, a dve 300.

(d) You are in a department store buying a jumper for a relative.
Complete the dialogue:

PRODAVACICA: Izvolite, mogu li da vam pomognem?
VI: _____

PRODAVACICA: Da li želite letnji ili zimski, topliji džemper?
VI: _____

PRODAVACICA: Kažete neki laganiji, da vidimo . . . Da li želite
neku posebnu boju?
VI: _____

PRODAVACICA: Imamo samo ove zelene džempere od
sintetike.
VI: _____

PRODAVACICA: Imamo lepe vunene džempere u plavoj ili
crvenoj boji.
VI: _____

PRODAVACICA: Koji broj džempera nosite?
VI: _____

PRODAVACICA: Možda će vam odgovarati ovaj plavi.
VI: _____

PRODAVACICA: Izvolite. Kasa je tu iza kabine za probanje.
VI: _____

PRODAVACICA: Nema na čemu. Do viđenja.

(e) Describe the contents of a large suitcase you are taking on
holiday, giving the colour of each item.

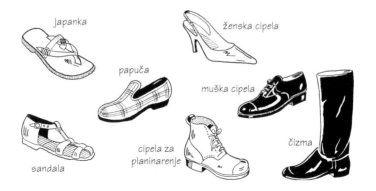

japanka

ženska cipela

papuča

muška cipela

sandala

cipela za
planinarenje

čizma

Dialogue 3

Екипа (14)

*Did Dado go to the cinema often when he lived in Bosnia? Does
Luka like sport? Does Filip like dancing? Who arrives just as Dado
and Jelena are leaving?*

Дади и Јелени се свидео филм, а онда су ушли у оnear ближњу
кафану на пиће.

– Јеси ли често ишао у биоскоп док си живео у Босни? –
упитала је Јелена.
– Како кад: прилично често, углавном зими кад је иначе
хладно и не можеш бити пуно напољу. А љети сам више
волио да се бавим спортом – одговорио је Дадо.
– Тако сам и мислила: јако си лепо развијен – рекла је Јелена.
А онда је брзо додала: – Мислим, сличан си Луки, који
обожава фудбал. Док је Филип више књишки тип: никад га
нисам чула да спомиње спорт. Иако много воли музику и
веома добро игра.

Дадо је ћутао, па је Јелена наставила:

– Да, Филип је један од најбољих играча које сам икада
видела. А кад смо већ код тога, сутра Маја прави журку,
па ако си расположен, дођи.
– Па, не знам. Морам да видим шта ради Сања.
– Не брини, сигурна сам да ће је Филип позвати. Хајде дођи,
биће весело!
– Не знам, видјећу. Могу ли да те отпратим кући?

Само што су устали, ушли су Маја и Лука. Дади је очигледно
одмах било лакше.

– Јелена, покушавам већ сатима да те добијем на мобилни,
али изгледа као да ти је искључен. Ипак, баш фино што
смо вас нашли заједно. Хтели смо да позовемо Даду на
забаву сутра, али нисмо знали како да га контактирамо.
Филип је већ позвао Сању, па ће нам бити јако драго ако
можеш и ти да дођеш.
– Хвала вам, у реду – рекао је Дадо, још увек помало збуњен.

Vocabulary

додати (pf.)	to add	**играти** (imp.)	to dance
изгледа	it seems		(also **играти**
искључен	switched off		(**се**) to play)
како кад	sometimes, it	**лакше**	easier
	depends when	**напољу**	outside
обожавати	adore	**подсећати** (imp.)	to remind
(imp.)		**споменути**	to mention
		(pf. **споменем**)	

15 Polazak

Departure

In this unit we will look at:

- demonstrative pronouns: 'this', 'that'
- possessive adjectives
- preparing for a car journey
- driving, route planning

Dialogue 1

Сопоћани

Why does Angela wake up excited? Who is navigating? Who was the ruler when the Serbian medieval kingdom reached its greatest territorial extent? When was Sopoćani founded?

Ујутру су се путници рано пробудили и кренули на пут.

Немања:	Знам да се манастир налази југозападно од града. Међутим, могу ли да вас замолим да ми дајете упутства куда да возим? Ево вам карте, Џоне.
Џон:	Како да не. Скрени лево на крају ове улице. Колико има до манастира?
Немања:	Око пола сата-сат вожње. Добро. Да ли је ово главни пут?
Џон:	Јесте. А сада, када дођемо до оног семафора, треба да видимо путоказ који показује путеве из града.
Анђела:	Тачно. Треба да кренемо оним путем, трећи излаз са велике раскрснице.
Немања:	Хвала, мислим да сада знам. Увек се збуним у граду јер тако ретко долазим овде. На срећу данас нема гужве у саобраћају.

После двадесетак минута су били ван града на путу према брдима где се налази манастир.

Немања: Да ли нешто знате о нашој средњовековној историји?
Џон: Знамо да је српска држава достигла врхунац своје моћи у четрнаестом веку.
Немања: Тако је, за време владавине Цара Душана.
Џон: Када је основан манастир Сопоћани?
Немања: У тринаестом веку. Манастир је познат по својим фрескама. А сада, погледајте иза те шумице на десној страни овог пута: ускоро ћемо уочити цркву.
Анђела: Ево је! Што је лепа! И какво предивно окружење!
Немања: Мораћемо да питамо да ли је паркирање овде дозвољено. Ето, стигли смо!

Vocabulary

брдо	hill	век	century
владавина	rule	врхунац	height
десни	right	достићи	to reach
дозвољен	permitted	(pf. **достигнем**)	
држава	state	**за време** (+ gen.)	during

Manastir Sopocani

збунити се (pf.)	to get confused	кренути (pf. кренем)	to set off
моћ (f.)	power	околина	surroundings
оснивати (imp. оснујем)	to found	паркирати (imp.)	to park
предиван	wonderful	путоказ	signpost
раскрсница	crossroads	средњовековни	medieval
таблица	board	ујутру	in the morning
уочити (pf.)	to catch sight of	упутство	instruction
шумица	copse		

Language points 1

Demonstrative pronouns

We have already come across the demonstrative pronouns **тај** and **овај** in the course of the units, in several different cases. Here is the declension of **тај** in full.

	Singular			Plural		
	m.	*n.*	*f.*	*m.*	*n.*	*f.*
nom.	тај	то	та	ти	та	те
gen.	тог(а)	тог(а)	те	тих	тих	тих
dat.	том(е)	том(е)	тој	тим(а)	тим(а)	тим(а)
acc.	тог(а)/тај	то	ту	те	та	те
loc.	том(е)	том(е)	тој	тим	тим	тим
instr.	тим(е)	тим(е)	том	тим	тим	тим

овај 'this' and **онај** 'that' (further away than **тај**) are declined on this model.

Exercise 1

(a) Answer the following questions:

1 Зашто је Анђела узбуђена?
2 Да ли Немања зна пут до манастира?
3 Где се налази путоказ који показује излаз из града?
4 Колико времена им је требало да изађу из града?

5 По чему је познат манастир Сопоћани?
6 Шта се Анђели свиђа?
7 Шта су морали да питају пре него што су се паркирали?

(b) Identify the odd one out:

1 манастир   књижара   фреске   задужбина
2 кухиња   саобраћај   семафор   раскрсница
3 краљ   цар   принц   стриц
4 окружење   паркинг   пејзаж   околина

задужбина foundation   **окружење** surroundings

(c)[†] Put the demonstrative pronouns into the correct case:

1 Да ли да пођемо _____ (ова) улицом?
2 Да, скрените лево код _____ (тај) семафора.
3 Проћићете поред _____ (она) велике зграде.
4 Онда продужите ____ (овај) путем до ____ (та) велике раскрснице.
5 На том путу ћете видети већину _____ (ти) познатих манастира.
6 Можете ићи до џамије _____ (она) малом улицом.
7 Где је _____ (тај) пут на овој карти?
8 Црква се налази на крају _____ (она) мале улице.
9 Видите ли _____ (тај) велики хотел на тргу?
10 Идите право до _____ (она) апотеке на углу.

Language points 2

Possessive adjectives

Possessive adjectives can be formed from proper nouns or nouns denoting people.

Masculine nouns ending in a consonant or **-o** have the ending **-ово**:

Војин	**Војинов**	**Војинов брат** Vojin's brother
Бранко	**Бранков**	**Бранков нови капут** Branko's new coat

путник	путников	путников шешир the passenger's hat

If the final consonant is soft, the suffix becomes **-ев**:

пријатељ	пријатељев	пријатељев пас (my) friend's dog
Ђорђе		Ђорђев мали син Djorđe's little son
Г. Петровић		Г. Петровићев стан Mr Petrović's flat

Feminine nouns ending in **-а** drop the final **-а** and replace it by **-ин**:

Марија	Маријин	Маријин брат Marija's brother
сестра	сестрин	сестрин муж (my) sister's husband

Note: The adjective for men's names with a feminine form is made in the same way:

Никола	Николин	Николин нећак Nikola's nephew

These possessive adjectives are then declined like regular definite[1] adjectives with the appropriate endings added to the new suffix:

Војинова сестра је овде.
Vojin's sister is here.

Видела сам Марковог брата.
I saw Marko's brother.

Да ли си то рекла професоровој сестри?
Did you tell that to the professor's sister?

1 You will also find indefinite endings for masculine possessives.

Note: These forms cannot be preceded by a qualifying adjective:

Ово је путникова торба.
This is the passenger's bag.

but **То је торба оног другог путника.**
This is that other passenger's bag.

Examples:

Да ли је Милош Јеленин муж?
Не, Милош је Маријин муж.

А како се зове Џонова жена?
Зове се Анђела.

Ко је Немања?
Он је Маријин нећак.

Где станује Маријина сестра?
У Подгорици, живи са Маријином старом мајком.

Да ли је то раније била Војинова кућа?
Да, на Његошевом тргу.

Exercise 2

(a) Make possessive adjectives from these names:

    Milan, Dragica, Ivan, Vesna, Đura

(b)[†]Translate the following sentences into Serbian:

  1 Is that Milica's husband?
  2 Where are the passenger's suitcases?
  3 They are travelling in Nemanja's new car.
  4 Will you be seeing Marija's daughter?
  5 The map is in Andjela's bag.
  6 Are you going to the monastery with Ivan's brother?
  7 Is that your friend's house?
  8 Nikola's jumper is here.
  9 When is Miloš's uncle (father's brother) arriving?
 10 Tijana's journey starts tomorrow.

Reading passage 1[†] (Audio 2: 11)

Try to translate the passage on your own. Be prepared to make informed guesses based on the context. You can check your version with the translation in the 'Key to exercises' when you are satisfied.

Od Beograda do Novog Pazara vodi magistralni put u pravcu jadranske obale. Ovaj put prolazi kroz živopisne gradove i krajeve Šumadije. Iznad Novog Pazara se uzdižu planine Golija i Rogozna kao i Pešterska visoravan. Grad se nalazi na dodiru reka Jošanice i Raške, u istoimenoj kotlini.

Podignut je u 15. veku, na teritoriji prestonice prve srpske države – Rasa. Geografski položaj je dosta povoljan. U samom novopazarskom polju sa okolnih planina se zvezdasto spušta 5 manjih reka. Ovu pojavu Jovan Cvijić, veliki srpski geograf i naučnik, označio je kao fenomen jedinstven na Balkanu. Prirodne lepote kojima se može pohvaliti Novi Pazar postale su privlačne i drugima. Lepota i turističke atrakcije Golije, naročito nakon što je sagrađen savremeni ski-centar, pa Sopoćanski kraj, blizina Peštara i Kopaonika . . . Prirodnom bogatstvu novopazarskog kraja treba dodati i dva lečilišta – Novopazarsku i Rajčinovića Banju u koje dolaze pacijenti iz svih krajeva Srbije i Crne Gore.

Pored spomenika pravoslavne – hrišćanske kulture Sopoćana, Petrove crkve i Djurdjevih stupova, asocijacija za Novi Pazar su i spomenici islamske kulture – džamije, hanovi, hamami, kao i nezaobilazna Gradska tvrđava u centru grada.

Dialogue 2 (Audio 2: 12)

Razgovor kod Beopetrolove benzinske pumpe

Conversation at the Beopetrol petrol pump

Mr Filipović is on the road and thinks he has lost his way. He goes to fill up with petrol.

F: Molim vas, gde je najbliža benzinska pumpa?
A: Kod prve velike raskrsnice.

* * *

B: Koliko litara želite?
F: Napunite, molim vas, i proverite ulje i vodu.
B: Da napunim akumulator destilovanom vodom?
F: Da, molim vas.
B: Da proverim gume?
F: Molim. Imate li dobru autokartu ovog područja?
B: Da, izvolite.
F: Da li možete da mi pokažete na karti tačno gde se nalazim?
   Mislim da sam na pogrešnom putu.
B: Idite pravo ovim lokalnim putem. Izaći ćete kod semafora na glavnom putu za centar grada.

Vocabulary

napuniti	to fill	**akumulator**	battery
kočnica	brake	**guma**	tyre
pritisak	pressure	**prednji**	front
zadnji	back	**autokarta**	road map
područje	region	**pogrešan**	mistaken, wrong

Exercise 3

(a) Put the following jumbled-up dialogue in order:

    Desno, odmah kod supermarketa.
    Vi ste odavde?

Molim vas, gde je najbliža benzinska pumpa?
Koliko ima kolima do tamo?
Ne, ja sam stranac.
Dobro, idite za ovim crvenim autobusom i pumpa je
odmah iza ćoška.
Iza ćoška levo ili desno?
Nema ni 500 metara do tamo.

(b) Match the questions with appropriate answers:

1 Srbija je bila na vrhuncu moći u vreme cara Dušana?
2 Vidimo se večeras ispred bioskopa.
3 Možda je ipak bolje da ostanemo kod kuće.
4 Da ponesem i mantile?
5 A posle svega idemo još i u klub.
6 On je svakako naš najbolji pisac.
7 Da li je Petar kupio karte za koncert?

(a) Nema potrebe.
(b) Tako je!
(c) Važi, vidimo se.
(d) To super zvuči!
(e) U pravu si.
(f) Valjda jeste.
(g) Ne slažem se.

(c)[†] Choose the appropriate word and put it in the correct form:

1 Не знам где да скренем. Не видим нигде _____ .
   (a) пошта   (b) пут
   (c) дрво   (d) путоказ

2 Мислим да смо кренули _____ путем. Идемо на
   запад уместо на исток.
   (a) прави   (b) погрешан
   (c) погрешити   (d) у праву

3 Скренућемо на тој _____ десно и наставити право
   том улицом.
   (a) семафор   (b) улица
   (c) раскрсница   (d) саобраћајни знак

4 Зими је овде тешко возити јер је због леда пут увек
   _____ .
   (a) клизав   (b) кратак
   (c) кривудав   (d) катастрофалан

5 Морам да станем на некој пумпи да _____ бензин.
   (a) направити   (b) наточити
   (c) научити   (d) наспрам
6 Требаће нам сат-два вожње да стигнемо јер је велика
  гужва у _____ .
   (a) продавница   (b) друштво
   (c) манастир   (d) саобраћај

🎧 Reading passage 2 (Audio 2: 13)

Kulturni život u Beogradu (15)

Who was reading at the literary evening? What were they called?
What did they invite Ben to do? Did Ben like their poetry?

Večeras su dve mlade pesnikinje imale književno veče. Obe su
Dejanove dobre prijateljice pa su pozvale Bena, kao uvaženog
gosta, da kaže nekoliko reči o savremenoj književnoj sceni u
Velikoj Britaniji. Ben je prihvatio njihov poziv, iako se malo bojao
jer nije navikao da javno govori. U svakom slučaju, želeo je da
upozna dve pesnikinje, jer ga posebno zanima žensko pismo, a
pogotovo poezija. Stigli su rano tako da je Ben imao priliku da
porazgovara sa Dejanovim prijateljicama – Tanjom i Ljiljanom –
pre nego što je počeo njihov nastup. Obe su veoma mlade, srdačne
i vesele. Benu su se mnogo svidele njihove pesme, pogotovo
Tanjine: bile su kratke i pune energije. Sam je Ben govorio na
zanimljiv način i na kraju je dobio aplauz od zadovoljne publike.
Uspeo je da odgovori na sva njihova pitanja i na kraju je bio
zapanjen njihovim poznavanjem britanske scene.

Vocabulary

javno	publicly	**književni**	literary
nastup	slot, appearance	**obe**	both (f.) (**oba** m.,
	(on stage)		**oboje** neuter,
pesnikinja	(woman) poet		mixed gender)
	(**pesnik**)	**pisanje**	writing
pre nego što	before	**prihvatiti**	to accept
publika	audience	**scena**	scene
srdačan	warm (cordial)	**uvažen**	respected
večeras	this evening	**zapanjen**	amazed

Exercise 4[†]

Translate the following dialogue into Serbian:

BEN: Where is your friend? I want to meet her.
DEJAN: You see that tall girl in a red T-shirt?
BEN: Oh, yes. I am going to introduce myself.

*   *   *

BEN: Hello, I am Dejan's friend, Ben.
LJILJANA: Nice to meet you finally, I have heard a lot about you.
BEN: I have heard a lot about you too. I can't wait for the
           reading to start.
LJILJANA: Neither can I. I am very excited. But, here comes
           Dejan and my friend Tanja. Let me introduce you.

čitanje reading

🎧 Dialogue 3 (Audio 2: 14)

Екипа (15)

*What does Maja live near to? Does Luka go on with the others when
Maja has turned off towards her flat? What does Jelena say her flat
is like?*

Маја и Лука су пошли са Јеленом и Дадом према Јелениној
кући.

– Можемо успут да вам покажемо где се налази Мајина
  кућа – рекао је Лука.
– Па да, није далеко одавде – приметила је Јелена.
– Ето, видиш ону улицу тамо, са малом самопослугом на
  ћошку? Идеш том улицом до првог семафора, па скренеш
  лево, мој стан са налази у првој згради на десној страни те
  улице, поред видео-клуба – рекла је Маја.
– Молим те, напиши адресу на овом комаду папира – рекао
  је Дадо.
– Дајем ти и број свог мобилног телефона – за сваки случај.
– Добро, другари, ми ћемо сада поћи овом улицом – рекао је
  Лука, који је такође ишао до Мајине куће.
– Лаку ноћ! До сутра – рекла је весело Маја.
– Лаку ноћ!

Дадо и Јелена су наставили пут.

- Ето, стигли смо, ово је моја зграда. Могу ли да те понудим кафом, или нечим другим? – питала је Јелена.
- Не, хвала – рекао је брзо Дадо. – Крајње је вријеме да пођем кући.
- Дакле, хвала што си ме отпратио.
- Нема на чему. Хвала на филму, био је баш добар. До сутра. Лаку ноћ!

И Дадо је пошао према свом крају града.

Vocabulary

комад	piece	крајње вр(иј)еме	high time
лаку ноћ	goodnight	самопослуга	supermarket

16 U kvaru

Breakdown

In this unit we will look at:

- possessive pronouns: 'my', 'your' etc.
- parts of a car

Dialogue 1

Проблеми са колима

What does Nemanja tell the Browns about during the drive? What struck Angela particularly about Sopoćani? Why do they think there is something wrong with the car? Does Nemanja think it will be easy to fix it?

На путу натраг у Нови Пазар, Немања је причао о улози манастира у српској историји.

Немања:	Били су од велике важности од самог почетка наше државе, а поготово за време турске владавине пошто су онда били једини културни центри.
Анђела:	Морам рећи да сам одушевљена предивним фрескама. Боје су просто невероватно јаке и живе после свих тих векова.
Немања:	Извините што мало скрећем са теме, али да ли чујете тај чудан звук у мотору? Бојим се да нешто није у реду са колима.
Анђела:	Да, и ја чујем нешто. Да ли знаш за неки сервис у граду?

Немања:	Знам за један сервис ту јако близу, и замислите, случајно је власник сервиса неки мој даљи рођак, па верујем да ће нам изаћи у сусрет. Не могу да верујем! Заборавио сам свој мобилни код куће па не можемо да га назовемо, али нема везе, он је сигурно тамо. Само да није нешто компликовано и да у сервису имају потребне резервне делове . . .
Анђела:	Док сте ви у сервису, ја ћу да пођем у пошту да купим марке и да пошаљем разгледнице које сам купила у Сопоћанима.
Немања:	Важи. Ето, ту ћемо се зауставити. Пошта се налази преко пута банке на ћошку главне улице. Само пређеш преко трга и видећеш банку испред себе.
Анђела:	Хвала. Доћи ћу за пола сата. Надам се да ће дотле мајстори да нађу проблем — па и његово решење!

Vocabulary

важност (f.)	importance	**власник**	owner
дотле	until then	**замислити** (pf.)	to imagine
зауставити се (pf.)	to stop	**звук**	sound
јак	strong	**изаћи (некоме) у сусрет**	to help
једини	single, only		
мотор	engine	**мајстор**	mechanic
пошто	since	**натраг**	back
резервни део	spare part	**пређи** (pf. **пређем**)	to cross
решење	solution	**сервис**	garage (repairs)
случајно	by chance	**чудан, -дна**	strange

Language points 1

Possessive pronouns

The declensions of possessive pronouns are straightforward and the endings are already familiar to you from those of adjectives and demonstrative pronouns.

мој, твој, свој

Singular

	m.	*n.*	*f.*
nom.	мој	моје	моја
gen.	мог(а)	мог(а)	моје
	мојег(а)	мојег(а)	
dat.	мом(е)	мом(е)	мојој
	мојем(у)	мојем(у)	
acc.	as nom. or gen.	моје	моју
loc.	as dat.		
instr.	мојим	мојим	мојом

Plural

	m.	*n.*	*f.*
nom.	моји	моја	моје
gen.	мојих	мојих	мојих
dat.	мојим(а)	мојим(а)	мојим(а)
acc.	моје	моја	моје
loc.	as dat.		
instr.	мојим(а)	мојим(а)	мојим(а)

Where there are alternative longer and shorter forms, the shorter form is always the more common. See 'Grammar summary', section 2 (p. 301).

Use of свој

Except in a few set phrases (e.g. **Он је свој човек** 'He is "his own" man'), this cannot be used in the nominative. It cannot *be* the subject as it is used to refer *to* the subject. It may be used of any person, singular or plural, to denote things pertaining to that person:

Видећу свог сина.	I shall see my son.
Били су у својој кући.	They were in their house.
Идемо својим колима.	We are going in (by) our car.

Exercise 1

(a) Mark the following statements **Tačno** (**T**) or **Netačno** (**N**):

1 Манастири су били једини културни центри
  у време турске владавине у Србији.   T/N

2 Анђела је разочарана фрескама у Сопоћанима. T/N

3 Немања мора да скрене са пута.   T/N

4 Немања познаје власника ауто-сервиса.   T/N

5 Немања нема код себе мобилни телефон.   T/N

6 Немања није забринут.   T/N

7 Анђела жели да пошаље разгледнице.   T/N

(b) Match the words/expressions on the right with words/
expressions on the left that have the equivalent meaning:

1 изаћи у сусрет некоме   (a) ако

2 разумети се у нешто   (b) није важно

3 за случај   (c) помоћи некоме

4 нарочито   (d) поготово

5 нема везе   (e) знати све о нечему

(c)† Translate into Serbian, using **moj, tvoj** or **svoj** as appropriate:

1 We'll get our things ready.

2 They were not in their car.

3 I saw your relative in the post office.

4 Are you travelling in your car?

5 My daughter has gone to England with some friends of
  hers.

6 I left my mobile at home.

7 Do you have your driving licence with you?

8 They are going to visit my parents.

9 They parked their car in front of the house.

10 When you turn left you will see my office.

vozačka dozvola   driving licence

Language points 2

More on possessive pronouns

наш, ваш 'our', 'your'

Singular

	m.	n.	f.
nom.	наш	наше	наша
gen.	нашег(a)	нашег(a)	наше
dat.	нашем(y)	нашем(y)	нашој
acc.	nom. or gen.	наше	нашу
loc.	нашем(y)	нашем(y)	нашој
instr.	нашим	нашим	нашом

Plural

	m.	n.	f.
nom.	наши	наша	наше
gen.	наших	наших	наших
dat.	нашим(a)	нашим(a)	нашим(a)
acc.	наше	наша	наше
loc.	нашим(a)	нашим(a)	нашим(a)
instr.	нашим(a)	нашим(a)	нашим(a)

његов, њен, њихов 'his', 'her', 'their'

These are easily remembered if you take the genitive (long form)
of each of **он**, **она**, **они** respectively as the starting point. (These
pronouns are often declined like indefinite adjectives, i.e. m. and
n, as are possessive adjectives formed from nouns, with endings
-ов and **-ин**.).

> gen. **његова, њена, њихова**
> dat. **његову, њену, њихову**

Exercise 2

(a) Write out the sentences choosing the appropriate word from
the alternatives given in **bold**:

1 Не могу да пронађем **моје/своје** кључеве од кола.
Моја жена мисли да су у **мом/свом** џепу јер их обично
ту држим.

2 Они не могу да нађу **њихову/своју** торбу. Нема је у
њиховом/свом пртљажнику.

3 Звала сам **своју/моју** пријатељицу телефоном. Међутим,
моја/своја пријатељица није била код куће.

4 Волим да се возим **мојим/својим** колима. Обично пустим
моју/своју омиљену музику и уживам у вожњи.

5 Ићи ћу да посетим **моје/своје** родитеље ускоро. Они живе
ван града. Имају **своју/њихову** кућу и малу башту.

(b) Replace the pronouns in the dative case in the following
sentences with the appropriate possessive pronoun, as in the
example:

Example: **Да ли ти је она девојка?**
Да ли је она твоја девојка?

1 Данас јој је седми рођендан.
2 Да ли знаш где ми је возачка дозвола?
3 Ово су му нова кола.
4 Хоће ли им се ћерка ускоро вратити са пута?
5 Недавно му је изашла прва књига.
6 Кафа вам је на столу, охладиће се.

(c) Match the two parts of the sentences:

1 Tek kad ju je policajac zaustavio,
2 Kola su nam u kvaru
3 Nikad ne vadim* svoju vozačku dozvolu iz novčanika
4 Nisam stigla na vreme na posao
5 Dok su automehaničari popravljali kola,

   (a) jer su se na glavnom putu sudarili* autobus i kamion.
   (b) jer sam jako zaboravan.*
   (c) ja sam zvala prijatelje telefonom.
   (d) i zato moramo da otkažemo* putovanje na more.
   (e) shvatila je da nije vezana.

sudariti se to collide **zaboravan** forgetful
otkazati to cancel **vaditi** to take out **vezan** tied, belted

(d) Using the details listed below write two emails explaining why you couldn't come to work that day.

1 auto u kvaru, iznenada, na putu na posao, servis daleko, ne razumete se u kola, šlep-služba* stigla tek kroz pola sata, komplikovan kvar, u servisu nisu imali rezervni deo
2 prvo sudar na putu, gužva u saobraćaju, onda se autobus pokvario, čekali sat vremena sledeći autobus, vratili se kući

šlep-služba towing service

🎧 Reading passage 1 (Audio 2: 15)

Kulturni život u Beogradu (16)

Where does Dejan take Ben and his family the next day? What does Ben find interesting about the journey? What do they stop to buy? Where is Dejan's friend's holiday home?

Sledećeg dana, Dejan je vozio Bena, Nadu, Anu i malog Janka na Frušku goru. Njegova kola su mala, ali su se svi nekako strpali unutra. Bili su pozvani na ručak u vikendici jednog Dejanovog prijatelja, koji stanuje u Novom Sadu, ali ima kućicu na brdu u kojoj provodi skoro svaki vikend.

Benu je put bio zanimljiv: u tom kraju su sva sela slična, sa širokim glavnim putem i niskim kućama sagrađenim sa svake strane puta. Te kuće imaju zatvorena dvorišta koja se ne vide sa ulice. U jednom od tih sela su stali ispred jedne kuće gde se prodavalo meso. Dejan je obećao svom prijatelju da će usput kupiti mesa za roštilj kod ovog mesara, jer znaju da je kod njega meso uvek sveže.

Uskoro su se vozili po šumama i brdima Fruške gore. Vikendica Dejanovog prijatelja kod koga su išli se nalazi na kraju dugačkog, uskog puta koji vodi prema manastiru, čija se kupola jedva videla iznad drveća. Nada je Benu objasnila da su ovi manastiri sagrađeni kasnije od onih u južnoj Srbiji, u sedamnaestom i osamnaestom veku, a da ih svakako vredi videti. Benu je veoma prijalo što je na svežem vazduhu i rekao je da želi da poseti manastir ako imaju vremena da pođu u šetnju pre ručka.

Vocabulary

čiji	whose	**dugačak**	long
iznad (+ gen.)	above	**južni**	southern
mesar	butcher	**nečiji**	someone's
nizak, niska	low	**obećati** (pf.)	to promise
posetiti (pf.)	to visit	**prijati**	to please,
		(**nekome** imp.)	to appeal to
roštilj	charcoal grill,	**sagrađen**	built
	barbecue	**stati** (pf. **stanem**)	to stop
strpati (imp.)	to squeeze,	**unutra**	inside
	shove into	**uzak** (**uska**)	narrow
vikendica	holiday home	**vredeti**	to be worth
zatvoren	closed	(imp. **vredim**)	

Exercise 3

(a) Answer the following questions:

1 Gde je Dejan vozio svoju porodicu i Bena?
2 Kakav su problem imali pre polaska i da li su ga rešili?
3 Gde živi njegov prijatelj?
4 Šta radi vikendom?
5 Šta Dejan misli o putovanju i zašto?
6 Gde su morali da svrate i zašto?
7 Da li su fruškogorski manastiri građeni u isto vreme kad i manastiri u južnoj Srbiji?
8 Šta će Ben da radi pre ručka?

(b)[†] Fill in the gaps with the appropriate preposition from the list below.

od   u   na   po   sa   za

Halo, šlep-služba, naš auto je ___ kvaru. Mi smo ___ autoputu Beograd-Niš, nekih 15 kilometara ___ Beograda. Da li možete da pošaljete mehaničara ili šlepera ___ nas? Izgleda da nešto nije ___ redu ___ motorom. Muž mi je ___ kolima, a ja sam ___ benzinskoj pumpi. Možete li doći ___ pola sata? Kasnimo ___ avion.

(c) You are in a town in the middle of central Serbia and you've broken down. Luckily a local woman walks past and you ask her for help:

🎧 **(Audio 1: 16)**

A: Gospodine, šta vam se desilo?

Vɪ: *You say that your car has broken down and that you don't know where the nearest garage is.*

A: Možete da nazovete Auto-moto savez Srbije i oni će vam sigurno izaći u susret.

Vɪ: *Ask for their number.*

A: Nemam ga kod sebe, ali tu iza ćoška je lokalna novinarnica i čovek koji tu radi sve zna.

Vɪ: *Ask her to repeat (**ponoviti**), you haven't understood where the newsagent is.*

A: Tu iza ćoška, pođite sa mnom ja ću vam pokazati.

(d)†Translate the following passage into Serbian:

– Hello, is that Marko? I'm phoning[1] to say that we're setting off to the coast on Saturday.

– Lucky you! I hope you will have good weather. Is there anyone to look after your cat?[2] I shall gladly come in from time to time.

– Thank you, it's nice of you. Veran's nephew will be here and he will probably bring some of his friends as well.

– Where are you going? Have you booked rooms somewhere?

– No, we haven't. We shall presumably find private accommodation without any problem. We don't know exactly where we shall be.

– And when are you coming back?[3]

– We can only stay five days. Will you be in Podgorica when we get back?[3]

– Yes, and then I'm going to Italy.

– Good, we'll see each other soon then.

– Have a good journey![4]

1 'to ring' **javljati se**. 2 'cat' **mačka**. 3 'to come back': think about which aspect to use in each case – **vraćati se** (imp.), **vratiti se** (pf.). 4 'good journey' **srećan put**.

(e) Look at the diagram of the car and describe the location of the various named parts and their relationship to the others:

Example: **Prtljažnik se nalazi iza sedišta.**
    Motor je ispod haube.

prednje svetlo/zadnje svetlo	light
guma	tyre

re̲gistarska ta̲blica/registra̲cija	registration plate
prednji/zadnji točak	front/back wheel
hauba	bonnet [hood]
ogle̲dalo	mirror
volan	steering wheel
sedište	seat
pr̲tljažnik/gepek	boot [trunk]
vrata	door

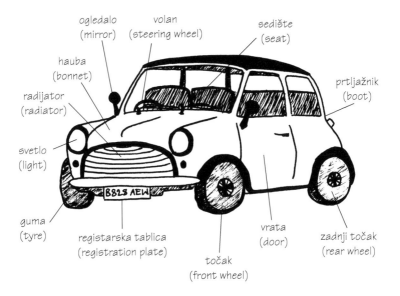

ogledalo (mirror) — volan (steering wheel) — sedište (seat) — hauba (bonnet) — prtljažnik (boot) — radijator (radiator) — svetlo (light) — guma (tyre) — registarska tablica (registration plate) — točak (front wheel) — vrata (door) — zadnji točak (rear wheel)

🎧 Dialogue 1 (Audio 2: 17)

Екипа (16)

What does Filip want to talk about as he walks Sanja home? Does Filip like sport? What do children in Bosnia learn to do? What do Filip and Sanja see?

Филип је пратио Сању кући. Успут су разговарали.

– Желим да знам што више о теби и твом животу, како си живела и чиме си се бавила тамо у твојој Босни – рекао је Филип.

–   Па живјели смо као млади људи свуда ... Бавила сам се
    активно скијањем. Али сам, нажалост, престала кад је
    почео рат. Да ли ти скијаш? – питала је Сања.
–   Нажалост, морам да признам да нисам спортски тип: више
    волим да седим у фотељи са књигом. Да ли се твоја кућа
    налазила на брду? Или можда не желиш да говориш о
    томе?
–   У реду је, не брини. Мислим често на ту нашу кућу, па ми
    се чини нормално да понекад и причам о њој. Иако то нисам
    до сада радила ... Није била нарочито лијепа, у новом
    насељу, али – била је наша.

Филип је осетио тугу у њеном гласу, па је пружио своју руку
према њеној и нежно је узео у своју.

–   Жао ми је, Сања, због тебе, због рата, због свега ...

Сања је чвршће држала Филипову руку.

–   Хвала, Филипе, знам. У реду је. Али је ипак можда боље
    да о томе не говорим, бар за сада.
–   Договорено. Видиш ли онај осветљен излог тамо? То је
    најбоља посластичарница у Београду. Идемо да се частимо
    нечим слатким.

Peciva

Vocabulary

глас	voice	излог	shop window
насеље	settlement, estate	нежно	tenderly
осветљен	lit	осетити (pf.)	to feel
посластичарница	confectioner's	признати (pf.)	to confess
пружити	to offer, extend	свуда	everywhere
скијање	skiing	туга	sadness
(скијати се)		у реду	OK

17 U kupovini

Shopping

In this unit we will look at:

- interrogative pronouns: 'who', 'what' etc.
- relative pronouns: 'who', 'which' etc.
- shopping for food
- aspect 2
- lost items, visiting a police station

 Dialogue 1 (Audio 2: 18)

Was it easy to have the car repaired? What did they all do while they were waiting? What did John buy? What about Angela? Where did they go when they finished shopping?

Немањин рођак је решио проблем са колима. Имао је потребни резервни део који је релативно брзо уградио. Док су чекали да се кола поправе, нису хтели да губе време, па су отишли у куповину јер је већ следећег дана требало кренути на море. Договорили су се са Маријом и Милошем да у Подгорици покупе њихову унуку и да је одведу са собом у Београд.

Анђела:	Шта ти највише волиш, Немања?
Немања:	Све волим! Увек сам гладан! Волим месо и воће, па колаче, бомбоне, сладолед. И наравно, чоколаду!
Џон:	Знаш шта сам ја јако заволео од када смо овде? Бурек са сиром. Мој омиљени доручак. Него, уђимо у ову самопослугу, ту ћемо вероватно да нађемо све што нам треба.

Анђела:	Џоне, да ли ти хоћеш да потражиш хлеб и поврће, док ја одем с Немањом да видим који сир и какво суво месо имају у овој радњи?
Џон:	Важи. Наћи ћемо се код поврћа кад завршите.
Анђела:	Узмимо двеста грама овог пршута и целу ову саламу. Прилично је скупа, али ће да траје. Онда, неки тврди сир.
Немања:	Да узмемо некакве конзерве за сваки случај? Рецимо ову паштету?
Анђела:	Може, што да не. Хајде да потражимо Џона.
Џон:	Ах, ево вас. Видите какав је одличан избор воћа.
Анђела:	Какве дивне брескве и кајсије!
Џон:	И сада, мислим да смо заслужили кафу!
Немања:	Свакако, знам за један врло пријатан кафић близу главне џамије.

Платили су све на каси и пошли на кафу.

Vocabulary

бомбон	sweet	**бурек**	pie (made with filo pastry)
губити (imp.)	to lose		
дека (abbrev. of **декаграм**)	10 grammes	**заволети** (pf.)	to come to love
		завршити (pf.)	to finish
заслужити (pf.)	to deserve	**избор**	choice
каса	till (cash register)	**конзерва**	tin, can (of food)
паштета	paté	**покупити** (pf.)	to collect, to pick up
потражити (pf.)	to look for	**претпоставити** (pf.)	to suppose
рецимо	let's say		
салама	salami	**сладолед**	ice cream
сув	dry	**уградити** (pf.)	to fit, build in
чоколада	chocolate	**џамија**	mosque

Language points 1

Interrogative pronouns

	ко 'who'	**шта** 'what'
nom.	**ко**	**шта**
gen.	**кога**	**чега**
dat.	**коме**	**чему**

acc.	кога	шта
loc.	ком, коме	чему
instr.	ким, киме	чим, чиме

Ко је на вратима?
Who's at the door?

С ким си путовала?
Who did you travel with?

Код кога сте преноћили?
At whose place did you spend the night?

Шта сте купили?
What did you buy?

Чега се боји?
What's he afraid of? (**бојати се** + gen.)

О чему се ради?
What's it about? (What's going on?)

The indefinite pronouns – **неко** 'someone' and **нико** 'no one' –
are declined like **ко**; **нешто** 'something' and **ништа** 'nothing' are
declined like **шта**.

Разговарала је с неким.
She was talking to someone.

Сетила сам се нечега.
I've remembered something.

Никога нисмо видели.
We didn't see anyone.

Нису се ничега бојали.
They weren't afraid of anything.

Note: But where negative compound pronouns occur with prepositions, the preposition is placed between the component parts:

Не виђа се ни с ким.
He doesn't see anyone.

Ни од кога немамо вести.
We've no news from anyone.

Узрујаваш се ни због чега.
You're getting upset about nothing.

◯ **Dialogue 2** (Audio 2: 19)

Two friends meet in the park.

A: Čekaj! Hoću nešto da te pitam!
B: Izvoli. O čemu se radi?
A: S kim si bio sinoć? Neko je nekome rekao da sam pobedio na lutriji!
B: E pa čestitam ti! Misliš da sam to ja? Nisam nikome rekao! Nisam ni znao!
A: Ali nije istina! Neko je to izmislio! Onda je moja žena od nekoga nešto čula.
B: Pa ja ništa ni od koga nisam čuo, nisam se ni s kim video!

Vocabulary

pobediti	to win	**lutrija**	lottery
istina	truth	**izmisliti**	to invent

Exercise 1

(a) Answer the following questions:

1 Шта су Немања и Браунови радили док су чекали да се кола поправе?
2 Ко ће се Брауновима придружити у Подгорици?
3 Шта је Џон заволео да једе од када је у Србији?
4 Шта ће Анђела и Немања да купе?
5 Какав је избор воћа?
6 Где ће на крају да попију кафу?

(b)[†]Choose the correct word from the list below for each question:

1 Нисмо хтели да _____ време па смо отишли у куповину.
    (a) губимо   (b) немамо
    (c) добијемо   (d) проведемо

2 Договорили смо се са њима да ми кренемо колима и да их _____ испред њихове куће.
    (a) купимо   (b) поведемо
    (c) пожуримо   (d) покупимо

3 Који сир и _____ суво месо имате?
   (a) како   (b) какво
   (c) колико   (d) ко

4 Није практично куповати пуно млека сада јер ће се
   _____ на овој врућини.
   (a) охладити   (b) узимати
   (c) покварити   (d) повећати

5 Нема _____ да у самопослузи купујемо хлеб. Боље да
   га купимо у пекари.
   (a) везе   (b) среће
   (c) случаја   (d) смисла

охладити to get cold   **повећати** to get bigger, to increase

(c)[†] Use the appropriate form of **ko, neko, niko** in the following
sentences:

A: S _____ ideš u bioskop večeras? (ko)
B: S _____ koga ti ne znaš. (neko)
A: Čula sam od _____ da u *Jadranu* igra film 'Zona
   Zamfirova' i da ga ne treba propustiti. (neko)
B: Meni _____ ništa nije rekao o tom filmu. (niko) U
   poslednje vreme se ne viđam _____ . (niko)

Language points 2

Relative pronoun који, које, која 'who', 'which'

	Singular			Plural		
	m.	*n.*	*f.*	*m.*	*n.*	*f.*
nom.	који	које	која	који	која	које
gen.	ког(а), којег(а)	којег(а)	које	којих	којих	којих
dat.	ком(е), којем(у)	којем(у)	којој	којим(а)	којим(а)	којим(а)
acc.	nom. or gen.	које	коју	које	која	које
loc.	ком(е), којем(у)	којем(у)	којој	којим(а)	којим(а)	којим(а)
instr.	којим	којим	којом	којим(а)	којим(а)	којим(а)

Notice that the declension is very similar to that of **мој**.

It is important to distinguish between the interrogative pronoun **ко** and the relative pronoun **који**. This is not always easy in practice as in some parts of the country the genitive and dative of **који** (m. and n.) are identical to the genitive and dative of **ко**. It is also awkward because English uses 'who' for both functions.

The relative pronoun cannot be omitted, as it might be in English, especially when it is used as an object, e.g. 'the man I saw', 'the town you visited'. In Serbian these must always be present:

the man whom I saw
човек кога сам видео

the town which you visited
град који сте посетили

Examples:

Ко је та дама са којом сам вас видео синоћ?
Who is that lady I saw you with last night?

То је мој пријатељ из Енглеске о коме сам ти причао.
That's my friend from England I told you about.

Воз којим су путовали касније је пола сата.
The train they travelled by was half an hour late.

Note: When you have to translate English sentences such as the above, first establish whether a relative pronoun has been omitted and then use the appropriate form of **који**.

In certain circumstances **што** can be used as a relative pronoun, and it must be used after neuter indefinite pronouns: **ово, то, оно, нешто, ништа, једино, прво, све.**

Свиђа ми се оно што сам видела.
I like what I have seen.

Да ли имате све што вам треба?
Have you got all you need?

Има нешто о чему морам да говорим са вама.
There is something I must speak to you about.

Нису разумели ни реч од онога шта смо им рекли.
They didn't understand a word of what we told them.

Exercise 2†

Translate the following sentences into Serbian:

1 The bread I bought this morning is on the table.
2 Where is the sandwich you prepared?
3 Is this the shop in which your sister works?
4 The meat he bought is not very fresh.
5 The friend I gave your address to is coming tomorrow.
6 The car they travelled by is very small and old.
7 What's it about?
8 Have you got all you need?

Language points 3

Relative pronoun чији, чије, чија **'whose'**

чији is declined like **који**, agreeing in all respects with the noun which follows it:

Чији је тај лепи шешир?
Whose is that nice hat?

Знаш ли чије су те наочаре?
Do you know whose those glasses are?

Чијим сте колима дошли?
Whose car did you come in?

У чијој смо кући били?
Whose house were we in?

🎧 Reading passage 1 (Audio 2: 20)

Mr and Mrs Jović are shopping.

Јовићеви су пошли у куповину. Госпођа Јовић ће да иде најпре у пекару. Тамо ће да купи хлеба и пецива. Купиће мали бели хлеб, четири кифле и пола килограма бурека са сиром. Затим ће да иде у млекару. Цела породица воли млечне производе па ће да купи јогурта, киселог млека, разне сиреве и слатку павлаку за колач који ће да пече после подне. Затим ће да пође код месара. Тамо ће да купи џигерице, млевене говедине, кобасица и сланине. У међувремену је њен муж пошао на пијацу. Он ће тамо да купи кромпира, лука, спанаћа, карфиола, патлиџана и белог лука. На крају ће муж и жена да се нађу у посластичарници где ће да се почасте порцијом сладоледа и капућином.

Vocabulary

јогурт	yogurt	бели лук	garlic
капућино	cappuccino	карфиол	cauliflower
кисело млеко	sour milk	кобасица	sausage
	(thicker than	кромпир	potatoes
	јогурт which is	лук	onions
	really a drink)	млевена	minced beef
млечни (adj.)	milk	говедина	
павлака	cream	патлиџан	aubergine
пекара	baker's shop	пећи (pf. печем)	to bake
пециво	roll	пијаца	market
сланина	bacon	спанаћ	spinach
џигерица	liver		

Exercise 3

(a) Mrs Jović is in the bakery.
Complete the following dialogue.

У пекари 'Центар'

Продавачица: Изволите, шта желите?
Госпођа Јовић: _____

Продавачица: Колико црног хлеба желите и колико кифли?
Госпођа Јовић: _____

Продавачица: Изволите, да ли желите још нешто?
Госпођа Јовић: _____

Продавачица: Колико сте рекли бурека?
Госпођа Јовић: _____

Продавачица: Још нешто?
Госпођа Јовић: _____

Gradska pekara

Продавачица:	Да, имамо и обичан јогурт и воћни јогурт. Који желите?
Госпођа Јовић:	_____
Продавачица:	То је све?
Госпођа Јовић:	_____
Продавачица:	Изволите рачун. Можете платити доле на каси.
Госпођа Јовић:	_____

(b) Now imagine that you are Mr Jović and that you are at the market:

На Бајлонијевој пијаци

Продавац:	Добар дан. Изволите, шта желите? *Greet the stallholder and ask for 250 grams of grapes and a kilo of bananas.*
Господин Јовић:	_____
Продавац:	Још нешто? *You want half a kilo of tomatoes.*
Господин Јовић:	_____

Продавац:	И још нешто?
	Say no, that's all, and thank the stallholder.
Господин Јовић:	_____
Продавац:	110 динара, молим.

Na pijaci

Dialogue 3

У полицији

At the police station

When they return from the shops, Angela discovers that she does not have her handbag. Where does she think she left it? What does the shop assistant suggest? Does Angela remember anyone else being in the shop at the same time? What was in the handbag?

Анђела:	Где ми је торба? Мора да сам је оставила у радњи.
Џон:	Да ли је било много тога у њој?

Анђела:	Нешто ситниша у новчанику, кључеви, такве ствари. Хоћеш ли да дођеш са нама, Немања? Хајде да пожуримо!

У радњи су питали продавачицу да ли је случајно неко нашао и предао црну женску торбу.

Продавачица:	Жао ми је, али ништа нисмо примили. Најбоље је да идете одмах у полицију да пријавите то што сте изгубили. Полицијска станица је иза првог ћошка десно.

У полицији.

Полицајац:	Треба да попуните овај формулар. Око колико сати сте изгубили торбу? Да ли сте приметили још некога у радњи у то доба?
Џон:	Била су двојица младића који су куповали жилете.
Полицајац:	Да ли можете да их опишете?
Џон:	Донекле. Један је био плав, један црн са дугом косом. Носили су фармерке и један је био у плавој мајици, други, чини ми се, у белој кошуљи.
Полицајац:	А шта сте имали у торби, госпођо?
Анђела:	Ништа од велике вредности – нешто ситног новца, кључеве, шминку, марамицу. Мени су најдрагоценије ствари у њој фотографија наше деце и нотес с адресама.
Полицајац:	Причекајте овде један тренутак.

Полицајац се вратио после неколико минута, с најлон кесицом у руци.

Полицајац:	Изгледа да имате среће, госпођо. Двоје деце је нашло ову торбу на улици пре неколико минута и предало је. Разуме се да нема новца, али је све остало унутра.

Vocabulary

описати	to describe	**вредност** (f.)	value
(pf. **опишем**)		**драгоцен**	precious
жилет	razor blade	**изгубљен**	(passive participle of
марамица	handkerchief		**изгубити** 'lost')

кесица	bag	најлон кесица	plastic bag
нотес	notebook	плав	blond
предати (pf.)	to hand in		(of hair)
пријавити (pf.)	to report	примити (pf.)	to receive
причекати (pf.)	to wait a moment	ситниш	change, loose
тренутак	moment		coins
установити(f.)	to ascertain,	фармерке	jeans
	to establish	шминка	make-up

🎧 Exercise 4 (Audio 2: 21)

You have lost your wallet. You are in the police station.

Полицајац: Добар дан. Шта желите да пријавите.

Ви: *Greet the policeman and say that your wallet was stolen while you were on the bus.*

Полицајац: Ево, испуните овај формулар. Када се то десило?

Ви: *This morning on your way to work. You only noticed that the wallet was missing an hour ago when you wanted to buy something for lunch.*

Полицајац: Да ли сте имали нешто вредно у новчанику?

Ви: *Credit cards and some money and a couple of photographs.*

Полицајац: Да ли сте приметили да вам неко узима новчаник?

Ви: *No, you were reading a newspaper. But now you remember that a tall man with dark hair was standing very close to you.*

Полицајац: Да ли сте звали банку?

Ви: *Yes, as soon as you noticed that you didn't have the wallet.*

Language points 4

Aspect 2

We touched on the question of 'aspect' in Unit 2. Now we should consider it in more detail. You have come across many examples of the use of aspect in the units and the reading passages. When you have worked through this section, it would be advisable to look back over all the earlier material, observing the use of aspect. The following are examples of aspect pairs:

Већ шест месеци купују нову кућу, и сад су је коначно купили.
They have been buying a new house for six months; now they've finally bought one.

Пијете ли увек хладан чај? Свој сам већ одавно попила!
Do you always drink cold tea? I drank mine long ago!

Путује се три сата до границе; кад намеравате да отпутујете?
One travels three hours to the border; when do you intend to leave?

Радо вам дајем те три књиге, али ову не бих никоме дала!
I gladly give you those three books, but I wouldn't give this one to anybody!

Ово дете страшно полако једе; биће довољно ако поједе месо.
This child is eating terribly slowly; it will be enough if he eats up the meat.

Notice that in each pair the first verb describes an open-ended action, while the second denotes an action conceived as finite, whether in the past, present or future.

Exercise 5[†]

Translate the following pairs of sentences, selecting the verbs from the list below (the imperfective is given first in each case):

(i)	**kasniti, zakasniti**	(ii)	**pisati, napisati**
(iii)	**piti, popiti**	(iv)	**sećati se, setiti se**
(v)	**jesti, pojesti**	(vi)	**otvarati se, otvoriti se**

1 The train is thirty minutes late.
   He was late for dinner.
2 I wrote this email last night and I still haven't sent it.
   She's in the living room writing a letter to her brother.
3 At last he has remembered where he parked the car.
   I don't remember this crossroads, are you sure this is the right way?

4 We never eat before 8.30 in the evening, so come when you can.
  Will he be able to eat this whole portion?
5 Drink up that red wine, then you can try this white.
  We are drinking home-made brandy, will you have some too?
6 The internet café opens at 8 o'clock.
  That new shop will open on the fifth of October.

Dialogue 4

Two friends are talking. One is being nosy and the other is out of sorts.

– Ko ti je došao?
– Niko, bio sam sam.
– Gde je onaj mladić koji je bio s vama u subotu?
– Ne znam; otišao je negde.
– Čija je ta lepa crna torba?
– Ne znam, mora da ju je neko zaboravio.
– Je li to kuća u kojoj si se rodio?
– Tako su mi rekli, ja se ne sećam!
– Kakav je bio grad u kom si odrastao?
– Malen i dosadan. Svako mlado stvorenje je htelo da pobegne odatle.
– Onda je valjda počeo da bude sve manji!
– Ne, u početku nam se činilo da grad nije ničiji, ali polako je postajao naš.
– Viđaš li se sa nekim starim prijateljima?
– Ni s kim.
– Kakvi su ti sada planovi?
– Nemam nikakvih planova.
– Zbog čega si tako neraspoložen?
– Ni zbog čega. Valjda zbog vremena!

Vocabulary

roditi se	to be born
dosadan	boring
stvorenje	creature
pobeći (pobegnem)	to escape, run away
odatle	from there
neraspoložen	in a bad mood

∩ Reading passage 2 (Audio 2: 22)

Kulturni život u Beogradu (17)

*What do they do when they first get there? Does Nikola go to the
monastery with them? Who meets them inside the monastery? Why
does the monastery need money? Who do the visitors meet? Are
there many young Orthodox monks and nuns nowadays?*

Konačno su stigli. Dejanov prijatelj, Nikola, je već radio oko
roštilja, a njegova žena, Mira, ih je pozvala u kuću, da se osveže i
popiju kafu. A onda je Dejan predložio da se prošetaju do manastira. Nikola je odlučio da ostane da se bavi ručkom, a ostali su
krenuli u lepu šetnju kroz šumu. Bio je prekrasan dan i svi su
uživali što hodaju pro prirodi. Uskoro su stigli do manastira. Mira
ih je zamolila da pričekaju dok je ona otišla da potraži igumana
koga dobro poznaje. Posle desetak minuta, pojavila se i rekla da
će iguman rado da ih primi. Ušli su u lepu kamenu zgradu gde im
je hladovina svima prijala. Iguman ih je srdačno dočekao i ponudio
ih šljivovicom koju su kaluđeri sami pravili. Pričao im je o istoriji
manastira i o tome kako su nedavno pokrenuli akciju za obnovu
crkve. Upoznali su dva mlada kaluđera, ali se iguman žalio da u
svim srpskim manastirima fale mladi ljudi: i žene i muškarci.
Razgovor s njim je bio vrlo prijatan: bio je blag i srdačan i imao
je prekrasan dubok glas. Ben je mogao samo da zamisli kako divno
peva tokom službe i jedino mu je bilo žao što to nisu mogli da
čuju. Onda ih je Mira odvela u crkvu i pokazala im sve stare freske
i ikone. Vratili su se vrlo zadovoljni i seli za sto pod vedrim nebom
da uživaju u ručku koji je Nikola pripremio.

Vocabulary

akcija	campaign	**blag**	gentle
dočekati (pf.)	to wait for, greet	**hodati** (imp.)	to go (on foot)
iguman	abbot	**kaluđer**	monk
kamen (noun	stone	**nedavno**	recently
and adj.)		**obnova**	renewal,
osvežiti (pf.)	to freshen up		restoration
pod vedrim	in the open air	**pojaviti se** (pf.)	to appear
nebom	(lit. 'under	**pokrenuti**	to launch,
	the clear sky')	(pf. **pokrenem**)	to set in motion
potražiti (pf.)	to look for	**šljivovica**	plum brandy
već	already	**žaliti se**	to complain, regret

Exercise 6†

Translate the following sentences into Serbian:

1 Someone has come to see you.
2 I don't want to see anyone.
3 Was anyone at home?
4 No, there was no one.
5 What where you talking about?
6 Who will they give the book to?
7 He was telling me about someone from the hotel.

Dialogue 5

Екипа (17)

What is Maja's flat like? What is the idea she suddenly has? How does Sanja react?

У суботу се цела екипа нашла код Маје. Лука је био домаћин и нудио је сваког госта пићем.

– Што ти је лијеп стан! – рекла је Сања чим су ушли.

– Имам среће: ово је наш породични дом, у којем сам одрасла. Родитељи су ми нажалост погинули у саобраћајној несрећи пре две године, тако да сам ту остала сама.

– Ох, баш ми је жао – рекла је Сања дирнута: имали су она и Дадо своје проблеме, али барем су им родитељи живи.

– Хоћеш ли да ти покажем? Ово је трпезарија, али се ретко користи осим кад има гостију. Више волим да једем у кухињи, која је сасвим довољно велика и за друштво од 5-6 људи. Дневна соба је још већа: тамо се налази клавир о којем ти је Филип причао. С једне стране ходника су две спаваће собе са купатилом, а с друге још две, од којих је највећа и најлепша моја. Моја соба има велики балкон са дивним погледом на Врачар.

– Прекрасан је – рекла је Сања. – Никад раније нисам била у таквом стану.

Одједном јој се Маја обратила, радосног лица.

– Знаш шта, Сања, синула ми је сјајна идеја! Како би било да се ти и Дадо преселите овамо код мене?

Сања је стала, широко отворених очију.

- Молим? – рекла је.
- Па да! Не знам како се нисам одмах сетила тога. Ја сам овде сама. Добро, Лука је често ту, али то не смета: он ионако спава у мојој соби. Заиста има много простора. А ти можеш да свираш клавир колико желиш! Реци да се слажеш да је идеја савршена!
- Заиста не знам шта да ти кажем. Бескрајно је лијепо од тебе што тако нешто предлажеш. Једва нас познајеш . . .
- Размисли, питај Даду. Али, молим те, ја то најозбиљније говорим. Сигруна сам да ћемо се одлично слагати.
- Потражићу одмах Даду. Онда морамо да се договоримо о новцу.
- Полако. Види најпре шта каже Дадо.

Vocabulary

бескрајно	endlessly, extremely	дирнут	touched
заиста	really	домаћин	host
лице	face	користити (pf.)	to use
обратити се	to turn to	несрећа	accident, misfortune
одједном	suddenly	одрастао,	grown up (past
око (gen. pl. очију)	eye	одрасла	participle of одрасти
погинути	perish	преселити се	to move
простор	space	радостан,	joyful
раније	earlier, before	радосна	
ретко	rarely	савршен	perfect
саобраћајни	traffic (adj.)	сасвим	quite, completely
сетити се	to remember, have an idea	синути	to flash
сметати	to disturb (imp. + dat.)		

18 Dolazak u Kotor

Arrival in Kotor

In this unit we will look at:

- the imperative
- negative imperatives
- adjective phrases expressed by verbs
- aspect 3
- parts of the body

Dialogue 1

Is Nemanja going to Kotor with the Browns? Does Nena know the way? Why does she advise them to wear their seat belts? What does the Bay of Kotor remind Angela of? Why did many buildings in Kotor have to be restored? Why doesn't John go to the Cathedral?

После пријатне вожње, стигли су у Подгорицу, где су се срели а Маријином унуком, Неном.

Немања:	Добро. Одвешћу вас до агенције где можете да изнајмите кола за остатак пута. Било ми је изузетно пријатно са вама. Дођите нам опет што пре!
Анђела:	Ти си заиста љубазан! Пуно ти хвала на свему.
Немања:	Бићемо у контакту. Џон ми је дао ваше мејл адресе и бројеве мобилних телефона. Сад вас напуштам. Нено, буди добра!

Изнајмили су кола и договорили су се са агенцијом да могу да их оставе у Бару, одакле им касније полази воз за Београд.

Џон:	И сада: кренимо у пустоловину! Знаш ли пут до Котора?

Нена:	О̲тприлике. По̲ђите овом ули̲цом да иза̲ђемо из града, па ћемо лако да на̲ђемо пут. Очекује нас пуно кри̲вина и не̲опрезних воза̲ча на путу па се боље ве̲жите и будите јако па̲жљиви док возите. Моји родитељи су прошле године имали саоб-ра̲ћајну несре̲ћу на овом путу. Тата је завршио у бо̲лници, где су му опе̲рисали ногу, а мама је поло̲мила руку и дуго јој је требало да се по̲врати од шока.

До̲везли су се без пробле̲ма до Котора, где су одлу̲чили да пре̲ноће. Нашли су собе и кренули у шетњу кроз стари град.

Анђела:	Оду̲шевљена сам целом Боком Которском. По̲дсећа ме на фјо̲рдове у Норвешкој, иако је пејзаж наравно сасвим дру̲кчији. Што је прекрасан тај мали манастир на си̲ћушнем о̲ствру у среди̲ни Боке!
Нена:	Слажем се! Хајде да вам по̲кажем Котор, који је за̲иста прелеп. Стра̲дао је од зе̲мљотреса, али су сада скоро све лепе венеци̲јанске зграде и цркве по̲тпуно рено̲виране, а у̲личице око њих по̲прављене. Гле̲дајте тамо десно: то вам је катедра̲ла.
Џон:	У̲ђите ви у катедралу. Незгодно ми је да уђем, јер носим шорц и мајицу са кратким рука̲вама, а мислим да није при̲стојно да се иде у цркву са голим ру̲кама и но̲гама. Хоћу ионако да купим да̲нашњу *Политику* и можда филм за фото-апа̲рат. Са̲чекајте ме овде испред цркве.
Анђела:	Добро. Немој да се и̲згубиш!
Џон:	Не брини! Сви ће знати да ми кажу где се налази катедрала.

Vocabulary

венеци̲јански	Venetian	**вожња**	drive
зе̲мљотрес	earthquake	**изна̲јмити** (pf.)	to hire
изузетан	exceptional	**нога**	leg, foot
оста̲так	remainder	**отприлике**	roughly
пејзаж	landscape	**поло̲мити** (pf.)	to break
пусто̲ловина	adventure	**рукав**	sleeve
саобраћајни	traffic (adj.)	**си̲ћушан**	tiny

средина	centre	**срести (се)**	to meet
страдати (imp.)	to suffer,	(pf., **сретнем**)	
	to be killed	**црква**	church

Language points 1

Formation of the imperative

To form the imperative, take the third person plural of the present tense and remove the final vowel. The stem will end either in **-j** or in a consonant.

(i)   If the stem then ends in **-j**, add nothing for 2nd pers. sing. and **-jмо, -jте** as below:

	(они)	чекају	пију	боје се
2nd pers. sing.	**-j**	чекај!	пиj!	боj се!
1st pers. pl.	**-jмо**	чекаjмо!	пиjмо!	боjмо се!
2nd pers. pl.	**-jте**	чекаjте!	пиjте!	боjте се!

(ii)   If the stem ends in a consonant, add the following endings:

	(они)	говоре	пишу
2nd pers. sing.	**-и**	говори!	пиши!
1st pers. pl.	**-имо**	говоримо!	пишимо!
2nd pers. pl.	**-ите**	говорите!	пишите!

(iii)   With verbs whose infinitive ends in **-ħи**, the formation of the imperative is not quite so straightforward: the endings are added not to the present tense stem, but to the infinitive stem. The original infinitive stem cannot easily be deduced and the imperatives should therefore be learned as they occur. A good dictionary will provide them. Examples:

реħи (derived from   **реци, рецимо, реците**
  рек-ти, к + и = ци):

помоħи (**помог-ти**, :   **помози, помозимо, помозите**
  г + и = зи)

Note: **иħи** and its derivatives form the imperative from the present tense stem:

| (они иду) | иди, идимо, идите |
| (они дођу) | дођи, дођимо, дођите |

There is also a colloquial form of **иди, идимо** which is in very common use:

Хајдемо!	Let's go!
Хајдемо напоље!	Let's go outside!
Хајдемо у биоскоп!	Let's go to the cinema!
Хајде да једемо!	Let's eat!
Хајде да идемо на море ове године!	Let's go to the sea this year!

You will also hear: **Ајдемо!/Ајде!**

(iv) Imperative of **бити**:

буди	2nd pers. sing.
будимо	1st pers. pl.
будите	2nd pers. pl.

Буди разуман!	Be sensible!
Будимо људи!	Let's be decent human beings!
Будите љубазни ...	Be so kind (as to ...)

(v) Imperatives of other persons: these are formed by using the present tense and **да** or **нека**:

First person singular **да** + present:

| Да видим! | Let me see! |

Third person singular and plural **нека** + present:

| Нека дође! | Let him come! |
| Нека чекају! | Let them wait! |

Exercise 1†

(a) Put the verbs in brackets into the imperative form and then translate the sentences into English:

1 А ти _____ да дођеш код нас у Енглеску! (гледати)

2 Нено и Анђела, _____ ми ваше ствари. (дати)

3 Другари, _____ у пустоловину! (кренути)

4 _____ пуно кривина и неопрезних возача на путу. (очекивати, ви)

5 _____ нам коначно свој нови ауто. (показати, ти)

6 _____ ме овде испред књижаре. (сачекати, ви)

7 Да ли сте чули за изреку: _____ игумане, за манастир не _____ ? (путовати, питати, ти)

8 _____ како је било у Котору. (причати, ти)

9 _____ ми да нећете возити пребрзо. (обећати, ви)

10 _____ спорије јер видиш да нас овај ауто претиче. (возити, ти)

> **изрека** saying
> **претицати** (imp. **претичем**) to overtake

(b) Choose the appropriate word:

1 Не _____! Све ће бити у реду са њима.
    (a) брини   (b) заборави
    (c) причај   (d) дај

2 Дођите нам опет _____!
    (a) било где   (b) што више
    (c) што касније   (d) што пре

3 Немој да се _____ у овој гужви!
    (a) отвориш   (b) изгубиш
    (c) збуниш   (d) јавиш

4 Гледајте да стигнете код њих _____!
    (a) у време   (b) на време
    (c) пре времена   (d) мало времена

5 Уђите _____ . Киша почиње да пада.
    (a) напоље   (b) изнутра
    (c) унутра   (d) напољу

6 _____ кола на два дана јер желим да преноћимо у Котору.
    (a) изнајми   (b) купи
    (c) паркирај   (d) опери

7   Децо, будите добра ако желите да вам касније
    _____ палачинке.
       (a) скувам   (b) урадим
       (c) поједем   (d) направим

8   Пођите овим путем па _____ десно.
       (a) стигните   (b) скрените
       (c) возите   (d) дођите

9   _____ се вежите и будите јако пажљиви док
    возите.
       (a) горе   (b) више
       (c) ниже   (d) боље

10 Послушај мој _____ и нећеш имати проблема.
       (a) савет   (b) глас
       (c) отац   (d) шеф

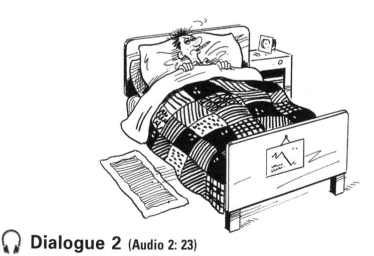

🎧 Dialogue 2 (Audio 2: 23)

Код лекара

At the doctor's

Before they leave Novi Pazar, John asks Nemanja whether it would be possible to visit a doctor. Why does John want to see a doctor? What about Angela? Is the doctor able to help them both?

Џон: Ако ти није тешко, Немања, треба да свратимо код
         лекара док смо још у Новом Пазару. На почетку
         нашег пута овамо, повредио сам лакат и повреда
         никако не иде на боље. Бојим се да ће ми то сметати
         док возим.

Немања: То није никакав проблем. Имам овде пријатељицу
         лекарку. Провериђу да ли је она вечерас у амб-
         уланти.

Анђела: Да ли и ја могу да пођем у исто време? Мене глава
         прилично гадно заболи ако сам предуго на сунцу и
         не знам да ли постоји лек против главобоље који ће
         моћи да ми помогне сада.

У амбуланти.

Лекарка: Добро вече, госпођо. Прегледала сам вам супруга
         и дала сам му рецепт за маст за лакат. Треба да
         га добро намаже кремом ујутру и пре спавања.
         Почеће одмах да делује. А вама треба неки прашак
         за главобољу, зар не? Даћу вам нешто јако, а
         препоручујем вам да пијете што више минералне
         воде и по могућности избегавате најјаче сунце.

Анђела: Где се налази најближа апотека?

Лекарка: Ту одмах поред дома здравља. Али пожурите,
         затвара се за пола сата.

Vocabulary

амбуланта	clinic	**болети**	to hurt
затварати се	to close	(imp. **болим**)	
(imp.)		**глава**	head
деловати	to act	**дом здравља**	health centre
(imp. **делујем**)		**избегавати**	to avoid
лакат	elbow	(imp.)	
(gen. **лакта**)			
лек	medicine	**лекар, -ка**	doctor
маст (f.)	ointment	**намазати**	to rub
прегледати (pf.)	to examine	(pf. **намажем**)	
повредити (pf.)	to injure	**пожурити** (pf.)	to hurry
прашак	powder	**сунце**	sun
(gen. **прашка**)		**супруг, супруга**	husband, wife

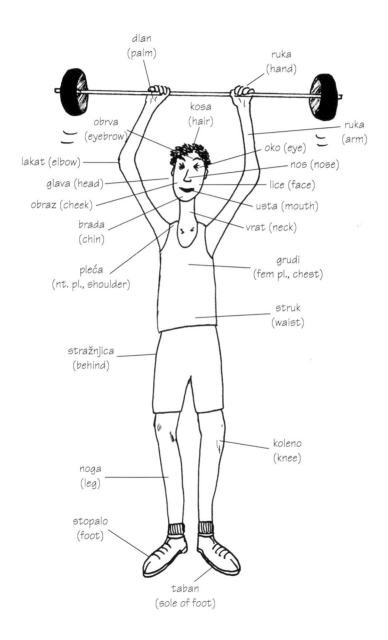

dlan
(palm)

ruka
(hand)

kosa
(hair)

obrva
(eyebrow)

ruka
(arm)

oko (eye)

lakat (elbow)

nos (nose)

glava (head)

lice (face)

obraz (cheek)

usta (mouth)

brada
(chin)

vrat (neck)

pleća
(nt. pl., shoulder)

grudi
(fem pl., chest)

struk
(waist)

stražnjica
(behind)

koleno
(knee)

noga
(leg)

stopalo
(foot)

taban
(sole of foot)

Exercise 2

(a) You feel like renting a car for the weekend. Speak to the assistant in the car rental agency.

(Audio 2: 24)

Службеник: Добар дан, изволите.
Ви: *Greet the assistant and say you want to rent a car for the weekend.*
Службеник: Нема проблема. Да ли желите већа или мања кола?
Ви: *Say that you would like a smaller car and ask how much it costs per day with insurance* (осигурање) *as well.*
Службеник: Имамо једног мањег реноа са клима уређајем (air-conditioning). Изнајмљивање кошта 200 долара на дан са осигурањем.
Ви: *Say that you will take it and ask until when you need to return it.*
Службеник: Вратите ауто до седам сати, иначе ћете морати да платите за још један дан. Дајте ми вашу возачку дозволу и личну карту или пасош.
Ви: *Say 'Here you are.'*

(b)†Translate the following text into Serbian:

Mrs Jović has taken her son to see the doctor. He has flu (**grip**). The doctor has examined him and is now advising Mrs Jović what to do: 'Let him eat a lot of fruit and vegetables. Prepare soups and light dishes if possible. Let him drink a lot of tea and juices. And finally let him sleep a lot. If he is not well after three days, bring him again.'

Language points 2

Negative imperative

There are two methods of forming the negative imperative:

(i) **не** + imperative:

Не брини!   Don't worry!
Не дирајте!   Don't touch!

In these sentences, the *imperfective* aspect *must* be used. The effect of this method is sometimes rather abrupt.

(ii)　This method should be used for 'softer' prohibitions. Either the imperfective or the perfective aspect may be used as appropriate. Examples:

немој (2nd pers. sing.)	**Немој да то једеш!**
	Don't eat that!
немојмо (1st pers. pl.)	**Немојмо да се бринемо!**
	Don't let's worry!
немојте (2nd pers. pl.)	**Немојте да закасните!**
	Don't be late!

(iii)　For 1st pers. sing. and 3rd pers. simply insert the negative particle **не** before the verb:

Нека не заборави!	Let him not forget!
Нека не чекају!	Let them not wait!
Да не закасним!	Let me not be late!

These may also be rendered by means of a request or command to a second person to intervene:

Немој да заборави!	Don't let him forget!
Немојте да закасним!	Don't let me be late!

Some useful imperative phrases

Бежи(те)!	Go away!
Губи(те) се!	Get lost! (*use this with care*)
Пусти(те) ме на миру!	Leave me alone!
Пази(те)!	Watch out!
Стани(те)!	Stop!
Држи(те) лопова!	Stop thief!
Дођи овамо!	Come here!
Пољуби ме!	Give me a kiss!

Exercise 4

Give the negative imperative of the following verbs:

заборавити (ти)　**закаснити** (ми)　**пити ту воду** (ти)
доћи рано (ви)　**мислити на то** (ви)

Language points 3

Vocabulary building

English adjective phrases expressed by a verb

Many expressions composed of 'to be '+ adjective in English are rendered by a verb in Serbian. These should be carefully noted as you come across them. Examples:

каснити, закаснити	to be late
љутити се, наљутити се	to be angry
стрпети се	to be patient
ћутати	to be quiet

 Reading passage 1 (Audio 2: 25)

Kulturni život u Beogradu (18)

Where did they go the following day? When was the Battle of Kosovo? Which empires ruled the Balkans? Who was the ruler of the second Yugoslavia, after the Second World War?

Bilo im je toliko prijatno na Fruškoj Gori da su odlučili da prenoće kod Nikole i Mire. Sledećeg dana, Dejan je Bena i svoju porodicu odveo u Smederevo da vide impozantnu tvrđavu na Dunavu. Usput je Dejan Benu pričao o srpskoj istoriji: kako se posle bitke na Kosovu (28. juni, Vidovdan) 1389, ostatak srpske države preselio severnije, najpre u Kruševac, pod vladarom Stefanom Lazarevićem, čiji je otac, Car Lazar, poginuo na Kosovu. Posle toga se država još više smanjila i, kako su osmanlijiski vladari ulazili sve dublje u balkanske zemlje, centar se pomerio ka Smederevu, gde se država konačno i ugasila.

Ben je želeo da zna šta se desilo u srpskoj istoriji posle kraja srednjevekovne države, pa su Dejan, Mira i njihova deca puno pričali o teškoćama pod turskom vladavinom, koje su opisane u čuvenoj narodnoj poeziji, i o prvom ustanku početkom devetnaestog veka, a onda o drugom ustanku i dugim pregovorima sa Turcima, koji su konačno doveli do samostalne kraljevine Srbije pred kraj devetnaestog veka. Mira mu je govorila o stvaranju prve Jugoslavije, posle prvog svetskog rata, kada su se raspale velike imperije na teritoriji Balkana: osmanlijska i austrougarska, u čijem su okviru bile Hrvatska i, od 1878, Bosna i Hercegovina (koja je ranije takođe bila pod turskom vlašću). A onda su Jugoslaviju u drugom svetskom ratu, okupirale sile Osovine, Nemačka i Italija. Partizani komunisti su vodili tešku i dugotrajnu borbu protiv okupacije, uz pomoć Saveznika i konačno stvorili komunističku državu sa Titom na čelu. Za vreme njegove vladavine, zemlja je bila nezavisna od Sovjetskog Saveza i od zapadnog bloka. Jugoslavija se brzo oporavila od rata i opstala kao federacija 6 republika sve do raspada komunističkog sistema u Evropi. Onda su, početkom 1990-ih, nacionalističke stranke došle na vlast u jugoslovenskim republikama i posle žestokih ratova jugoslovenska federacija se raspala na samostalne države.

Vocabulary

bitka	battle	**čelo**	head (lit. 'forehead')
čuven	famous	**dugotrajan**	lengthy
kraljevina	kingdom	**okvir**	framework
oporaviti se	to recover	**opstati**	to survive
Osmanlijski	Ottoman	(pf. **opstanem**)	
Osovina	Axis	**pomeriti se** (pf.)	to shift
pregovor	negotiation	**raspad**	break-up
raspasti se (pf.)	to break up	**samostalan**	independent
Saveznici	Allies	**smanjiti se**	to be reduced
stranka	(political) party	**stvoriti** (pf.)	to create
stvaranje	creation	**teškoća**	difficulty
tvorevina	creation	**ugasiti se**	to be extinguished
ustanak	uprising	**vladavina**	rule
vlast (f.)	power, government	**žestok**	cruel, vicious

Exercise 5

Answer the following questions:

1 Зашто су Бен, Дејан и Дејанова породица одлучили да остану на Фрушкој Гори?
2 Где су отишли следећег дана?
3 Зашто је Смедерево битан град у српској историји?
4 Шта је опевано у народној поезији?
5 Када се десио први српски устанак?

6 Када се српска држава ослободила турске владавине?
7 Када је створена прва Југославија?
8 Шта се дешавало са Југославијом током другог светског рата?
9 Какав положај је имала Југославија током хладног рата?
10 Шта се десило са Југославијом након распада комунистичких система у Европи?

Language points 4

Aspect 3

This is a large and complex subject and we can do no more than touch on one or two features in these units. We have already looked at many examples of the practice, so we should now consider some features of the theory.

In attempting to formulate a useful description of aspect it is best to start with the more clearly marked quality of perfective verbs. Their function is to express a single finite action which cannot be divided into phases:

Појео сам сладолед.   I ate up the ice cream.

This sentence does not refer to the beginning, middle or end of the action or the process of eating the ice cream. It describes the totality of the action. Another example:

Дошли смо да те видимо.   We have come to see you.

Again there is no reference here to the business of arriving, the speaker's concern is entirely with the fact of having arrived. This is the clearest use of the perfective.

The function of imperfective verbs is vaguer, they express an action which *may* have various different qualities. It may be:

gradual: **Једем сладолед и гледам море.**
           I am eating ice cream and looking at the sea.

repeated: **Долазимо често на ову плажу.**
           We often come to this beach

general: **Воле да читају стрипове.**
           They like to read comic strips.

We have described this function earlier as 'open-ended' and 'on-going'. All of these terms are impressionistic and vague. The closest we can get is perhaps to say that the imperfective describes an action which is not conceived as an indivisible total. Another example of this open-endedness is the use of the imperfective to describe an action which was not actually brought to completion:

Неколико дана се одлучивао да отпутује.
He had been deciding to leave for several days.
or   He spent several days trying to make up his mind to leave.

This can be contrasted with the perfective:

Већ се неколико пута одлучио да отпутује.
He has already decided several times to leave.

It should be clear that in the first instance the subject did not actually make the decision, in the second he did, but something evidently prevented him carrying it out. Again:

Цео дан је гледала излоге и куповала нове хаљине, али ниједна јој није одговарала.
She spent the whole day looking in shop windows and buying new dresses, but she did not like a single one.

In this case she bought the dresses in her imagination only.

Тог дана је купила три нове хаљине.
That day she bought three new dresses.

In this case, it might have taken her all day, but she did buy the dresses in the end.

Since the perfective is conceived as an indivisible totality, it will be obvious that verbs such as **почети** 'to begin', **наставити** 'to continue', **завршити** 'to finish' etc., which refer specifically to the phases of a process (the beginning, the middle and the end, respectively), must be followed by the imperfective:

Почела сам да учим ваш језик; ко зна да ли ћу икад да га научим!
I have begun to study your language; who knows if I'll ever learn it!

Пробудићемо комшије, ако наставимо да певамо овако гласно!
We'll wake the neighbours, if we carry on singing so loudly!

Language in action

Translation of 'it depends'

This is usually rendered by **зависи од** + genitive:

> **Зависи од времена.**   It depends on the weather.

A useful way of expressing English 'it depends when' etc. is to add the conjunction **како** to the adverb or pronoun you wish to qualify:

> **Да ли волите хладно пиво? Како кад.**
> Do you like cold beer? It depends, sometimes.

> **Да ли ваша породица воли лигње? Како ко.**
> Does your family like squid? It depends, some do.

> **Може ли да се купа у топлесу на Јадрану? Како где.**
> Is there topless bathing on the Adriatic? It depends, in some places.

Exercise 6†

(a) Translate into Serbian:

It is difficult to be a child. Your parents and teachers all keep telling you (**stalno govoriti**) what you have to do: 'Get up, get dressed, clean your teeth, make your bed, don't be late for the bus, eat it all up, be home at seven latest, telephone as soon as you arrive, don't be rude (**biti bezobrazan**), don't speak to me like that!' I wonder (**pitati se**), shall I talk to my children like that.

(b) Fill in the blanks in the following instruction on how to prepare Turkish coffee:

_____ (узети) џезву. _____ (напунити) је водом. Ако правиш кафу само за себе, онда _____ (сипати) само једну шољицу воде. Када вода проври _____ (сипати) једну кашику кафе и добро _____ (промешати). Онда _____ (вратити) џезву на шпорет и сачекај један минут. Када кафа проври, _____ (скинути) је са шпорета.

> **џезва**   pot for Turkish coffee
> **проврети** (pf.)   to come to the boil   **промешати** (pf.)   to stir
> **скинути** (pf. **скинем**)   to take off

(c) Answer the following questions with: **kako gde** 'it depends where, in some places', **kako kad** 'it depends when, sometimes' or **kako ko** 'it depends who, some people', as appropriate, and then translate the dialogues:

1 Да ли се у свакој самопослузи могу купити лекови?

   _____ .

2 Да ли сви ви волите да читате новине?

   _____ .

3 Да ли пијеш кафу свако јутро? _____ .

🎧 Dialogue 3 (Audio 2: 26)

Екипа (18)

Who did Jelena want Dado to meet? What does Vedran suggest? What does his company do? What does Dado have to drink? What is the black-haired girl called?

На забави, Дадо је гледао кроз прозор на осветљен град.

– Дадо – пришла му је Јелена. – Дођи овамо.
– Добро – рекао је, помало збуњено, као и увек у Јеленином друштву.
– Желим да те упознам са својим момком – објаснила је. Дади је одједном било лакше.
– Ево долазим – рекао је, уз осмех.
– Ево га. Ведране, ово је наш нови пријатељ, Дадо, о коме сам ти причала. Дадо, мислим да ћеш се одлично слагати са Ведраном, јер и он много воли спорт. Зар не, Ведране?
– Апсолутно. Мораш да дођеш да играш фудбал са мојим другарима – рекао је Ведран.
– То би било сјајно, рекао је Дадо, чији је осмех постајао све шири. Како то да те нисам раније упознао? – питао је.
– Био сам на пословном путу – објаснио је Ведран.
– Ведране, понуди Даду неким пићем: чаша му је празна – рекла је Јелена.
– Изволи, Ведран је пружио Дади чашу пива. А сада, хајде, Јелена, дај да играмо!

Дади је пришла непозната црнокоса девојка са живим очима и ведрим осмехом.

- Здраво – рекла је. – Ја сам Ивана. Мора да си ти Дадо из Босне, Сањин брат.
- Тако је, рекао је и руковао се са њом. Драго ми је. Нисам одавно видио Сању.
- Ено је, види, код врата, сад сам била са њом. Али немојмо је прекидати: мислим да води важан разговор са Филипом.
- Добро – насмејао се Дадо. – Волиш ли плесати?
- Много!
- Онда, хајде да плешемо! И кренули су према трпезарији и музици.

Vocabulary

ведар	bright
момак	boy (friend), young man
олакшати (pf.)	to ease, become easier
плесати (imp. плешем)	to dance (used in Bosnia-Herzegovina and Croatia)
пословни пут	business trip
постајати (imp. постајем)	to become
прекидати (imp.)	to interrupt
прићи (pf. приђем)	to approach, come up to
руковати се (imp. рукујем се)	to shake hands
црнокос	black-haired

19 U Kotoru

In Kotor

In this unit we will look at:

- the conditional: 'I would' etc.
- conditional clauses
- hypotheses
- reflexive phrases

 Dialogue 1 (Audio 2: 27)

What was the weather like when they woke up? What did they decide to do? What did John do first? What happened when they were returning from the island? Who is buried on Mount Lovćen? Where does the road with all the hairpin bends go to?

Следећег дана, кад су се пробудили, било је о̲блачно. Киша није падала али је дувао ветар.

Нена:	Какво грозно време! Облачно је и дува ветар. За сада не пада киша, али нема купања у мору данас! Погледајте те таласе! А бојим се да не би имало смисла ни да се возимо на Ловћен ако се време не по̲прави.
Анђела:	Видећемо, може увек и̲зненада да се ра̲зведри. Но ипак би било добро да поне̲семо кишобране, у случају да почне да пада киша.
Нена:	Морали бисмо ипак одмах да кренемо, јер се иначе б ојим да нећемо имати времена да све у̲радимо.
Џон:	У праву си. Ја ћу сад брзо да одем до реце̲пције да о̲дјавим собе и да платим рачун. Хајде ви купите неко пециво у граду па можемо да једемо успут.

Ulica u Kotoru

Срећом, док су се жене враћале из града, облаци су се разишли и сунце је почело да греје.

Нена:	Красно! Сада можемо да пођемо на Цетиње да бисте видели двор краљева Црне Горе.
Анђела:	Да ли морамо да се возимо овим кривудавим путем?
Нена:	Нажалост, да. То су серпентине, мислим да их има преко двадесет!
Џон:	Ништа се не бојте, даме, кола су јако добра. Биће узб удљиво!
Нена:	Исплати се, свакако: Цетиње је мали, али дивно очуван стари град. Док се шетате његовим уским улицама, поготово око краљевског дворца, лако

можете да замислите како су људи тамо живели у ранијим вековима, без много додира са светом.

Провели су се одлично. Онда су се спустили низ планину и стигли без проблема у Бар, где су оставили кола.

Vocabulary

ветар	wind	**грејати**	to heat
гроб	grave	(imp. **грејем**)	
грозан, -зна	dreadful	**двор**	castle
дворац	palace	**додир**	contact, touch
дувати (imp.)	to blow	**замислити** (pf.)	to imagine
изненада	suddenly	**имати смисла**	to have a point
исплатити се	to be worth	**киша**	rain
(imp.)	(doing	**краљ**	king
	something)	**кривудав**	winding
купање	bathing	**низ** (+ acc.)	down, along
(**купати се**)		**облачан**	cloudy (**облак**
ојачати (imp.)	to strengthen		cloud)
очуван	preserved	**поправити се**	to improve
разведрити		(pf.)	
се (pf.)	to clear up	**разићи**	to part,
серпентина	hairpin bend	(pf. **разиђем**)	to disperse
спустити се (pf.)	to go down	**срећом**	luckily
талас	wave	**узбудљив**	exciting

Language points 1

Formation of the conditional (1)

This mood expresses such statements as 'I would like to live here', 'That really could not happen'. In Serbian it is a compound tense composed of the active present participle (the same as that used for the perfect) and the aorist of **бити**.

Generally speaking, the auxiliary is placed in the same position as other auxiliary (enclitic) verbs (**сам** etc. and **ћу** etc.). There are therefore two possible positions for the participle, depending on whether or not the pronoun, or other preceding word, is used.

читати

Pronoun	Auxiliary	Participle	or	Participle	Auxiliary
ја	бих	читао/ла		читао/ла	бих
ти	би	читао/ла		читао/ла	би
он	би	читао		читао	би
она	би	читала		читала	би
оно	би	читало		читало	би
ми	бисмо	читали		читали	бисмо
ви	бисте	читали		читали	бисте
они	би	читали		читали	би
оне	би	читале		читале	би
она	би	читала		читала	би

Negative

The negative particle **не** is placed immediately before the auxiliary:

Ја не бих читао.   Не бих читао.

Не бих никад од њега купио кола.
I'd never buy a car from him.

Не би ме послушала.
She wouldn't listen to me.

Не бисте стигли на време.
You wouldn't get there in time.

Interrogative

Question marker	Auxiliary	Participle	
Зашто	бисте (ви)	стајали?	Why should you stand?
Колико	бих (ја)	платила?	How much would I pay?
Где	би (они)	ручали?	Where would they have lunch?
Када	би (она)	дошла?	When would she come?
Да ли	бисмо (ми)	закаснили?	Would we be late?

Exercise 1

(a)† Translate the following sentences into Serbian:

1 Where could we stay in case it starts raining?
2 I wouldn't want to go out today.
3 Would you like to travel with them?
4 It would be better for us to have lunch here.
5 Bad weather could change everything.

(b) Have a look at the following weather expressions, check what they mean and put them into lists under the appropriate heading:

ЛЕПО ВРЕМЕ	ЛОШЕ ВРЕМЕ

1 време се пролепшало
2 дува јак ветар
3 сија сунце
4 време се погоршало
5 хладно је
6 пада снег
7 ведро је
8 пљушти киша и грми

пролепшати се to get nicer   **дувати** to blow
погоршати се to get worse   **снег** snow   **пљуштити** to pour
грмети (грми) to thunder

(c)† Translate the following conversation into Serbian:

A: What's the weather like today? It looks nice.
B: Why do you ask?
A: I thought we could go out somewhere, if it's not raining.
B: It's cold and I would prefer to stay at home.
A: You can't stay inside all day!
B: Why not?
A: Come on, the sun's shining. We could go to Košutnjak.
B: It's always windy there.
A: Rubbish!
B: You go then!
A: It would be nicer if we were together.
B: I agree. How would it be if we walked together to our local café?

Language points 2

Formation of the conditional (2)

As a rule, English 'would' may be translated by **бих** etc. In addition
to conditionals, it is used to express:

(a) *habitual actions*

> **Прочитао би по пет књига сваке недеље.**
> He would read some five books each week.

(b) *'softened' requests, statements and commands*

> **Да ли бисте отворили прозор?**
> Would you open the window?

> **Нешто бих вас питао.**
> I would (like to) ask you something.

> **Не бих то препоручила.**
> I wouldn't recommend that.

> **Не бих то радио.**
> I wouldn't do that.

Conditional clauses (1)

In Serbian you must distinguish between *real* conditions and *unreal*
conditions. In real conditions 'if' is translated by **ако** and the tenses
are the same as in English:

> **Ако нађенмо смештај, преноћићемо овде.**
> If we find accommodation, we'll spend the night here.

> **Ако је (буде)**[1] **лепо време, увек вечерају напољу.**
> If it's nice weather, they always have dinner outside.

> **Ако је он то рекао, можемо да му верујемо.**
> If he said that, we can believe him.

---

1 The perfective form of **бити** is often used in this situation.

Exercise 2

(a) Complete the dialogue:

> A: Хајде да останемо у Котору још један дан.
> B: Ако _____ , преноћићемо овде.
> A: Да нађемо смештај? Али зар нисмо остали без пара?
> B: Немамо пара али, ако _____ , моћи ћемо да узмемо неку јефтину двокреветну собу.
> A: Картицом? Нисам знала да си понео кредитну картицу.
> B: _____ . А ако ми не _____ , погледај у мој новчаник.

(b) John listened to the weather forecast on the radio. This is what it said:

СРБИЈА И ЦРНА ГОРА: Умерено и потпуно облачно, местимично са кишом, а локални пљускови са грмљавином се очекују углавном после подне. Ветар слаб до умерен, источни и југоисточни. Најнижа температура од 14 до 17, на југу Црне Горе око 19 степени, а највиша од 21 до 28 степени.

Look at the weather signs and write a forecast for the destinations John and Angela are going to visit soon.

Нови Пазар 25°–28°	
Котор 20°–24°	
Ловћен 19°–21°	

Dialogue 2 (Audio 2: 28)

Домаће, свакодневне теме

Homely everyday topics

The Browns arrive in Budva and meet up with their friends Mihajlo and Mara, whom they had got to know the previous year in England. What does Mihajlo think is most important about being on holiday? When does he start work? Do the children go to school as early as that? What do you think 'baka-servis' is?

Џон:	Ето, мислим да смо вам испричали све у вези са путовањем овамо. Углавном је све прошло без већих проблема.
Михајло:	За мене је на одмору увек најбитније да не морам да устајем у одређено време, да могу да радим шта хоћу и кад хоћу.
Анђела:	Да ли имаш строго одређено радно време?
Михајло:	Прилично. Сваког радног дана устајем рано, у пола шест, а онда можете да замислите колико ми је тешко да се отарасим ове навике кад сам на одмору.
Џон:	Да ли ти посао почиње баш тако рано?
Михајло:	У канцеларији сам у седам. Човек се навикне. Може да буде чак и пријатно. Поготово лети. А још је згодније што посао завршавам у рано поподне. Тада сам слободан да на миру ручам, да мало одспавам, па да после подне радим шта желим.
Анђела:	Да ли деца иду у школу тако рано ујутру?
Михајло:	Већина наших школа ради по систему смена. То значи да дете иде у школу једне недеље пре, а једне после подне. То је понекад компликовано, ако је обоје родитеља запослено и ако та породица нема 'бака сервис'!
Мара:	Мени је најдраже на одмору то што не морам да мислим на куповину и кување, нити на плаћање рачуна.
Џон:	Да ли су плин, струја, телефон код вас скупи?
Мара:	Па знаш како је, све ти се чини много кад ти је плата мала.

Vocabulary

ве̲ћина	majority	испри̲чати (pf.)	to relate
на миру	in peace	на̲вика	habit
на̲викнути се (pf.)	to get used	одмор	rest, holiday
одсп̲авати (pf.)	to take a nap	одре̲ђен	specific, fixed
плин	gas	от̲арасити се (pf. + gen.)	to shake off
посао (gen. посла)	work, job	сва̲кодневни	everyday
строг	strict, severe	смена	shift
		стру̲ја	current, electricity

Language points 3

Conditional clauses (2)

Unreal conditions

These are statements in which the condition has not been or will not be met, such as:

> If you were here, you would see him.
> (But you are not, so you cannot.)

> If it had not been raining, we would have gone out.
> (But it was, so we did not.)

In such sentences in Serbian, the verb in the main clause is in the conditional, as you would expect. What is different is the 'if' clause. The two sentences above could also be expressed:

> Were you here, . . .
> Had it not been raining, . . .

In this case the unreality of the propositions is more obvious. When you need to translate an English 'if' clause, then, you should see whether the 'if' can be omitted in this way. This does not always work, but it is a useful rough guide.

The subordinate clause in such cases is introduced by the conjunction **да** + appropriate tense:

> **Да си овде, видео би га.**
> **Да није падала киша, изашли бисмо.**

Realizable conditions

There is also a category of potentially realizable conditions, e.g. 'If he were to come on time, we would be able to see him.' The subordinate clause in such sentences in Serbian is introduced by кад or **ако** + *conditional*:

> **Кад би дошао на време, могли бисмо да га видимо.**

Also

> **Ако би се јавила, рекао бих да ниси ту.**
> If she were to phone, I'd say you weren't here.

Exercise 3

(a) Match the two halves to make complete sentences, taking one part from numbers 1 to 5, and the other from (a) to (e):

1 Ako ne ustanem na vreme,
2 Da nisam otišao sad na odmor,
3 Kad bi hteo da dođe u Beograd,
4 Išli bismo na planinarenje,
5 Da si ovde,

  (a) video bi kako je Kotor predivan grad.
  (b) zakasniću na posao.
  (c) da je vreme bilo lepo.
  (d) ubila bi me kolotečina.
  (e) mogao bi da živi sa nama.

(b)† Use **ako, kad** or **da** to complete the following:

1 _____ bih imao mnogo novca, obišao bih ceo svet.

2 Videli biste odličnu predstavu _____ ste imali vremena da dođete.

3 _____ imaju slobodnu dvokrevtenu sobu, rezerviši je.

4 _____ sam znao da se skupljate u 'Manježu', došao bih tamo.

5 Pozvao bih ga telefonom _____ imam njegov broj.

6 _____ ne poneseš kišobran sa sobom, pokisnućeš.

> **pokisnuti** (pf.)   to get wet (in the rain)

Language points 4

Language in action

Reflexive passive

One of the main methods of conveying passivity in Serbian is the use of the reflexive form of verbs, which are otherwise transitive. The object of the transitive verb becomes the subject of its reflexive form:

Да ли се код вас пуно пије пиво?
Is beer drunk a lot in your country?

Овде се не говори енглески.
English is not spoken here.

Где се купују карте?
Where does one buy tickets? (Where are tickets bought?)

Како се каже . . .?
How do you say . . .? (lit. 'How is it said?')

Овде се примају странке.
Clients are received here.

Exercise 4†

Translate into Serbian using the reflexive passive:

1 I hear that very good coffee is made here.
2 Can radio B92 be heard via the internet?
3 His books are read throughout the world.
4 The cathedral can be clearly seen on the hill.
5 One could say that it is expensive to live here.

Language points 5

Expression of 'whoever', 'whatever' etc.

The addition of the particle **било** to various pronouns and adverbs conveys English '-ever': **било ко** 'whoever'; **било шта** 'whatever'; **било где** 'wherever'; **било кад** 'whenever'.

Донеси ми било какву књигу.
Bring me any kind of book whatever.

Уради то на било који начин.
Do that in any way whatever.

🎧 Reading passage 1 (Audio 2: 29)

Kulturni život u Beogradu (19)

*How many people came to Ben's meeting with journalists? What did
they talk about? Why did Ben keep a diary during his trip? How
had he prepared for the meeting?*

Približava se kraj Benove posete Srbiji. Ali pre nego što ode, Dejan
se dogovorio sa nekim svojim kolegama, novinarima, da se nađu u
Klubu novinara kako bi Ben mogao da im postavi još neka pitanja,
sad kada zna nešto više o kulturnom životu u Srbiji. Došlo je
desetak ljudi, iz različitih medija.

Vodili su veoma živ razgovor o uslovima u kojima rade i o tome
šta bi želeli da promene. Razume se da su se svi složili da bi njihov
život bio daleko lakši kada bi više zarađivali i kada bi uslovi za
bavljenje novinarstvom bili bolji. Neki su rekli da bi mnogo voleli
da rade neko vreme u inostranstvu kao dopisnici. Najčešće su se
spominjali Nju Jork i Pariz kao najpoželjniji gradovi, kada bi
njihove novine ikada imale sredstava za tako nešto.

Tokom svog boravka, Ben je vodio detaljni dnevnik da bi mogao
da napiše seriju članaka. Sada je imao sjajnu priliku da kompletira
svoju sliku kulturnog života u Srbiji i Crnoj Gori, pa je prethodno
zabeležio čitav niz pitanja. Želeo je da njegovi članci budu što
potpuniji i tačniji.

Vocabulary

čitav	whole	članak	article
dnevnik	diary	dopisnik	correspondent
ikada	ever	izveštaj	report
niz	series	postaviti	to ask a
poželjan	desirable	pitanje (pf.)	question
prethodno	in advance	promeniti (pf.)	to change

sp<u>o</u>minjati (imp.)	to mention	**u inostr<u>a</u>nstvu**	abroad
uslov	condition	**zab<u>e</u>ležiti**	to note,
zarađivati	to earn		make a note
(imp. **zar<u>a</u>đujem**)			

Exercise 5

Read the text above once again and complete the dialogues between Ben and Dejan and Ben and the journalists:

(i) Дејан: Бене, Хајде да се вечерас нађемо са мојим
     пријатељима новинарима.

   Бен: Важи. _____?

   Дејан: Налазимо се у клубу новинара, а онда идемо у
     кафану 'Мањеж'.

   Бен: _____?

   Дејан: Биће ту новинара из различитих медија. Позвао
     сам другаре из *Политике, Бете, Нина,* са
     радија *Б92* и са разних телевизија.

(ii) У "Мањежу"

   Бен: Шта бисте рекли, какви су услови за бављење
     вашом професијом сада у Србији?

   Марко: Наши животи _____ .

   Иван: Ја бих лично много волео _____ .
     На пример, у Њу Јорку или у Паризу.

Language points 6

Aspect 4

Features of English as a guide to choosing aspect

(i) The meaning of a given verb: the *nature* of some types of action suggests a particular aspect:

– *imperfective*: verbs such as: 'to rest', 'to sleep', 'to listen', 'to watch', 'to study', 'to walk', 'to talk' etc.
– *perfective*: 'to say', 'to learn' (as opposed to 'to study'), 'to switch on/off', 'to glance', 'to catch sight of' etc.

(ii) Verbs expressing sense impressions such as 'to see' and 'to hear' may be followed by either an infinitive or a participle in English. For the participle construction Serbian requires **како** + *present*:

Чуо сам га како прилази.
I heard him approaching.

Видели су их како се играју лоптом.
They saw them playing ball.

These constructions require the *imperfective*. However, English infinitive constructions tend to indicate the *perfective*:

Чини ми се да сам чуо како је ушао.
I think I heard him come in.

Видео је како је председник предао документе.
He saw the president hand over the documents.

(iii) Progressive tenses in English *must* be translated by the *imperfective* in Serbian.

I am sitting by the window thinking.
Седим крај прозора и размишљам.

He was reading a newspaper.
Читао је новине.

She will be waiting on the platform.
Чекаће на перону.

Note: This does *not* mean that simple tenses in English denote the perfective.

Adverbs and conjunctions as determining factors

(i) Adverbs: some adverbs clearly indicate one or other aspect:

– *imperfective*: **непрестано** 'constantly'; **стално** 'all the time'; **редовно** 'regularly'; **дуго** 'a long time'; **цео дан** 'all day long'; **неко време** 'some time'; etc.
– *perfective*: **коначно** 'at last'; **одједном** 'all at once'; **изненада** 'suddenly'; **одмах** 'immediately'; **нагло** 'abruptly'; etc.

(Of course some flexibility will be required according to context:

e.g. 'At last they are on their way' obviously refers to an 'ongoing' action.)

(ii)   Conjunctions: some may denote either aspect, depending on context:

> You ought to nibble something *when* you drink strong drinks.
> **Морате да грицкате нешто *кад* пијете жестока пића** (imp.).

> *When* you've finished your wine, try our coffee.
> ***Кад* попијете вино, пробајте нашу кафу** (pf.).

> They took off their shoes *when* they entered the mosque.
> **Изули су ципеле *кад* су ушли у џамију** (pf.).

Some indicate the imperfective:

> She knitted this jumper *while* she was (lying) in hospital.
> **Исплела је овај џемпер док је лежала у болници.**

> As we came I noticed your new car.
> **Док смо долазили приметила сам твоја нова кола.**

Others the perfective:

> I shall telephone *as soon as* I arrive.
> **Телефонираћу чим стигнем.**

(iii)   Phrases introduced by 'for' and 'in': time phrases introduced by 'for' tend to lay emphasis on the *process* of the action:

> We wrote letters *for* three hours.
> **Писали смо писма три сата.**

The imperfective is used to express this emphasis. On the other hand, phrases introduced by 'in' emphasize the totality of the action:

> We wrote the letters *in* three hours.
> **Написали смо писма за три сата.**

Exercise 6[†]

Translate the following passage into Serbian, selecting from the verbs below and paying particular attention to aspect. The verbs are given in the order in which they occur in the text and the first verb in each pair is the imperfective.

The Browns arrived at the hotel. When he came to the reception desk to book a room, John realized that he had left his wallet in the car. He went outside to fetch it. He returned in five minutes and finally began to talk with the receptionist. While John was talking, the receptionist suddenly interrupted him because he recognized Nena. She always stays in this hotel when she comes with her parents to Kotor.

изненада   suddenly

Verb list

стизати, стићи; долазити, доћи; резервисати; схватати, схватити; заборављати, заборавити; одлазити, отићи; узимати, узети; враћати се, вратити се; разговарати, поразговарати; прекидати, прекинути; препознавати, препознати; одседати, одсести; долазити, доћи

Dialogue 3 (Audio 2: 30)

Екипа (19)

How did Dado react to Maja's suggestion? What did Dado and Sanja agree to do? Why does Sanja like the idea of being in Maja's flat? Why would Filip be pleased as well?

Одмах после разговора са Мајом, Сања је попричала са Дадом. Био је одушевљен идејом да се преселе у овај прекрасни, пространи стан. Договорили су се са Мајом да ће да јој се јаве чим буду имали прилику да попричају са Бранком.

Филип је пратио њихов разговор са друге стране собе. Кад је Дадо отишао да потражи Ивану да је поново позове да плеше, пришао је Сањи.
    – Било би заиста предивно, када бисте били овде! – рекао је.
    – Знам, што више мислим, све ми се више свиђа идеја. Могла бих да се заиста посветим свирању, што нисам радила већ годинама. А Дадо би био у друштву које се бави спортом . . .
    – Све је то истина. Али знам шта је за мене лично највећа предност.
    Сања је знала отприлике шта ће да каже, али ништа није рекла. Чекала је да се Филип изјасни.

– Мислим да већ знаш – почео је Филип. – Мени је то важно јер бих се осећао слободније, када не би била више код Бранка. Знам да је изузетно љубазан, али свеједно, не могу сваки час да те видим.

– Ко ти је рекао да би могао "сваки час" и да смо овдје! – насмејала се Сања.

– Знаш шта желим да кажем – рекао је Филип. – Желим да што чешће и што дуже будем са тобом — уколико и ти то желиш, разуме се.

– Ајде, Филипе, доста си причао. Хоћеш да плешемо?

– Хоћу! Ајдемо!

Vocabulary

изјаснити се	to express oneself	посв(ј)етити се	to devote
сваки час	all the time,		oneself to
	at any time	свеједно	all the same
слободан	free	трошак	expense

20 Kraj

The end

In this unit we will look at:

- participles: 'being', 'having been' etc.
- verbal nouns
- word order

Dialogue 1

What did the Browns do when they reached Bar? How did they spend the time in the train? What most impressed John? What impression does Nena have of the English countryside? Why did Angela like Serbian villages?

Преноћили су у Бару, пошто су резервисали возне карте за следеће јутро. Платившри хотел, узели су такси до станице и сели у воз.

Анђела:	Седећи овако, мирно, у возу, не могу а да не размишљам о целом нашем дивном боравку у Србији и Црној Гори.
Џон:	Тачно. И баш смо имали среће што смо успели толико да видимо . . ., а све захваљујући пријатељима и свим љубазним људима које смо успут срели.
Нена:	Има још шта да се види, узгред буди речено!
Анђела:	Сигруно, и то нас радује. Доћи ћемо опет!
Нена:	Баш ме занима који су вам утисци најупечатљивији . . .
Џон:	За мене ће мислим најупечатљивији утисак бити природа. Само погледајте овај предиван пејзаж! Није ни чудо што имате тако сјајне песнике и певаче!

Анђела: То свакако, али за мене је овај пејзаж више од тога: препун је подсећања на важне моменте из историје.

Нена: Нисам била у Енглеској, али судећи по сликама и филмовима које сам видела, пејзаж је код вас углавном питомији него што је код нас.

Џон: У праву си. Овде има великих планина, река, клисура и густих, старих шума.

Анђела: Да и ваша земља није тако густо насељена. Мени се много свиђају ваша села, у којима се очигледно још увек може наићи на бројне старе обичаје.

Нена: Да, слажем се, села су врло живописна, али није увек лако живети тамо.

Џон: Приближавамо се Београду. Као да се враћамо кући!

Нена: Баш ми је драго да то чујем! Сигурно сте приметили да су Срби и Црногорци гостопримљив народ. Желим да однесете најлепше успомене одавде и да нам се вратите што пре!

Vocabulary

бројан, -јна	numerous	**гостопримљив**	hospitable
густ	dense	**живописан, -сна**	picturesque

Železnička stanica Beograd

клисура	gorge	насељен	inhabited
питом	tame	радовати (се)	to be glad
судити (imp.)	to judge	(imp. радујем)	
узгред буди	incidentally,	упечатљив	indelible
речено	by the way	успомена	memory
чудо	surprise, wonder		

Language points 1

Participles (1) (verbal adverbs or gerunds)

There are four participles in Serbian, of which two are verbal adjectives and two verbal adverbs.

We have already met the active past participle (**био, имао** etc.), and know that this is one of the adjectival forms. We shall come to the other adjective form, the passive past participle, later – it is not in very common use.

There are two verbal adverbs or gerunds, one denoting simultaneous action and the other past action: (i) 'seeing' and (ii) 'having seen'.

Present gerund

This is formed by adding the suffix **-ћи** to the third person plural of the present tense of the *imperfective*:

(они) говоре	**говорећи**	speaking
(они) пишу	**пишући**	writing
(они) имају	**имајући**	having

The gerund is infrequently used, even in the written language, except in certain situations.

The present gerund of **бити** is based on the perfective third person plural **буду** = **будући**. This is used frequently as a conjunction with **да**:

Будући да смо у Србији ...
Since we are in Serbia ...

Будући да је лепо време ...
Since it is nice weather ...

Strictly speaking, the gerund is, indeclinable, like all adverbs. But, increasingly, certain gerunds are becoming used as adjectives:

будући   **Да те упознам са својим <u>будућим</u> мужем!**
Let me introduce you to my future husband!

идући   **Вратиће се сигурно <u>идуће</u> године ако могу.**
They will certainly come back next year if they can.

следећи   <u>**Следећег**</u> **дана смо се рано пробудили.**
We woke up early the following day.

текући   **Колико имаш на <u>текућем</u> рачуну?**
How much have you got in your current account?

(**тећи**, 3rd. pers. pl. **теку**: 'to flow')

Past gerund

This is formed by adding the suffix **-в** or **-вши** (after a vowel) or **-авши** (after a consonant) to the infinitive stem:

уста-ти	уставши	рек-ти (рећи)	рекавши
виде-ти	видевши	мог-ти (моћи)	могавши
сети-ти се	сетивши се		

Again, the past gerund is rarely used. It is more common to find a whole clause where such a participle is used in English:

Having started the book I'd like to finish it.
Кад сам већ почео да читам књигу, хтео бих да је завршим.
or   **Будући да сам почео ...**
or   **Почео сам, па бих хтео ...**

As in the case of the present gerund, we find that the past gerund of **бити, бивши**, is in common use as an adjective:

Да те упознам са својом бившом супругом!
Let me introduce you to my former wife!

Та кућа припада бившем председнику.
That house belongs to the former president.

Note: The common English construction with the active present participle ending in '-ing' can cause problems in translating, e.g. 'I heard the birds singing'. Such sentences should be rendered by **како** + present (imperfective) tense: **Чуо сам како птице певају.**

Exercise 1†

(a) Put the verbs in brackets into the past or present gerund, as appropriate:

   1 _____ (седети) у возу, причали су о утисцима са путовања.

   2 _____ (враћати се) кући, размишљао је о најупечатљивијим успоменама са летовања.

   3 Узео је да погледа фотографије _____ (написати) писмо пријатељу.

   4 _____ (изаћи) из хотела, позвали су такси.

   5 _____ (бити) да смо устали касно, мораћемо да јуримо на воз.

(b) Translate the following sentences into Serbian:

   1 I think I saw them coming.
   2 Have you heard her singing?
   3 We found them playing in the park.
   4 He didn't notice me going out.
   5 She stood by the window and watched people passing by.

Language points 2

Participles (2)

Passive past participle

The passive past participle is the other verbal adjective. Passive participles are formed from the infinitive stem of either aspect. Most verbs with the infinitive ending in **-ати** have the passive participle in **-ан**:

читати	читан, читана, читано
позвати	позван, позвана, позвано

Most verbs with infinitive ending in **-ити** or **-ети** have **-jен** (see 'Grammar summary', section 6 (p. 306) for the rules of effect of **j** on the preceding consonant):

видети	виђен, виђена, виђено
учинити	учињен, учињена, учињено

Verbs with the infinitive ending in **-нути** have **-нут**:

прекинути **прекинут**
to interrupt

Verbs with infinitive ending in **-ети** and present **-мем** or **-нем** have **-ет**:

заузети (**заузмем**) **заузет**
to occupy

проклети (**прокунем**) **проклет**
to curse

These are the most common regular patterns.

Examples are:

Да ли је овај хлеб добро испечен?
Is this bread well baked?

Сто је прострт, хлеб је нарезан, вино је охлађено, рижа је скувана. Дођите да ручате!
The table is laid, the bread is cut, the wine chilled, the rice boiled. Come and have lunch!

Verbal nouns

Many of these passive participles may be made into nouns by the addition of the suffix **-је**:

ослободити to liberate	**ослобођен** liberated	**ослобођење** liberation
читати	**читан**	**читање** reading
проматрати	**проматран**	**проматрање** observation, watching
учити	**учен**	**учење** learning

Intransitive verbs cannot have a passive participle. In such cases the endings **-ање** or **-ење** are added to the infinitive stem:

купати се	**купање**	bathing
седети	**седење**	sitting
путовати	**путовање**	travelling, journey

Exercise 2

(a) John is leaving the hotel in Bar and is giving instructions to a taxi driver. Put the sentences in the jumbled-up dialogue in order:

Џон:	Добро јутро.
Таксиста:	Ево стигли смо.
Џон:	До железничке станице. И ако можете да пожурите. Каснимо на воз.
Таксиста:	800 динара.
Џон:	Хвала.
Таксиста:	Нема проблема господине. Даћу све од себе, али јутро је, и велика је гужва у саобраћају. . . . Надам се да вам не смета што пушим.
Џон:	Колико смо дужни?
Таксиста:	Добро јутро, господине.
Џон:	Ни најмање, и ми смо пушачи.

дати све од себе   to do one's best
ни најмање   not at all, not remotely

(b) John has arrived at the railway station in Bar and is trying to purchase tickets. Put the sentences in the jumbled-up dialogue in order:

Службеник:	2 сата.
Џон:	Не, у једном смеру. Идемо после одмах на аеродром.
Службеник:	Добро јутро, изволите.
Џон:	Имам резервације за воз Бар-Београд који креће у 10:35 сати.
Службеник:	Дајте ми да погледам. Желите повратне карте?
Џон:	Да ли могу да платим картицом?
Службеник:	У реду. Цена карте је 1,523 динара.
Џон:	Ево новца. Колико касни?
Службеник:	Не примамо картице, само готовину. Узгред буди речено, воз за Београд касни.

(c) Now *you* take a taxi: 🎧 (**Audio 2: 31**)

Таксиста:	Добро вече, господине/госпођо.
Vɪ:	*Say hello and where you want to go.*

VOZNA KARTA   *ŽTP BEOGRAD*
- prvi razred -

BEOGRAD – BAR   datum: 23.08.2003.
polazak: 08:25 dolazak: 09:55
rezervacija: sedište 36D

Таксиста:	У центру је гужва па ћемо се возити мало спорије.
Vɪ:	*Say that it doesn't matter since you are not in a hurry.*
Таксиста:	Ево стигли смо.
Vɪ:	*Ask how much it is.*
Таксиста:	580 динара.
Vɪ:	*Say 'Here is 600 dinars and you can keep the change.' Just say 'It's all right.'*

Reading passage 1 (Audio 2: 32)

Kulturni život u Beogradu (kraj)

Why does Ben feel indebted to Dejan? What does he feel is the only way he can thank him? How is he going to send Dejan the articles he writes? Why do both Dejan and Ben feel it is important that people read about cultural life in Serbia and Montenegro?

Vrativši se kući, Ben je seo da napiše Dejanu pismo, da mu se zahvali na svemu što je učinio za njega.

Dragi Dejane,
   Ne znam kako da ti se z<u>a</u>hvalim na svemu. Bio si najljubazniji mogući dom<u>a</u>ćin, vodič i prijatelj. Mnogo sam video, čuo i naučio i sve što sam s<u>a</u>znao o b<u>o</u>gatom kulturnom životu Srbije i Crne Gore dugujem tebi. Upoznao sam velik broj izuzetno pr<u>i</u>jatnih i dragih ljudi, koji su me srdačno primili u svoju sredinu, i u svoje kuće, a i u svoj život. To je dug koji se teško može otplatiti. Jedini

pravi dokaz moje zahvalnosti biće moji članci. Poslaću ih tebi mejlom pre nego što ih predam novinama, da budem siguran da nisam negde pogrešio ili nešto bitno izostavio. Naravno, sve samo u slučaju da si spreman da mi učiniš još i ovu dodatnu uslugu. Ali znam da ti je stalo do toga da Srbija i Crna Gora budu poznate u svetu po nečem drugom, a ne samo po ratu i atentatima i burnom političkom životu.

Ovo pismo ti dolazi običnom poštom, jer sam hteo da vam pošaljem i neke slike za koje se nadam da će da vas sve obraduju. Konačno sam prebacio sve svoje beleške sa laptopa na veliki kompjuter i od sada ću moći redovno da ti se javim mejlom.

Najsrdačnije pozdravi Nadu i zagrli decu,
        Od sveg srca te pozdravlja
        tvoj Ben

Vocabulary

atentat	assassination	**beleška**	note
buran	stormy	**dodatan**	additional
dokaz	proof	**dug**	debt
dugovati	to owe	**izostaviti** (pf.)	to leave out, omit
(imp. **dugujem**)		**mejl**	email
obradovati (imp.	to please,	**otplatiti** (pf.)	to pay, repay
obradujem)	delight	**pogrešiti** (pf.)	to be mistaken
poslati (pf. **pošaljem**)		to send	
pozdravljati, pozdraviti		to greet	
prebaciti (pf.)		to transfer	
predati (pf.)		to hand over	
stalo je (nekome) do		someone cares (about something,	
(nekoga, nečega)		someone)	
učiniti uslugu (pf.)		to do (someone) a favour	
vodič		guide	
zagrliti (pf.)		to embrace, hug	
zahvaliti se (pf.)		to thank	

Exercise 3

Now you try to write a letter about your holiday to a friend. This is the information you need to include:

– where you are
– how long you have been there and when you are coming home

- you've met many people who are very hospitable and helpful
- the country is beautiful
- you have visited both the coast and the mountains
- stayed in various hotels
- everything is so cheap
- for that reason you never rented a car but took taxis everywhere
- you haven't had any problems
- you want to come back next year

Language points 3

Word order 1

This is another area that can cause some difficulties for English speakers. Some of these considerations are basic to correct grammar, and some are more subtle and largely stylistic. It is important to be aware of differences in word order between the two languages, both in composing correct and informative utterances in Serbian and in translating from Serbian into English.

Difficulties arise for two main reasons: (i) the presence of *enclitics*, for which there is no equivalent in English; (ii) the fact that English speakers are familiar with a system in which word order indicates syntactic relations between the main elements of a sentence and only secondary elements (adverbs, preposition phrases) normally vary in position.

We shall look at these two areas of difficulty in turn.

Enclitics

We are already quite familiar with the basic rules governing the placing of enclitics and with the order in which they come when there are several of them. Where there is a group of enclitics they must all come together in the order:

> interrogative particle **li**; verbal; dat. acc./gen. (of pronouns); **se**; **je**

The enclitic group is normally placed after the first element in the sentence or clause. This may be *a single word*:

***Ivan* mi je kupio kartu.**
Ivan bought me a ticket.

Note: **ne** + verb count as a single word:

Ne mogu ti ga odmah dati.
I can't give it to you immediately.

Remember also that the linking conjunctions **i**, **a** and **ni** do not count as separate words in this context.
The first element may also be a phrase:

Jedan moj prijatelj **mi je rekao da imate stan.**
A friend of mine told me you had a flat.

Prošle nedelje **su nas pozvali na večeru.**
Last week they invited us to dinner.

In general, it is considered literary or pedantic to break up a phrase by putting the enclitics strictly after the first word. But notice the following interrogative words which do not form a phrase with the words they govern:

Koliko je sati?
What's the time?

Koliko ima godina?
How old is he/she?

Koje su boje tvoja nova kola?
What colour is your new car?

The conjunctions **ali**, **ili** and **jer** may be treated as the first word in the sentence or simply as linking words.
But some other conjunctions never count as the first word because they are followed by a pause, sometimes an actual comma:

Dakle **nisam mu ga dao.**
So I didn't give it to him.

Prema tome, **javiće ti se sutra.**
Consequently he'll ring you tomorrow.

The most important thing to remember is that if a sentence or clause starts with a 'clause introducer', the enclitics must follow immediately after it. Consequently when you are composing a clause in Serbian and come to such a word you must immediately work out which enclitics will be required later in the sentence and put them in straightaway. All the other elements in the sentence must then be fitted in. This necessity is the cause of frequent mistakes for English speakers.

Such 'clause introducers' are **da**, **što**, **ako**, relatives and inter-rogatives.

Rekao je *da* će mi ga odmah vratiti.
He said (*that*) he would give it straight back to me.

Drago mi je *što* ste nam opet došli.
I'm glad (*that*) you've come to us again.

***Pre nego što* smo mu objasnili o čemu se radi, izašao je.**
Before we had explained to him what it was about,
he went out.

***Ako* mi je vrati, daću ti knjigu.**
If he returns it to me, I'll give you the book.

To je prijatelj *koji* mi je pričao o tebi.
That's the friend *who* told me about you.

To je prijatelj *o kom* sam ti pričala.
That's the friend I told you about (*about whom* I told you).

Više ne znam ni *kako* se zvao.
I no longer even know *what* he was called.

Moram da znam *kad* ćeš da mi ga daš.
I must know *when* you're going to give it to me.

Care must be taken with subordinate clauses, which behave like independent units. Enclitics from the main clause are not usually placed immediately after them and never inside them. This presents no difficulty if the main clause comes first:

Jasno mi je da si ga tajno viđala.
I realize that you've been seeing him secretly.

When the subordinate clause comes first the enclitics from the main clause follow the first word in the main clause: **Da si ga tajno viđala, jasno mi je**. This construction can be awkward, so often the pronoun **to** is added to take over the role of the subordinate clause: **Da si ga tajno viđala, to mi je jasno**. Such constructions are far more frequent in Serbian than their equivalent would be in English.

Infinitives can behave either as separate clauses or as parts of the main clause:

Mira te želi videti.
Mira wants to see you.

If the main clause contains enclitics, they are all put together:

Mira te je želela videti.
Mira wanted to see you.

Exercise 4

(a) Some of the sentences in this dialogue are jumbled up. Put the
words in the jumbled-up sentences (shown in bold) in order
and translate the dialogue:

Tomo and his sister Ana are talking on the phone.

A: Halo, Tomo ovde Ana.
B: Hej, zdravo Ana. Kako si, šta ima novo?
A: Dobro sam, hvala. **pitam / da / sam / Htela / te / da / znaš /
li kad / na / mama i tata / sleću / aerodrom.**
B: **znam / tačno / Ne / mislim / ali / proverim / mogu / da /
da.** zašto / a / pitaš?
A: **Pa / sam / mislila / da / od / neko / nas / ode / po / aero-
drom / na / njih.**
B: Hajde, ja ću da proverim kada sleće avion i otićiću da ih
pokupim. **bez / budi / brige!**
A: **ti / hvala / puno.**

Language points 4

Word order 2

Apart from the strict rules governing the placing of enclitics, word
order in Serbian is relatively free. The existence of cases makes it
possible to place subject verb and object in any order:

I gave the porter the luggage.   **Dala sam nosaču prtljag.**
                                   Prtljag sam dala nosaču.
                                   Nosaču sam dala prtljag.

All of these sentences are equally acceptable. Their order is not
random, however: each sentence conveys a slightly different emphasis. It is important to distinguish first of all between basic, grammatical word order in Serbian and order which is determined by
context and which conveys meaning in itself.

Basic, neutral, word order, independent of context, is on the whole similar to English: subject – verb – object.

In word order conditioned by context, however, there are various differences. These seem to stem from the fact that in Serbian, as a rule, the less informative part of the sentence comes before the more informative part. (This is related to the question of enclitics, in that stress tends to build up over the sentence with increasing emphasis on the end. Consequently the enclitics must be placed as far as possible from this inherent emphasis.) Examples:

Prošle nedelje nismo uopšte izašli.
We didn't go out at all last week.

This order emphasizes the fact that the speaker stayed at home.

Nismo uopšte izašli prošle nedelje.

This order, on the other hand, stresses the fact that the speaker usually goes out a lot in any given week but did not this particular week. This means that in Serbian if the object is of less informational value (perhaps because it has already been mentioned) it may be placed first in the sentence:

Tu kuću je sagradio poznati arhitekta.
A famous architect built that house.

It is possible for the Serbian order to be preserved in English by using a passive construction: 'This house was built by a famous architect.' This is a very important device, which works both ways: Serbian generally avoids the passive, but English passive constructions can usually be rendered by placing the object first in the sentence, as in the example above.

The principle is, then, that new information or the more informative part of the sentence tends to follow other elements in the sentence:

Ovi stanovi su sagrađeni pre deset godina. U stanovima žive uglavnom mladi ljudi.
These flats were built ten years ago. On the whole young people live in the flats.

Adverbial 'scene setting' phrases

These phrases are placed at the beginning of a neutral sentence in Serbian: their function is to 'set the scene' for the main information. In English, on the other hand, they are normally at the end:

Na plaži **je bilo mnogo meduza.**
There were a lot of jellyfish *on the beach.*

Po povratku **smo bili vrlo zauzeti.**
We were very busy *after we got back.*

Za vreme odmora na ostrvu, **nismo mnogo čitali.**
We didn't read much *during our holiday on the island.*

In Serbian adverbs which qualify or quantify the action of the verb generally precede it:

Veoma **lepo svira klavir.**
She plays the piano very well.

Prebrzo **govore. Ništa ne razumem!**
They speak too fast. I don't understand a thing!

So, English speakers should take care over the placing of adverbs and adverbial phrases: it will help to make a note of instances you come across in your reading.

Adverbs and pronouns with low informational value

As a general rule, objects, pronouns and adverbs which carry little information precede the verb. To put them after the verb would give them special emphasis, altering the meaning of the sentence:

Daj da ti *nešto* **pokažem.**
Let me show you *something.*

Daj da ti pokažem *nešto.*
Let me show you *at least something*, even if you don't want to see everything.

Negde **smo ga videli.**
We saw him *somewhere.*

Videli smo ga *negde.*
We saw him *somewhere*, I'm just trying to think where it was.

Such 'low prominence' words include: **nešto, negde, nekako, nekud, tu**, **ovde**, **juče**, **danas**, **sutra**, **ovo**, **to**, **sad**, **često**, **stalno.**

Phrases with fixed word order

There are a few more or less fixed patterns which should be learned:

Vocative phrases

In these the neutral order of adjective–noun is often reversed:

Budalo jedna!	**Bože dragi!**
You fool!	Dear God!
Mili moj!	**Zlato moje!**
My darling!	My treasure (gold)!

Possessive phrases

taj moj prijatelj	**ovi njegovi prijatelji**
that friend of mine	these friends of his
jedan moj poznanik	**dva naša poznanika**
an acquaintance of	two acquaintances of
mine	ours

Exercise 5†

Translate the following passage into Serbian, paying particular attention to word order:

Last week John and Angela left Serbia and went back to England. After a month-long holiday in Serbia it wasn't easy to go home. They had a wonderful time there and would really love to visit the country again next year.

This week they want to organize a party for their friends and tell them about their trip. They want to show them photographs and give them presents from Serbia. Angela plans to impress everyone with some Serbian dishes which she learned how to prepare when they were staying in Sirogojno. But before that, John will offer plum brandy to his friends since he brought a bottle with him. He would also like to tell everyone about the series of articles about cultural life in Belgrade that a local newspaper has started to publish.

Dialogue 2

Екипа (крај)

Who telephoned Branko's flat the next day? What did he suggest?
Why was Dado especially pleased? Why does Vedran like living on
a barge? What does Sanja offer to do? Did they have a good day?

Сви су се сложили да је журка била сјајна и било је прилично
касно када су се разишли. Следећег јутра, телефон је зазвонио
код Бранка, Сањиног и Дадиног рођака. Јавио се Ведран и позвао
их да дођу са целом екипом да проведу остатак дана код њега
на сплаву на Сави, близу Аде Циганлије. Дан је био сунчан и
ведар, па су се Сања и Дадо брзо спремили.

– Здраво, другари! викнули– су кад су стигли до обале.
– Еј, добро дошли! – рекао је Ведран и помагао Сањи да се
   попне на брод.

Дадо се посебно обрадовао кад је видео да је и Ивана у друштву.
А и Филипу је било очигледно драго што је Сања стигла.

– Што ти је диван брод! – рекла је Сања.
– Да ли овде живиш? – питао је Дадо, такође одушевљен.
– Па да, ово ми је дом – одговорио је Ведран. – Много путујем,
   пословно, а онда спавам по разним хотелима, па заиста
   уживам кад год се вратим овамо, у овакав једноставан и
   опуштен начин живота.
– Зими, понекад ипак зна да се појави код пријатеља! –
   Насмјала се Јелена.
– Шта ћете да пијете? Пиво се хлади у реци, а има наравно и
   вина и свега и свачега.
– Лука и Маја се баве роштиљем. Ено их, под дрвећем – рекао
   је Филип. – А ја сам задужен за салату.
– Могу ли да ти помогнем? – понудила је Сања.
– Ако те не мрзи, можеш. Хвала на понуди. Биће брже готово.
   Одвео ју је доле у малу кухињу.
– Сјајно, ту има све што је потребно! – рекла је Сања.
– Има, само фали мало више места! Али нема везе. Можеш
   ли исецкати овај парадајз? Даћу ти даску.

Радили су тихо, а онда је Филип стао и погледао Сању.

– Баш ми је супер, овде сам са тобом, заједно радимо у кухињи, као да смо прави пар.
– Филипе, молим те, не претеруј! Уживајмо данас, има времена за те ствари – рекла је Сања одлучно.

Сви су провели диван дан заједно и на крају су се разишли срећни, одморни и спремни за понедељак: неко за посао, а неко за факултет.

Vocabulary

Ада Циганлија	island on the Sava river in Belgrade	**брод**	boat
доле	down, below	**викнути** (pf. **викнем**)	to shout
задужен	in charge of, responsible for	**дом**	home
одлучан	decisive	**мрзети** (imp.)	to hate (*here* 'if you don't mind')
одморан	rested		
понуда	offer	**опуштен**	relaxed
претеривати (imp. **претерујем**)	to exaggerate	**пословно**	on business
		сецкати (imp.)	to chop
		сплав	barge
ступити (pf.)	to step	**хладити се** (imp.)	to get cool

Grammar summary

1 Noun declensions

Masculine

Singular

nom.	prozor	prijatelj	sto	muž	čitalac
gen.	prozora	prijatelja	stola	muža	čitaoca
dat.	prozoru	prijatelju	stolu	mužu	čitaocu
acc.	prozor	prijatelja	sto	muža	čitaoca
voc.	prozore	prijatelju	stole	mužu	čitaocu
loc.	prozoru	prijatelju	stolu	mužu	čitaocu
instr.	prozorom	prijateljem	stolom	mužem	čitaocem

Plural

nom.	prozori	prijatelji	stolovi	muževi	čitaoci
gen.	prozora	prijatelja	stolova	muževa	čitalaca
dat.	prozorima	prijateljima	stolovima	muževima	čitaocima
acc.	prozore	prijatelje	stolove	muževe	čitaoce
voc.	prozori	prijatelji	stolovi	muževi	čitaoci
loc.	prozorima	prijateljima	stolovima	muževima	čitaocima
instr.	prozorima	prijateljima	stolovima	muževima	čitaocima

Note: soft consonants: **c, č, ć, dž, đ, j, lj, nj, š, ž**

1 Masculine nouns with soft consonant ending preceded by **e** usually have instrumental singular **-om**: **Beč** 'Vienna', **Bečom**; **padež** 'case', **padežom**. Masculine nouns ending in **-c** usually have instrumental **-om**; but if **-c** follows mobile **a**, then instrumental always ends **-em**: **stranac** 'foreigner', **strancem**; **novac** 'money', **novcem**; **otac, ocem**.

2 Masculine nouns ending in **-anin** (e.g. **građanin, Dubrovčanin**) have plural **-ani: građani** etc.

Neuter

Singular

nom.	selo	more	vreme[1]	dete[2]
gen.	sela	mora	vremena	deteta
dat.	selu	moru	vremenu	detetu
acc.	selo	more	vreme	dete
voc.	selo	more	vreme	dete
loc.	selu	moru	vremenu	detetu
instr.	selom	morem	vremenom	detetom

Plural

nom.	sela	mora	vremena	deca
gen.	sela	mora	vremena	dece
dat.	selima	morima	vremenima	deci
acc.	sela	mora	vremena	decu
voc.	sela	mora	vremena	deco
loc.	selima	morima	vremenima	deci
instr.	selima	morima	vremenima	decom

1 Most neuter nouns ending in **-me** follow this pattern.

2 Some neuter nouns have the infix **-et-**. These are usually the words for young animals and they have an irregular plural (usually a feminine singular collective form, e.g. **tele** 'calf' has gen. sing. **teleta** and n. pl. **telad**).

Feminine

Singular

nom.	žena	stvar
gen.	žene	stvari
dat.	ženi	stvari
acc.	ženu	stvar
voc.	ženo	stvari
loc.	ženi	stvari
instr.	ženom	stvari

Plural

nom.	žene	stvari
gen.	žena	stvari
dat.	ženama	stvarima
acc.	žene	stvari
voc.	žene	stvari
loc.	ženama	stvarima
instr.	ženama	stvarima

Feminine nouns ending in **-a** preceded by two or more consonants may have genitive plural in **i**: **torba**, gen. pl. **torbi** (see also section 5.)

2 Adjective declensions

	Masculine	*Neuter*	*Feminine*

Singular definite

nom.	mladi	mlado	mlada
gen.	mladog(a)	mladog(a)	mlade
dat.	mladom(e)	mladom(e)	mladoj
	mladom(u)	mladom(u)	
acc. (inan.)	mladi	mlado	mladu
(an.)	mladog(a)		
voc.	mladi	mlado	mlada
loc.	mladom(e)	mladom(e)	mladoj
	mladom(u)	mladom(u)	
instr.	mladim	mladim	mladom

Plural

nom.	mladi	mlada	mlade
gen.	mladih	mladih	mladih
dat.	mladim(a)	mladim(a)	mladim(a)
acc.	mlade	mlada	mlade
voc.	mladi	mlada	mlade
loc.	mladim(a)	mladim(a)	mladim(a)
instr.	mladim(a)	mladim(a)	mladim(a)

	Masculine	*Neuter*

Indefinite (singular only)

nom.	mlad	mlado
gen.	mlada	mlada
dat.	mladu	mladu
acc. (inan.)	mlad	mlado
(an.)	mlada	
loc.	mladu	mladu
instr.	mladim	mladim

Soft stem, definite (singular)

nom.	sveži	sveže
gen.	svežeg(a)	svežeg(a)
dat.	svežem(u)	svežem(u)
acc. (inan.)	sveži	sveže
(an.)	svežeg(a)	
loc.	svežem(u)	svežem(u)
instr.	svežim	svežim

Alternative longer form. The shorter forms are normally used, however, there are three situations in which the longer forms should be used:

1 If the adjective is used on its own, without a noun: **Uzmi hleba, ako ima svežega**.

2 If several adjectives qualify the same noun, the first will usually be long: **Sećam se tvoga simpatičnog strica**.

3 If the adjective follows the noun it qualifies: **Ni imena svoga se nije više sećao**.

The last example is not so much a grammatical rule as a stylistic preference, and it is on the whole for stylistic purposes that the longer forms are used.

3 Personal pronoun declensions

Singular

nom.	ja	ti	on	ono	ona	
gen.	mene, me	tebe, te	njega, ga	njega, ga	nje, je	sebe, se
dat.	meni, mi	tebi, ti	njemu, mu	njemu, mu	njoj, joj	sebi, si
acc.	mene, me	tebe, te	njega, ga[1]	njega, ga[1]	nju, ju, je	sebe, se
loc.	meni	tebi	njemu	njemu	njoj	sebi
instr.	mnom(e)	tobom	njim(e)	njim(e)	njom(e)	sobom

Plural

nom.	mi	vi	oni	ona	one
gen.	nas	vas	njih, ih	njih, ih	njih, ih
dat.	nama, nam	vama, vam	njima, im	njima, im	njima, im
acc.	nas	vas	njih, ih	njih, ih	njih, ih
loc.	nama	vama	njima	njima	njima
instr.	nama	vama	njima	njima	njima

1 The alternative short form **nj** may be used after a preposition which carries stress. You may come across examples, particularly in literary texts.

4 Verb types

Verbs are divided into several classes, with subdivisions according to their infinitive stem. There are three main sets of endings, however, as seen in Unit 2:

	I	*II*	*III*
1st pers. sg.	-am	-im	-em
3rd pers. pl.	-aju	-e	-u

It is important to be aware that some forms of the verb are based on the infinitive stem, and some on the present tense stem. In many verbs these are the same, but in others they are not and the present tense stem of such verbs must therefore be learned. A good dictionary will supply the first person of the present tense whenever this cannot be deduced from the infinitive. Here are a few guidelines.

Infinitives ending in -ti

The infinitive and present tense stems of these verbs are usually the same:

      čitati   to read   **čitam**

Usually the vowel preceding **-ti** will indicate which set of endings the verb takes, but not always:

1 Verbs ending in **-ati** take Type I endings, unless:

  (a) the last consonant of the infinitive stem is **č**, **ž** or (sometimes) **j**, then Type II:

trčati	to run	**trčim**
držati	to hold	**držim**
stajati	to stand	**stojim**
bojati se	to be afraid	**bojim se**

  (b) the stem ends in **-nj**, **-lj** or (sometimes) **-j**, then Type III:

počinjati	to begin	**počinjem**
ostajati	to remain	**ostajem**

Note: Also, in some instances when the last consonant of the infinitive stem is **s**, **z**, **t**, **c**, **k** or **ks**, the present tense stem may be different and Type III endings will be added:

pisati	to write	**pišem**
kazati	to say	**kažem**

2 Verbs ending in **-iti** always take Type II endings:

      govoriti   to speak   **govorim**

3 Verbs ending in **-uti** always take Type III:

      krenuti   to move   **krenem**

4 Verbs ending in **-eti** may take Type II or III (in this case the present tense stem is usually different): **uzeti** 'to take', **uzmem**. The present tense of each of these must therefore be learned.

Infinitives ending in -ivati, -ovati

Again, the infinitive and present tense stems are usually the same, but in these cases the syllable **-iv**, **-ov** is replaced by **-uj-** before the Type III endings:

stanovati	to reside	**stanujem**
pokazivati	to show	**pokazujem**

Infinitives ending in -avati

In these verbs **-j** is added to the first **a** of the suffix, before Type III endings:

davati	to give	**dajem**
prodavati	to sell	**prodajem**

Note: Care should be taken with these verbs as sometimes the syllable **-av-** is part of the stem and retained in the present tense:

pokušavati	to try	**pokušavam**

Infinitives ending in -ci

Verbs ending in **-ći** *never* have the same infinitive and present tense stem:

reći	to say	**reknem**
pomoći	to help	**pomognem**
ići	to go	**idem**
doći	to come	**dođem**

Infinitives ending in -sti

(a) vowel + **-sti**: the present tense stem will be different (usually **t**, **d**, **p** or **b**):

jesti	to eat	**jedem**

(b) consonant + **-sti**: the infinitive and present stems may be the same, but if the final consonant is unvoiced it may change to its voiced equivalent (see p. 306):

iscrpsti	to exhaust	**iscrpim**

but

grepsti	to scratch	**grebem**

5 Mobile a

Nouns

(a) Masculine nouns ending in two consonants other than **st**, **zd**, **št** and **žd** have the letter **a** inserted between these consonants in the nominative singular and genitive plural.

	Gen. sing.	*Gen. pl.*	
momak	**momka**	**momaka**	lad
pas	**psa**	**pasa**	dog
borac	**borca**	**boraca**	warrior, soldier

(b) Masculine nouns ending in **l** which has become **o** in the nominative:

ugao	**ugla**	**uglova**	corner
posao	**posla**	**poslova**	work, job

(c) Neuter nouns with their stem ending in a consonant cluster may also have mobile **a** in the genitive plural:

pismo	**pisma**	**pisama**	letter
društvo	**društva**	**društava**	society

(d) Feminine nouns ending in **-a** preceded by two consonants may take mobile **a** in the genitive plural:

devojka	**devojaka**	girl
sestra	**sestara**	sister

but the alternative genitive plural ending in **-i** has replaced this in many such feminine nouns:

legenda	**legendi**	legend

Adjectives

Adjectives with their stem ending in two consonants other than **st**, **zd**, **št** and **žd** may take mobile **a** to form the indefinite masculine singular:

Definite	*Indefinite*	
dobri	**dobar**	good
kratki	**kratak**	short
radosni	**radostan**	joyous
topli	**topao**[1]	warm

1 All adjectives with final **l** derived from **o**, including active past participles, are in this category.

The **a** in the following adjectives is also mobile: **sav**, **kakav**, **takav**, **nikakav** etc.

6 Consonant changes

We have seen that the combination of certain consonants and vowels leads to changes:

(a) **k + i** = **ci**   **momak, momci**
     g + i = **zi**   **kovčeg, kovcezi**
     h + i = **si**   **muha, musi**

These changes occur in the masculine plural and feminine dative/ prepositional of nouns; and the imperative (**pomoći** – **pomog-ti** – **pomozi**, **pomozite**). Note that this rule does not apply to adjectives. Exceptions include proper names and feminine nouns with stem ending in **-tk** (**tetka**), **-čk** (**mačka**) and **-zg** (**tezga**).

(b) **k + e** = **če**   **momak, momče**
     g + e = **že**   **Bog, Bože**
     h + e = **še**   **duh, duše**

These changes occur in the vocative singular of masculine nouns; and in the present tense of verbs with infinitive in **-ći** derived from **k + t**, **g + t** and **h + t**:

peći (pek-ti)	**pečem**	to roast
strići (strig-ti)	**strižem**	to shear
vrći (vrh-ti)	**vršim**	to thresh

(c) Consonant + **j**. These changes occur mostly in the comparison of adjectives:

p + j	=	**plj**	**skup**	**skuplji**	expensive
b + j	=	**blj**	**riba**	**riblji**	fish
v + j	=	**vlj**	**krv**	**krvlju**	blood
m + j	=	**mlj**	**razum**	**razumljiv**	reason, comprehensible
t + j	=	**ć**	**smrt**	**smrću**	death
d + j	=	**đ**	**mlad**	**mlađi**	young
s + j	=	**š**	**visok**	**viši**	tall
z + j	=	**ž**	**brz**	**brži**	fast

k + j	=	č	jak	jači	strong
h + j	=	š	tih	tiši	quiet
g + j	=	ž	drag	draži	dear
st + j	=	šć	čest	češći	frequent
zd + j	=	žđ	grozd	grožđe	grapes

Assimilation

As Serbian spelling is phonetic, any consonant assimilations that occur are recorded in writing.

(a) Alternation of voiced/unvoiced consonants. The following consonants are 'paired':

| unvoiced: | č | ć | (f) | k | p | s | š | t |
| voiced: | dž | đ | (v) | g | b | z | ž | d |

If one of the following consonants is placed immediately next to one of the others it may be replaced by its pair so that they are both either voiced or unvoiced, according to the last consonant in the group:

sladak	slatko	sweet
težak	teško	difficult
Englez	engleski	

(b) Alternation of s and z with š and ž. When s, z are placed next to a palatal or palatalized consonant, they change to their palatalized equivalent š and ž:

| misliti | to think | mišljenje | opinion |
| paziti | to take care | pažnja | attention care |

7 Formation of questions

In Unit 1 you met all the most common ways of asking questions. There are three more:

(a) Questions may be formed by the addition of **zar ne?** 'isn't it so?' at the end of the sentence. This usually implies the expectation of a positive answer:

> **Vaš stric je bogat, zar ne?**
> Your uncle is rich, isn't he?

(b) The words **je li?** or **je l' da?** may also be added, but in this case the expectation may be slightly different:

> **Vaš stric je bogat, je li?**
> So, your uncle is rich, is he?

(c) **Zar** used with an affirmative verb conveys a note of surprise:

> **Zar učiš srpski?**
> You don't really mean you're learning Serbian,
> do you?

8 Other tenses

There are four tenses that you have not yet encountered: the aorist, imperfect, pluperfect and future perfect. Of these, the future perfect is the only one you are likely to use with any frequency, but you should be able to recognize the others, particularly in certain stock phrases.

Aorist

You have already come across the aorist of **biti** (**bih** etc.). Apart from this, you are most likely to meet it in dialogue involving the verb **reći** 'to say':

> **Doći ću, reče.**
> 'I shall come,' he said.

or in reported speech:

> **Rekoh da ću doći.**
> I said I would come.

So, the aorist endings of **reći** are: **(ja) rekoh, (ti) reče, (on) reče, (mi) rekosmo, (vi) rekoste, (oni) rekoše**

In the modern language, however, the past perfect tense has virtually replaced the aorist. In narration, its place is frequently taken by the *historic present*, i.e. the present tense used with past meaning to convey speed or suddenness of action.

> **Pokupiše sav novac i pobjegoše.**
> **Pokupe sav novac i pobjegnu.**
> They collected all the money and ran away.

Imperfect

Again, this tense has been virtually replaced by the perfect. You may sometimes hear the imperfect of **biti**, however, so it is as well to be able to recognize it: **(ja) bejah/beh**, **(ti) bejaše/beše**, **(on) bejaše/beše**, **(mi) bejasmo/besmo**, **(vi) bejaste/beste**, **(oni) bejahu/behu**.

Pluperfect

This is a compound tense, consisting of either the imperfect of **biti** and the active past participle (**bejah došao**) or the perfect tense of **biti** and the past participle (**bio sam došao**). The second method is more common.

Future perfect

While still not very common, this tense is in far more general use than the others and you should therefore learn its formation and usage. It is composed of the present perfective of **biti** and the active past participle:

(ja) budem pisao/pisala	**(mi) budemo pisali**
(ti) budeš pisao/pisala	**(vi) budete pisali**
(on) bude pisao	**(oni) budu pisali**
(ona) bude pisala	**(one) budu pisale**

This tense is used to express an action in the future, which precedes another action in the future:

Javiće ti se čim se bude vratio.
He'll ring you as soon as he gets back.

Pročitaću tvoju knjigu kad budem imala vremena.
I shall read your book when I have time.

The verb in the main clause need not be in the future tense in Serbian: a relatively frequent use is in expressing requests which refer to the future:

Kupi mi novine kad se budeš vraćao.
Buy me a newspaper on your way home.

Ako budete našli kafe, uzmite pola kile za mene.
If you find any coffee, get half a kilo for me.

9 Collective numerals

Neuter collective numerals

Where English has a limited number of collective numerals –
'pair', 'trio', 'quartet', 'quintet' etc. – it is possible to make a collective neuter form of virtually any number in Serbian: **dvoje**,
troje, **četvoro/četvero**, **petoro**, **šestoro**, **sedmoro** ... **jedanaestoro**,
dvanaestoro etc. As in English ('a pair of ...') these numerals take
the genitive:

> **Desetero putnika je došlo na izlet.**
> Ten passengers came on the outing.

They are used in two main situations:

(a) When the numeral refers to a group of mixed gender:

> **Troje nas je sedelo na terasi.**
> Three of us were sitting on the terrace.

> **Ima šestoro gostiju na večeri.**
> There are six guests for dinner.

(b) With collective nouns, whether or not they refer to the same
gender: **deca** (which may be mixed or not), **braća** (which is
obviously all male):

> **Imamo troje dece: dva sina i ćerku.**
> We have three children: two sons and a daughter.

> **Karte za četvoro odraslih i dvoje dece, molim.**
> Tickets for four adults and two children, please.
> (In this case the children could be two boys or two girls
> or mixed.)

> **Zamisli, ona ima sedmoro braće!**
> Imagine, she has seven brothers!

There are declensions for these numerals, but they are virtually
obsolete:

gen.	**dvoga**, **troga**, **četvorga** etc.
dat./loc./instr.	**dvomu/dvoma**, **tromu/troma**, **četvormu/četvorma** etc.

These forms are never used in the modern language after a preposition, but you will find them occasionally in oblique cases when there is no preposition:

> **Putovaću s dvoje prijatelja.**
> I shall travel with two friends.

but **Nama dvoma je govorio.**
He spoke to the two of us.

Masculine collective numerals

These are used to refer to a group of males. They have a feminine singular form, but are followed by a plural verb. If the verb is in the past tense, the participle may be either masculine plural or feminine singular:

> **Dvojica su došla** (or **došli**).
> Two men came.

They are formed by the addition of the suffix **-ica** to the collective stem, giving: **dvojica, trojica, četvorica, petorica, šestorica** etc. They are generally used when the men they refer to have already been mentioned:

> **Ona ima sedmero braće: trojica su lekari, dvojica su inženjeri, a dvojica su još uvek na fakultetu.**
> She has seven brothers: three are doctors, two engineers and two are still at university.

'Both'

English 'both' may be expressed in each of these ways:

oboje: **Imam sina i ćerku, oboje su kod bake.**
I have a son and a daughter, they are both at their grandmother's.

obojica: **Poznajem njena dva brata, obojica su zgodna.**
I know her two brothers, both are good-looking.

Distributive numerals

There are adjectival forms of the neuter collective numerals, which agree in all respects with the noun they qualify. They must be used in the following situations:

(a) With those nouns that have only plural forms:

dvoja vrata   two doors
troje pantalona   three trousers

(b) With nouns denoting pairs of things:

Kupila sam dvoje cipela.
I bought two pairs of shoes.

On treba troje novih čarapa.
He needs three new pairs of socks.

Morate otvoriti četvore oči.
You must have your eyes wide open.

	Masc.	*Neut.*	*Fem.*	*Masc.*	*Neut.*	*Fem.*
nom.	dvoji	dvoja	dvoje	petori	petora	petore
gen.	dvojih	dvojih	dvojih	petorih	petorih	petorih
dat.	dvojim	dvojim	dvojim	petorim	petorim	petorim
acc.	dvoje	dvoja	dvoje	petore	petora	petore
loc./instr.	dvojim	dvojim	dvojim	petorim	petorim	petorim

Čitali smo istu vest u trojim novinama.
We read the same piece of news in three papers.

Brava na dvojim vratima se slomila.
The lock on two doors is broken.

Note: These forms are virtually obsolete, but you may come across them in written texts.

Key to exercises

The following answers are for the main exercises only.

Unit 1

Exercise 1

(a) 1 sam; je; 2 su; smo; 3 su; su; 4 stc; 5 su
(b) 1 Mi; 2 Ti; 3 Vi; 4 Oni; 5 Ja

Exercise 2

1 Jeste; 2 Jesu; 3 Jesmo; 4 Jeste; 5 Jesam

Exercise 3

1 nismo; 2 nisu; 3 nisi; 4 nije; 5 nisam

Exercise 7

(b) 1 b; 2 a; 3 d; 4 c

Unit 2

Exercise 1

(a) 1 govoriš; 2 preporučujem; 3 kupim; 4 voze; 5 ideš
(c) 1 Mi; 2 ti; 3 Oni; 4 Ja; 5 On/Ona

Exercise 2

(a) 1 promenim, imam, nalazi; 2 vidiš
(b) 1 upozna; 2 putuje; 3 ostaje; 4 dešava; 5 kupim

Exercise 5

(b) 1 ponekad; 2 odlično; 3 rado; 4 brzo; 5 dobro
(c) Ana: Umorna sam. I pored toga, ne volim da putujem autobusom. Marko: Taksi puno košta, ali ... Okej, možemo da
idemo taksijem. Ana: To zvuči odlično. Želim samo da kupim
novine i cigarete. Marko: Dobro, ali moramo prvo da nađemo
djuti-fri.

Unit 3

Exercise 1

(c) 1 stižu; 2 je; 3 večera; 4 kaže; smo; 5 kaže; moram; jedem

Exercise 2

(a) 1 prijatelji; 2 aerodrom; 3 knjižara; 4 novinari; 5 Amerikanci;
6 kombi

Exercise 4

(a) Ivane, Marko, Milane, Zorice, Dragane, Majo, Svetlana,
Đorđe, Vera

Exercise 6

(c) 1 d; 2 b; 3 c; 4 a; 5 c

Unit 4

Exercise 1

1 (a) Beograd; 2 problem; 3 Dejana; Janka; 4 Kalemegdan; 5 ključ;
6 Anđelu; Knez Mihjlovu ulicu; 7 večeru; 8 čokoladu; 9 torbu;
10 more

Exercise 3

(a) 1 u; 2 na; 3 za; 4 kroz; 5 na; 6 u; 7 u; 8 na; 9 za; 10 kroz

Exercise 5

1 Zemuna; 2 trga; 3 kuće; 4 pošte; 5 problema

Exercise 6

(a) Džona; Engleske; Engleske; Londona; znamenitosti; Beograda; mapu; grada; karte; Kalemegdan; Knez Mihajlovu ulicu

(b) 1 vrlo rado; 2 lepo se provedite; 3 nema na čemu; 4 sledeći put

Unit 5

Exercise 1

1 Džonu; 2 Anđeli; 3 novinama; 4 roditeljima; 5 deci

Exercise 2

(c) A: Zdravo, da li možete da nam kažete gde je glavni trg? B: Glavni trg? Nije daleko. Da li imate mapu? A: Imamo. Evo je. B: Da li vidite ovu ulicu? Treba samo da idete pravo. Glavni trg je na kraju ulice, preko puta crkve. A: Hvala B: Nema na čemu.

Exercise 3

(b) 1 moru; 2 Hrvatsku; 3 Beogradu; 4 Zemunu; 5 stanu; 6 banku; 7 torbi; 8 Trgu Republike; 9 autobusu; putu; centru; 10 početku ulice

Exercise 5

(b) 1 prijateljima; 2 mužem; 3 drugaricom; 4 decom; 5 recepcionarom

Unit 6

Exercise 5

(b) 1 Da li je tvoja soba udobna? 2 Da li je tvoj stan moderan? 3 Njihova kuća je velika. 4 Žive blizu centra. 5 Idu na posao autobusom. 6 Rade puno, ali nisu umorni. 7 Ona je lepa i vrlo elegantna žena. 8 On viđa mnoge zanimljive ljude.

Unit 7

Exercise 2

(b) 1 dve; 2 tri; 3 pet; 4 dva; 5 četiri; 6 jednu; 7 dve; 8 sto
1 We have to reserve two rooms at the hotel. 2 In the office

we buy three postcards. 3 I need to send five letters. 4 You must invite two more friends. 5 Where can I hand in these four forms? 6 We have to buy a bar of chocolate as well. 7 We need two more chairs. 8 You can change $100 in the bank.
(c) 1 U ovom hotelu ima dvadeset pet soba. 2 Marko ima dva brata. 3 Molim vas tri boce vina. 4 Na putu planiraju da vide dva sela. 5 On ima preko hiljadu knjiga. 6 Ostajemo sedam dana. 7 Kupujem četiri rečnika. 8 Kupuju dvadeset dve karte za pozorište. 9 Večera u restoranu košta sedam sto četrdeset dva dinara. 10 Ja sam već petnaest dana na putu.

Exercise 3

1 umorna putnika; 2 crvene vaze; 3 ozbiljna studenta; 4 crna kofera; 5 prostrane sobe; 6 udobna stana; 7 ukusna jela; 8 važna pisma; 9 telefonska razgovora; 10 ljuta gosta

Exercise 5

(a) 1 Koliko ona ima godina? 2 Kolika je kirija? 3 Koliko košta stan na Dorćolu?/Da li je stan na Dorćolu skup/jeftin? 4 Kako se on preziva? 5 Koliko košta taksi do centra? 6 Gde oni odsedaju? 7 Koliko ostajete u Srbiji? 8 Zašto ne možete da dođete?/Da li ćete da dođete? 9 Šta ste vi/si ti po zanimanju? 10 Kako/čime ideš na posao?

Unit 8

Exercise 1

(a) 1 mog dobrog prijatelja; 2 nekog novosadskog hotela; 3 domaćeg vina; 4 narodnih specijaliteta; 5 ovog malog restorana; 6 riblje čorbe; 7 odličnih palačinki; 8 sveže, domaće hrane; 9 mojih roditelja; 10 sveže ribe

Exercise 3

(a) voćni sok, belo vino, kiselu vodu, kolače, pitu od jabuka, sladoled, palačinke sa džemom, čokoladnu tortu

Exercise 4

(b) Ne viđam svog dobrog prijatelja Ivana baš često jer on živi u Novom Sadu. Ali volim da putujem u Novi Sad kad imam vremena. Kad sam tamo uvek izađemo na večeru zajedno. Ima jedan odličan restoran blizu Ivanovog stana. Ima malu terasu sa prelepim pogledom na Dunav. Restoran služi tradicionalna jela, a moja omiljena su teleća čorba, meso na roštilju i krompiri, mešana salata i palačinke na kraju. Ivan više voli ribu. On uvek uzme šarana na roštilju i krompir salatu. Ali i on voli palačinke. Nikad iz Novog Sada ne odem gladan!

Exercise 6

(b) 1 b; 2 c; 3 a; 4 d; 5 c; 6 c

Unit 9

Exercise 1

(b) A: Da li mi možete reći gde je železnička stanica? B: Idite pravo do kraja ulice Srpskih vladara i tu skrenite levo. Idite opet pravo još 100 metara i, ili skrenite desno i idite niz Nemanjinu ulicu do stanice, ili odatle uzmite tramvaj. A: Koji tramvaj? B: Svi tramvaji koji staju tu idu do stanice. A: Hvala najlepše. B: Nema na čemu.

(c) (i) 1 starom profesoru; 2 Ani; 3 vašoj deci; 4 grupi turista; 5 dobrom prijatelju; (ii) 1 ovom gradu; 2 jednom starom univerzitetu; 3 jednom popularnom pozorištu; 4 lepom plavom Dunavu; 5 našoj kući

Exercise 2

Miloš T., tram driver:

Is it possible not to love Belgrade? My love of this city has lasted from my first boyhood days, from when my memories of red trams and trolleybuses, the Danube and Kalemegdan zoo date. I remember also the legendary bookshop in the Yugoslav Drama Theatre, Duško Radović's radio programmes and concerts at the Dom Omladina (Youth Centre).

But of course these are not the only things I love in Belgrade. This city has many faces and changes constantly. It is impossible not to mention how beautiful Kalemegdan is in the aututmn, Košutnjak in winter and the Botanical Gardens and Tašmajdan in spring.

I love Belgrade also because of its openness, because of the paradoxical contrasts created by the old and the new: old Belgrade and New Belgrade, the National Theatre and Staklenac (the Glass Building), trolleybuses and buses.

My favourite place in the city is the little café in the City Cultural Centre on Republic Square. Some people call it Republic Square, and some Freedom Square. This is where everything I love most in the city is situated. Here is the National Theatre. Beside the theatre on the right is the Staklenac commercial centre, while opposite the theatre is the National Museum. On the square there is a statue to Prince Mihailo. Opposite the statue is the Boško Buha children's theatre and the 'At the Horse' café. Near the square are also Skadarlija and Bajlonijeva market.

Exercise 3

(a) 1 od; 2 o; na; 3 pored; sa; 4 na; pored; 5 ka; 6 na; 7 u; sa; 8 pod; 9 kroz; 10 blizu
(b) 1 Pred crkvom se nalazi lepi mali park. 2 Vodim prijatelja na Kalemegdan. 3 U tom selu ima jedna lepa crkva. 4 Idu prema stanici ovim putem. 5 Pod brdom je reka.

Exercise 5

predstavu; režiji; glumci; pozorište; predstavom

Unit 10

Exercise 1

(a) 1 ste čuli; 2 smo čitali; 3 su saznali; 4 je bila; 5 je prodavala; 6 su prošli; 7 je imao; 8 ste došli; 9 je rekla; 10 je jeo

Exercise 2

(a) 1 Da li ste stigli u Novi Sad juče? 2 Da li je naručio ribu i krompir? 3 Da li su videli crkvu i pozorište? 4 Da li je otišla da poseti prijatelje? 5 Da li su pili crno vino i jeli kolače? 6 Da li si hodao/hodala ceo dan? 7 Da li sam došao/došla u Beograd pre nedelju dana? 8 Da li smo čitali o ovom mestu u turističkom vodiču?
(b) 1 On je bio ovde juče. 2 Išli smo svi zajedno u Užice. 3 Drago mi je što ste mogli da dođete. 4 Rekao je da je bio na selu sa prijateljima. 5 Da li si video gde sam ostavila mobilni telefon?

Unit 11

Exercise 1

(d) 1 mnom; 2 mi; 3 mene; 4 mi; 5 mene; 6 meni; 7 mi; 8 meni; 9 mnom; 10 mene; 11 mi

Exercise 2

(a) 1 sebi; 2 se; 3 sebi; 4 sebe; 5 sebe
(c) 1 ih; 2 ih; 3 je; 4 nju; 5 njima; 6 njima; 7 njih; 8 njim; 9 je; 10 ga

Exercise 3

(b) 1 Oni su sedeli iza tebe. 2 Da li me je video? 3 Dao/Dala sam ti ključeve. 4 Ona mi je sestra. 5 Ona ide u pozorište sa njim. 6 Sećamo je se sa uživanjem. 7 Upoznala sam ih prekjuče. 8 Razgovarali smo o njemu u autobusu. 9 Šta sam ti rekao/rekla?

Exercise 4

(a) 1 igrane; 2 glavnu ulogu; 3 snima; 4 premijera; 5 karte
(b) A: Upravo sam video odličan dokumentarac u bioskopu! Baš mi se svideo. B: Stvarno! Koji film? A: Zove se *Super 8* B: Nisam nikad čuo za njega. Ko je režiser? A: Emir Kusturica. B: A, Sad se sećam. Čitao sam puno o njemu u novinama. Ne slažem se da je to dobar film. A: Kako možeš to da kažeš kad ga nisi video?

Unit 12

Exercise 2

(a) (i) 1 na severu; 2 na jugu; 3 na jugozapadu; 4 na zapadu; 5 na jugoistoku. (ii) 1 severno od; 2 južno od; 3 južno od; 4 istočno od

Exercise 4

(b) Moram da isplaniram odmor. Želim da putujem u Srbiju početkom juna. Posetiću prijatelje u Beogradu. Ostaću par dana sa njima. Onda ću da odem na planinu, na Taru, da posetim svoju tetku. Mislim da ću putovati vozom do Užica. A onda ću da idem autobusom. Volim da putujem vozom jer mogu da vidim mnogo toga kroz prozor. Na Tari ću da uživam u dobroj hrani, svežem vazduhu, i gostoljubivosti ljudi. Tara je prelepa planina i idem tamo svake godine. Ove godine ću ostati samo jednu nedelju. A onda ću da idem u Kotor. Rezervisaću privatnu sobu pored mora. Moji prijatelji će već biti tamo.

Unit 13

Exercise 1

(b) 1 radili; 2 odveli; 3 vole; 4 postoji; 5 sluša; 6 imati; 7 obnavljaju; 8 čuli; 9 propustite; 10 održava; 11 pevaju, sviraju

(c) 1 Soba je na drugom spratu. 2 Pošta je iza prvog ugla sa desne strane. 3 Ovo mu je peta knjiga. 4 Treća vrata sa desne strane je kupatilo. 5 Da li ti je ovo prva večera u restoranu 'Dalmacija'?

Exercise 2

(b) 1 petkom; 2 u petak; 3 prošlog petka; 4 u sredu; 5 sredom; 6 sledeće srede
(c) 1 Ne idem na posao nedeljom. 2 Šta radiš ovog vikenda? 3 Moj otac svira trubu svake srede. 4 Koncert je u ponedeljak uveče. 5 On gleda televiziju ceo dan.

Exercise 3

(a) 1: 100 godina; 2: 3 sata; 3: 15. jula; 4: za mesec dana; 5: pre dve nedelje

Unit 14

Exercise 1

(b) 1 duže; 2 skuplje; 3 poznatijih; 4 starije; 5 lepša, novija; 6 veselije; 7 pametniji; 8 ukusnije; 9 mlađa
(c) 1 nije preporučljivo; 2 nema potrebe; 3 u međuvremenu; 4 imati pri ruci; 5 imati na umu

Exercise 2

1 bliži; reðe; 2 dalji; 3 višoj; 4 kraćeg; 5 dublje

Exercise 3

(a) 1 teže; 2 skuplje; 3 radije; 4 bliže; 5 lakše; 6 bolje
(b) 1 najviši; 2 lepše; 3 zanimljivija; 4 najbolja; 5 najudobnije

Exercise 4

Idemo na odmor u subotu, prekosutra! Ne želimo da nosimo puno stvari, tako da ćemo poneti samo najpotrebnije. Imam jedan mali kofer i jednu veliku torbu. Poneću pantalone i džemper jer je ponekad hladno uveče, tri haljine, suknju, dve majice, dve bluze, cipele, čarape i veš. Moj muž će poneti pantalone, pet košulja, tri majice, šorc i dva džempera. On može da nosi kupaće kostime i peškire u svom koferu.

Exercise 5

(b) 1 knjižari; 2 biblioteke; 3 bestseleri; 4 omotu; 5 naslov; 6 pisca; 7 poglavlja

Unit 15

Exercise 1

(c) 1 ovom; 2 tog; 3 one; 4 ovim, te; 5 tih; 6 onom; 7 taj; 8 one; 9 taj; 10 one

Exercise 2

1 Da li je to Milicin muž? 2 Gde su putnikovi koferi? 3 Putuju Nemanjinim novim kolima. 4 Da li ćeš videti Marijinu ćerku? 5 Mapa je u Anđelinoj torbi. 6 Da li ideš u manastir sa Ivanovim bratom? 7 Da li je to kuća tvog prijatelja? 8 Nikolin džemper je ovde. 9 Kada stiže Milošev stric? 10 Tijanino putovanje počinje sutra.

Reading passage 1

From Belgrade to Novi Pazar the main road leads towards the Adriatic coast. This road passes through the picturesque towns and regions of Šumadija. Above Novi Pazar rise the mountains of Golija and Rogozna and also the Pešter plateau. The town is situated at the contact of the Jošanica and Raška rivers, in the valley of the same name.

It was raised in the 15th century, on the territory of the capital of the first Serbian state – Ras. Its geographical position is quite favourable. From the surrounding mountains 5 smallish rivers fall into the Novi Pazar field itself. This phenomenon was designated by Jovan Cvijić, the great Serbian geographer and scholar, as a feature unique to the Balkans.

The natural beauties which Novi Pazar can boast of have become attractive also to others. The beauty and tourist attractions of Golija, particularly since the modern ski centre was built, and the Sopoćani area, the proximity of Peštar and Kopaonik ... To the natural wealth of the Novi Pazar region one should add also two spas – Novi Pazar and Rajčinović Spa to which patients come from all regions of Serbia and Montenegro.

In addition to the monuments of Orthodox Christian culture of Sopoćani, Petrova Crkva and Djurđevi stupovi, another association

322   Key to exercises

with Novi Pazar are also the monuments of Islamic culture – mosques, inns, baths, as well as the unmissable city fortress in the centre of the town.

Exercise 3

(c) 1 d putokaza; 2 b pogrešnim; 3 c raskrsnici; 4 a klizav; 5 b natočim; 6 d saobraćaju

Exercise 4

B: Gde je tvoja prijateljica? Hoću da je upoznam. D: Da li vidiš onu visoku devojku u crvenoj majci? B: A, da. Idem da se predstavim. B: Zdravo, ja sam Dejanov prijatelj, Ben. LJ: Drago mi je da sam vas konačno upoznala, mnogo sam čula o vama. B: I ja sam o vama puno čuo. Jedva čekam da čitanje počne. LJ: I ja. Vrlo sam uzbuđena. Ali evo Dejana i moje prijateljice Tanje. Da vas upoznam.

Unit 16

Exercise 1

1 (c) Spremićemo svoje stvari. 2 Nisu bili u svojim kolima. 3 Video sam tvog rođaka u pošti. 4 Da li putujete svojim kolima? 5 Moja ćerka je otišla u Englesku sa nekim svojim prijateljima. 6 Ostavio sam svoj mobilni kod kuće. 7 Da li imaš svoju vozačku dozvolu kod sebe? 8 Posetiće moje roditelje. 9 Parkirali su svoja kola ispred kuće. 10 Kad skrenete levo videćete moju kancelariju.

Exercise 3

(b) 1 u; 2 na; 3 od; 4 za; 5 u; 6 sa; 7 u; 8 na; 9 za; 10 na

(d) – Halo, da li je to Marko? Zovem da ti kažem da odlazimo na more u subotu. – Blago vama! Nadam se da ćete imati lepo vreme. Da li imate nekog ko će vam paziti mačku? Rado ću da svratim s vremena na vreme. – Hvala, baš lepo od tebe. Veranov nećak će biti ovde i verovatno će dovesti još nekoliko prijatelja. – Gde idete? Da li ste rezervisali sobe negde? – Nismo. Valjda ćemo naći privatni smeštaj bez problema. Ne znamo tačno gde ćemo biti. – A kad se vraćate? – Možemo da ostanemo samo 5 dana. Da li ćeš biti u Podgorici kad se vratimo? – Da, a posle idem u Italiju. – Dobro, onda se vidimo uskoro. – Srećan put!

Unit 17

Exercise 1

(b) 1 a; 2 d; 3 b; 4 c; 5 d

(c) A: kim; B: nekim; A: nekoga; B: niko; ni s kim

Exercise 2

1 Hleb koji sam kupio jutros je na stolu. 2 Gde je sendvič koji si spremila? 3 Da li je ovo prodavnica u kojoj radi tvoja sestra? 4 Meso koje je kupio nije baš sveže. 5 Prijatelj kome sam dao tvoju adresu dolazi sutra. 6 Kola kojima su putovali su vrlo mala i stara. 7 O čemu se radi? 8 Da li imaš sve što ti je potrebno?

Exercise 5

1 Voz kasni 30 minuta. On je zakasnio na večeru. 2 Napisao sam ovaj mejl sinoć ali ga još uvek nisam poslao. Ona je u dnevnoj sobi i piše pismo svom bratu. 3 Konačno se setio gde je parkirao kola. Ne sećam se ove raskrsnice, da li si sigurna da je ovo pravi put? 4 Nikad ne jedemo pre 8.30 uveče, tako da dođi kad možeš. Da li će on moći da pojede celu ovu porciju? 5 Popij to crno vino pa onda možeš da probaš ovo belo. Pijemo domaću rakiju, hoćeš i ti malo? 6 Internet kafe se otvara u 8 sati. Ta nova prodavnica će se otvoriti 15 oktobra.

Exercise 6

1 Neko je došao da te vidi. 2 Ne želim nikoga da vidim. 3 Da li je neko bio kod kuće? 4 Ne, nije bio niko. 5 O čemu ste pričali? 6 Kome će dati knjigu? 7 Govorio mi je o nekome iz hotela.

Unit 18

Exercise 1

(a) 1 gledaj; And you be sure to come and see us in England! 2 dajte; Neno and Angela, give me your things. 3 krenimo; Friends, let's go on an adventure! 4 Očekujte; expect a lot of bends and careless drivers on the road. 5 Pokaži; At last, show us your new car! 6 Sačekajte; Wait for me here in front of the bookshop. 7 Putuj, pitaj; Have you heard of the saying: 'travel, abbot, don't ask about the monastery'? 8 Pričaj; Tell (me) how it was in Kotor. 9 Obećajte; Promise me you won't drive too

fast. 10 vozi; Drive more slowly because you can't see that this car is overtaking us.
(b) 1 a; 2 d; 3 b; 4 b; 5 c; 6 a; 7 d; 8 b; 9 d; 10 a

Exercise 2

(b) Gospođa Jović je odvela svog sina kod doktora. On ima grip. Doktor ga je pregledao i sada savetuje gospođu Jović šta da radi: 'Neka jede puno voća i povrća. Spremajte supe i lagana jela ako je moguće. Neka pije puno čaja i sokova. I na kraju neka puno spava. Ako mu nije dobro posle tri dana, dovedite ga opet.'

Exercise 6

(a) Teško je biti dete. Roditelji i nastavnici ti stalno govore šta moraš da radiš: 'Ustani, obuci se, operi zube, spremi krevet, nemoj da zakasniš na autobus, pojedi sve, dođi kući najkasnije do sedam, javi se telefonom čim stigneš, nemoj biti bezobrazan, nemoj sa mnom tako da razgovaraš! Pitam se, da li ću ja tako razgovarati sa svojom decom?'
(b) 1 uzmi; 2 napuni; 3 sipaj; 4 sipaj; 5 promešaj; 6 vrati; 7 skini
(c) 1 Kako gde; 2 Kako ko; 3 Kako kad

Unit 19

Exercise 1

(a) 1 Gde možemo da odsednemo ako počne kiša? 2 Ne bih želeo/želela da idem napolje danas. 3 Da li bi voleo/volela da putuješ sa njima? 4 Bilo bi bolje da ručamo tamo. 5 Loše vreme bi moglo da pokvari sve.
(c) A: kakvo je vreme danas? Izgleda lepo. B: Zašto pitaš? A: Mislila sam da bismo mogli da izađemo negde, ako ne pada kiša. B: Hladno je i ja bih radije da ostanem kod kuće. A: Ne možeš da budeš unutra ceo dan! B: Što da ne? A: Hajde, sunce sija. Mogli bismo da idemo u Košutnjak. B: Tamo uvek duva. A: Gluposti! B: Ti idi onda! A: Bilo bi lepše da smo zajedno. B: Slažem se. A kako bi bilo da prošetamo do našeg lokalnog kafića?

Exercise 3

(b) 1 kad; 2 da; 3 ako; 4 da; 5 da; 6 ako

Exercise 4

1 Čujem da se ovde pravi dobra kafa. 2 Da li se radio B92 čuje preko Interneta? 3 Njegove knjige se čitaju u celom svetu. 4 Katedrala se jasno može videti na brdu. 5 Moglo bi se reći da je skupo živeti ovde.

Exercise 6

Braunovi su stigli u hotel. Kad je došao do recepcije da rezerviše sobu, Džon je shvatio da je zaboravio novčanik u kolima. Otišao je napolje da ga uzme. Vratio se za pet minuta i konačno počeo da razgovara sa recepcionarom. Dok je Džon govorio, recepcionar ga je iznenada prekinuo jer je prepoznao Nenu. Ona uvek odseda u ovom hotelu kad dođe u Kotor sa roditeljima.

Unit 20

Exercise 1

(a) 1 Sedeći; 2 Vraćajući; 3 napisavši; 4 Izavši; 5 Budući
(b) 1 Mislim da sam ih video kako dolaze. 2 Da li se je čuo kako peva? 3 Našli smo ih u parku kako se igraju. 4 Nije primetio kako izlazim napolje. 5 Stajala je pored prozora i gledala kako ljudi prolaze.

Exercise 5

Prošle nedelje su Džon i Anđela otputovali iz Srbije i vratili se u Englesku. Nakon jednomesečnog u Srbiji odmora nije bilo lako vratiti se kući. Odlično su se proveli i zaista bi želeli da ponovo posete zemlju sledeće godine. Ove nedelje žele da organizuju zabavu za svoje prijatelje i da im pričaju o svom putovanju. Žele da im pokažu fotografije i da im daju poklone iz Srbije. Anđela planira da impresionira sve srpskim jelima koja je naučila da kuva dok su bili u Sirogojnu. Ali pre toga, Džon će da ponudi šljivovicu svojim prijateljima pošto je doneo flašu sa sobom. Takođe bi želeo da svima kaže za seriju članaka o kulturnom životu u Beogradu koja je počela da izlazi u lokalnim novinama.

Translations of main texts

Below are given translations of the main dialogues of Units 1 to 5 and also of 'Kulturni život u Beogradu' and 'Ekipa'.

Translations for Units 1 to 5

Unit 1

(A)

MILAN:	Good day.
ANGELA:	Good day.
MILAN:	I am Milan Jovanović.
ANGELA:	I am Angela Brown, and this is my husband, John.
MILAN:	Pleased to meet you. Welcome to Belgrade!

(B)

JOHN:	You're Serbian (lit. 'a Serb'), aren't you?
MILAN:	Yes, I'm Serbian. What about you?
JOHN:	We are English.

Unit 2

MILAN:	You are in Belgrade for the first time?
ANGELA:	Yes. Do you live here?
MILAN:	No, I live in Niš, but I'm staying a few days in Belgrade.
ANGELA:	Can you tell us how to get to the city?
MILAN:	You can go by bus or taxi. But I recommend a *kombi*.
ANGELA:	What's that?
MILAN:	It's a little bus that goes to hotels and private addresses, which is very convenient. Plus, it's not as expensive as a taxi.
JOHN:	Thank you, that sounds excellent!

Unit 3

RECEPTIONIST:	Good day, how can I help you?
JOHN:	We are John and Angela Brown. We have reservations.
RECEPTIONIST:	Welcome! Let me just have a look ... What is your surname?
JOHN:	Brown.
RECEPTIONIST:	Ah, yes. A double room. May I have your passport, Mr Brown. Thank you. And yours, Mrs Brown. Here you are, this is your key. Do you wish to have dinner?
ANGELA:	Gladly, thank you! I'm really hungry!
RECEPTIONIST:	No problem! The restaurant is there, opposite. My colleague can take your luggage. I wish you a pleasant evening!
JOHN AND ANGELA:	Thank you!

Unit 4

ANGELA:	Good day, we want to go into the city and see the main sights of Belgrade.
AGENT:	Fine, madam. You have a bus from here which goes to Branko Bridge. It stops in front of the hotel.
JOHN:	Is Branko Bridge near Kalemegdan? We want to go to Kalemegdan.
AGENT:	Yes. You can easily reach the park on foot from there. Just ask for Knez Mihailo St. It's a very beautiful street, where there are no vehicles.
ANGELA:	Wonderful! Thank you!
AGENT:	You're welcome! Have a good time!

Unit 5

ANGELA:	Excuse me, madam, can you tell us how to get to Knez Mihailova St.?
PASSER-BY:	You have to go straight to the post office and then turn left. But I'm going in that direction as well. We can (go) together.
JOHN:	We want to go to Kalemegdan, to see the confluence of the Sava and the Danube.
PASSER-BY:	You should certainly see that. But go slowly along Knez Mihailo St.: there are some very interesting buildings and shops there.
ANGELA:	Can we have a coffee somewhere on the way?

PASSER-BY: Certainly: there are several restaurants and many cafés in Knez Mihailova St.

JOHN: There's a Turkish fortress in Kalemegdan, isn't there?

PASSER-BY: Yes, that is worth seeing as well. Here, I work in this building. This is the beginning of Knes Mihailo St.

ANGELA: Thank you for your help!

PASSER-BY: You're welcome.

Translations of 'Cultural life in Belgrade'

Unit 1

Ben Wilson is from London. He's a journalist by profession. Now he's in Belgrade. His friend Dejan is waiting at the airport. Ben comes out. 'Hey, hi, Ben, welcome!' 'Thanks, Dejan! All the better to have found you!' Dejan takes Ben to his car and they go to Zemun.

Unit 2

As they drive to Zemun, they talk. Dejan wants to know what Ben is supposed to see while he is in Serbia. Dejan asks whether Ben wants to travel round Serbia or whether he wants to stay in Belgrade. Ben wants to get to know artistic life in Serbia. But he thinks that a lot of things happen precisely in Belgrade. Dejan agrees and says that he can make a nice programme. Ben is very pleased.

Unit 3

Soon they reach Zemun, where Dejan introduces Ben to Nada and the children Ana and Janko. Ben takes (some) English chocolate from his bag and gives it to the children. Nada tells the children that they have to say 'thank you'. They say 'thank you, uncle Ben!' Dejan shows Ben where (his) bedroom and the bathroom are. Nada prepares dinner. Dejan asks Ben whether he wants to drink wine or beer. Ben says he prefers wine, and asks for a glass of water as well.

Unit 4

As they eat their dinner, Ben and Dejan make plans for the following day. They agree that it is a good idea to go straight away into town – although Dejan says there is plenty to see in Zemun as well. Dejan suggests that they go to a café on the main square where his friends, journalists, are often to be found, and then they can discuss things all together.

Unit 5

Ben and Dejan are going by bus into town. It is very interesting for Ben in the bus: first they go through the old centre of Zemun, then they cross the Sava river and make their way towards the white city on the hill. Dejan explains to Ben that the city acquired its name because the white colour of the city can be seen from a long way off. They get off at Zeleni venac (square), where there are a lot of buses and people.

Unit 6

Dejan and Ben go to the National Museum. The Museum is on Trg republike (Republic Square), not far from Knez Mihailo St. It is a large, old building on several floors. Here there are exhibits from various areas and periods of Serbian culture. There are national costumes, village carvings, paintings and modern sculpture. While they are looking at the spacious halls accompanied by the Director of the Museum, Dejan explains some important events in Serbian history.

Unit 7

Dejan takes Ben to the Fresco Gallery and explains the important role of Orthodox churches and monasteries in Serbian culture. The frescoes in the museum are copies of the frescoes on the walls of churches, but they are very faithful and in the museum it is possible to look over them in detail. Ben is deeply impressed by the beauty, colour and liveliness of the paintings. They are lucky that Dejan knows the curator of the museum: he is able to explain to them everything that interests Ben. The visit to the museum takes 2 hours. After that, tired and full of impressions, Ben and Dejan go to a nearby café for a coffee. The Fresco Gallery is on the Dorćol slope. This is a very popular part of Belgrade full of charming old houses, modern cafés and little, independent galleries. Dorćol is a place where the old and modern merge in a unique way.

Unit 8

The next day, after an abundant lunch, Dejan takes Ben to the Museum of Modern Art, which is situated on the bank of the Sava river, opposite old Belgrade, near Branko Bridge and the confluence (of the rivers). It is a nice day so they walk to the Museum from the centre of Zemun beside the Danube: here, beside the river, is a nice place to walk, where people walk, take their dogs and ride bicycles. The Museum is a fine, modern building with many interesting and unusual works by contemporary Serbian painters and sculptors. Ben is particularly interested in the paintings by the youngest generations of painters and impressed also by the building itself, which has a wonderful position, it is surrounded by a park.

Unit 9

In the evening Dejan and Ben go, with Nada, to the theatre. Dejan explains that the Yugoslav Drama Theatre burned down several years before and now it has been completely rebuilt. The new building looks impressive: it is all (made) of glass and metal.

They see the performance of 'A Barrel of Gunpowder', [with a] script by Dejan Dukovski, and directed by Slobodan Unkovski. The performance is lively, with realistic decor and excellent actors. Ben is not sure that he understands everything the actors say, but he makes an effort. Nada is delighted by the performance and talks about individual scenes and the direction in a way that is very interesting for Ben. They are all very pleased with the performance.

Unit 10

The next day, Dejan took Ben to meet some of his friends in the 'Atelje 212' theatre. They talked about a famous festival of international theatre, BITEF, which is held every year in Belgrade. The festival promotes new theatrical trends and groups from all over the world participate in it.

Ben follows theatre life in Britain and he is interested in bringing some British theatre group to Belgrade. However, Ben is surprised how come (lit.) there are so many theatres in Belgrade. And how come people are so interested in theatre. They explained to him that theatre is a very important and popular cultural institution in Belgrade: it was incredible, but even during the difficult years of Serbian history, the theatres did not stop working.

Unit 11

On the way home, Dejan told Ben that the next day he must introduce him to his friends who worked in film. First they had to go to the studio of a film school, where on the whole short films and documentaries were shot, to see how films were made. In the last couple of years, several film schools had been opened in Belgrade. Lovers of film and enthusiasts were working quite a lot on popularizing film so from the beginning of the 1990s there were even several festivals of amateur film in Belgrade.

Dejan hopes that this way Ben will be able to hear something about the history of the feature film in former Yugoslavia and the newly formed states as well. The only directors from these parts that he had heard of were Kusturica and Makavejev. Since at the moment only

American films were being shown, Dejan planned to show him some classics of local film, which he had on video cassettes. The first film that occurred to him was 'Who's that singing over there?' by the director Slobodan Šijan, and it usually bowled everyone over. It was a question of a comedy in which the humour was very specific and hard to translate. Dejan wasn't sure whether Ben could understand the film, but he could try to explain some things in the course of the film, It didn't matter, they had the whole evening in front of them!

Unit 12

Dejan and Ben decided to have a bit of a rest today. They had had too intense a programme recently and it was the right time to organize their impressions a bit. In the evening they would just go to the Kinoteka to see the film 'The Marathonists run a lap of honour' about the legendary Topolović family.

During the day Dejan will try to arrange a trip to Fruška gora. He will call his friends who have a house there. He must check that they will be there when they want to visit them. Ben will write emails to his friends and his editorial board. He must read through everything he has written so far and write his first article about cultural life in Belgrade. He will also try to telephone his parents if he gets the time. He hasn't called them for a really long time. They will certainly be interested to hear how Ben is getting on in Serbia.

Unit 13

Ben is walking through town. Dejan telephoned him to inform him that on the fifteenth of July there would be a nice chamber concert. The concert will be held in the exhibition rooms of the Serbian Academy of Science and Arts and will begin at half past seven. Ben had to check that that meant seven thirty, just in case, and he replied that he would be very glad to come. He had heard that the light exhibition hall, with its modern equipment, was on the corner of Knez Mihailo and Vuk Karadžić St. Exhibitions were regularly held in those rooms. That concert was being held on Tuesday, while on Saturday an exceptionally talented young violinist from Japan would be playing. Ben is beginning to think about how much more he can see and hear: he's already been in Belgrade for some ten days, he's got another week at his disposal and he wants to spend a couple of days in Fruška gora as well. His diary is already pretty full.

Unit 14

Dejan invited Ben to the Writers' Union to a delicious lunch and a conversation with some of the best-known contemporary writers. This was exceptionally interesting for Ben: he is a passionate reader and before his trip he had read everything he could find of contemporary Serbian writers in translation. He was surprised when in the course of conversation with the writers he heard that there are a large number of small private publishers in Serbia and that books are bought and read in quite large numbers, given the on the whole modest salaries and considerable number of unemployed. He gained the impression that reading serious literary works was a more popular activity in Serbia and Montenegro than in Great Britain, although the writers warned him that the print-runs were usually far smaller. All the same, it was obvious that these writers were well known and on the whole prominent members of society, while some of them were real media stars! As far as styles and tastes were concerned, there was all and sundry on the agenda: from traditional approaches to the most avant garde, particularly among the youngest.

Unit 15

This evening two young women poets had a literary evening. Both are good friends of Dejan's so they invited Ben, as a respected guest, to say a few words about the contemporary literary scene in Great Britain. Ben accepted their invitation, although he was a little afraid because he was not used to speaking in public. In any case, he wanted to meet the two women poets, because he was particularly interested in women's writing, and especially poetry. They arrived early so that Ben had an opportunity to have a chat with Dejan's friends – Tanja and Ljiljana – before they came on stage. They were both very young, warm and cheerful. Ben liked their poems very much, especially Tanja's: they were short and full of energy. Ben himself spoke in an interesting and accessible way and at the end he was applauded by the satisfied audience. He succeeded in answering all their questions and in the end he was astonished by their knowledge of the British scene.

Unit 16

The next day, Dejan drove Ben, Nada, Ana and little Janko to Fruška Gora. His car was small, but they all managed to squeeze inside somehow. They were invited to lunch at the holiday home of one of Dejan's friends, who lived in Novi Sad, but had a little house on a hill in which he spent almost every weekend.

Ben found the journey interesting: in this region all the villages are similar, with a broad main street and low houses built on either side of the road. These houses have closed courtyards, which cannot be seen from the road. In one of these villages they stopped outside a house where meat was sold. Dejan had promised his friend that on the way he would buy meat for the charcoal grill at this butcher's, because they knew that his meat was always fresh.

Soon they were driving through the woods and hills of Fruška Gora. The holiday house of the friend of Dejan's they were going to was situated at the end of a long, narrow road which led to a monastery, whose cupola could barely be seen above the trees. Nada explained to Ben that these monasteries were built later than the ones in southern Serbia, in the seventeenth and eighteenth centuries, but that they were certainly worth seeing. Ben was very pleased to be in the fresh air and said that he certainly wanted to visit the monastery if they had time to go for a walk before lunch.

Unit 17

At last they arrived. Dejan's friend, Nikola, was already working round the grill, and his wife, Mira, invited them into the house, to refresh themselves and have a coffee. And then Dejan suggested that they take a walk to the monastery. Nikola decided to stay to occupy himself with the lunch, while the others set off on a pleasant walk through the wood. It was a beautiful day and they all enjoyed the fact that they were walking in the country. Soon they arrived at the monastery. Mira asked them to wait while she went to look for the Abbot, whom she knew well. After about ten minutes, she appeared and said that the Abbot would be glad to receive them. They went into a beautiful stone building where the cool appealed to them all. The Abbot greeted them warmly and offered them plum brandy which the monks themselves made. He told them about the history of the monastery and about the fact that they had recently launched a campaign for the restoration of the church. They met two young monks, but the Abbot complained that in all the Serbian monasteries there was a lack of young people: both women and men. The conversation with him was very pleasant: he was gentle and warm and had a beautiful deep voice. Ben could just imagine him singing wonderfully during the service and he was only sorry that they weren't able to hear that. Then Mira took them into the church and showed them the old frescoes and icons. They returned very satisfied and sat down at the table in the open air to enjoy the lunch Nikola had prepared.

Unit 18

It was so pleasant for them all in Fruška gora that they decided to spend the night at Nikola and Mira's. The next day, Dejan took Ben and his family to Smederevo to see the imposing fortress on the Danube. On the way Dejan talked about Serbian history: how after the Battle of Kosovo (28 June, St Vitus Day), 1389, the remainder of the Serbian state moved further north, first to Kruševac, under the ruler Stefan Lazarević, whose father, Tsar Lazar, had been killed at Kosovo. After that the state was still further reduced in size and, as the Ottoman rulers were advancing ever more deeply into the Balkan lands, the centre moved to Smederevo, where the state was finally extinguished.

Ben wanted to know what had happened in Serbian history after the end of the medieval state, so Dejan, Mira and their children talked a lot about the difficulties under Turkish rule, which are described in the famous traditional poetry, and about the first uprising at the beginning of the nineteenth century. And then about the second uprising and the long-drawn out negotiations with the Turks, which finally led to the independent kingdom of Serbia towards the end of the nineteenth century. Mira told him about the formation of the first Yugoslavia, after the First World War, when the large empires on the territories of the Balkans collapsed: the Ottoman and Habsburgs, in whose framework were Croatia and, from 1878, Bosnia and Herzegovina, which had previously also been under Turkish rule. And then, in the Second World War, Yugoslavia was occupied by the Axis powers, Germany and Italy. The communist Partisans waged a difficult and long drawn-out struggle against the occupation, with the help of the Allies and finally created a communist state with Tito at its head. Under his government, the country was independent of both the Soviet Union and the Western bloc. Yugoslavia quickly recovered from the war and survived as a federation of 6 republics right up until the collapse of the communist system in Europe. Then, at the beginning of the 1990s, nationalist parties came to power in the Yugoslav republics and after vicious wars the Yugoslav federation broke up into independent states.

Unit 19

The end of Ben's visit to Serbia is coming near. But before he leaves, Dejan arranged with some of his colleagues, journalists, to meet in the Journalists' Club so that Ben would be able to ask them some more questions, now that he knew more about cultural life in Serbia. Some ten people came, from various media.

They had a very interesting conversation about the conditions in which they worked and what they would like to change. Of course they all agreed that their life would be far easier if they earned more and if the conditions for being involved in journalism were better. Some said that they would very much like to work for a time abroad, as correspondents. New York and Paris were most frequently mentioned as the most desirable cities, if their newspapers ever had the funds for something like that.

During his stay, Ben had kept a detailed diary, in order to be able to write his series of articles. Now he had a splendid opportunity to fill out his picture of cultural life in Serbia and Montenegro, so he had noted down in advance a whole series of questions. He wanted his articles to be as full and accurate as possible.

Unit 20

Having got home, Ben sat down to write Dejan a letter, to thank him for everything he had done for him.

Dear Dejan,

I don't know how to thank you for everything. You were the kindest possible host, guide and friend. I saw, heard and learned a lot, and everything I got to know about the rich cultural life of Serbia and Montenegro I owe to you. I met a large number of exceptionally pleasant and dear people, who received me warmly into their surroundings, their houses and their lives. That is a debt which it would be hard to repay. The only real proof of my gratitude will be my articles. I shall send them to you by email before I submit them to the paper, to be certain that I have not made a mistake somewhere or left out something essential. Of course, only in the event that you are prepared to do me also this additional favour. But I know that you care about Serbia and Montenegro being known in the world by something else, and not only war and assassinations and a stormy political life.

This letter is coming to you by ordinary post, because I wanted also to send you some pictures which I hope will please you all. Otherwise I have at last transferred all my notes from my laptop to the big computer and from now on I shall be able to contact you regularly by email.

Warmest greetings to Nada and a hug to the children,

Greetings from the bottom of my heart to you,

Yours,

Ben

Translations of 'The gang'

Unit 1

Maja calls her friend Luka on her mobile phone.

'Hi, Luka, what are you up to?'

'Nothing. What about you?'

'Nothing.'

'Let's go to the club!'

'OK!'

Unit 2

'Hi, mates! How are you?' asks Luka.

'Great! We're celebrating!' replies Jelena.

'What are you celebrating?' asks Maja.

'It's my birthday today,' explains Filip.

'Congratulations! Let's order some drinks! It's my treat!' says Luka.

Unit 3

'Filip,' says Jelena, 'these are my new friends.'

'Hi, I'm Sanja, and this is my brother Dado.'

'Pleased to meet you. Please, sit down,' says Filip.

'Maja, is there any space beside you?'

'Of course. Sit here, Sanja.'

'Are we all for red wine?' asks Luka.

'Yes, thank you, Luka!' they all reply.

Unit 4

'Where are you from, you two?' asks Filip.

'From Bosnia, from Zenica. What about you, are you all from Belgrade?'

'No,' replies Filip. 'I'm from Novi Sad, and Jelena's Montenegrin.'

'That's right,' says Jelena. 'I'm from Podgorica.'

'And I'm from Kruševac,' says Maja.

'At least I'm a real Belgrader!' says Luka.

'Welcome to Belgrade!' says Jelena.

Unit 5

Sanja sits beside Maja, opposite Jelena and Luka.

'Luka, serve our new friends some wine!' says Jelena.

Luka pours wine for Sanja and Dado.

'How long have you been in Belgrade?' asks Maja.

'Since the winter,' answers Dado.

'Are your parents still in Bosnia?'

'Yes, but they're not in Zenica any more. Now they're in Banja Luka, at our grandmother's.'

'Welcome and cheers!' says Filip. 'To new friendship!'

'Cheers!' they all reply.

'Cheers!' say Dado and Sanja.

Unit 6

Filip turns to his friends. 'I have a suggestion: let's all go to my place. Mum has baked a wonderful cake.'

'Filip has a beautiful bachelor flat in the attic of a building in Kondina St.,' Jelena explains to Sanja and Dado. 'We often meet up there.'

Luka asks for the bill and pays. The others get up from the table and set off towards the door.

'It's a lovely evening! Let's go on foot,' suggests Jelena.

'OK, it's not far.'

'Do you live in the centre?' asks Sanja.

'Yes, I'm really lucky!' replies Filip, with a cheerful smile.

Unit 7

'I'm sorry I don't have any more comfortable chairs,' says Filip.

'No problem, I like sitting on the floor,' replies Sanja.

'Me too,' agrees Maja, 'you come as well Luka, sit beside me on this beautiful carpet!'

'What can I offer you? I have red and white wine, of course. There's fresh bread, hard cheese and some fruit, if anyone feels like it,' Filip offers them.

'Let me give you a hand,' says Jelena. 'Does anyone want to try my great coffee?'

'Certainly,' says Luka. 'What do you have in the way of music, Filip?'

'You can take a look: the CDs and cassettes are over there.'

'It's really nice here at your place!' says Sanja.

They all agree that it is exceptionally pleasant and continue to enjoy a good time.

Unit 8

Filip asks Sanja where they live.

'Let me see you home,' he says to Sanja.

'Thanks, Filip, but it's not far,' replies Sanja.

'I know, but all the same, you might get lost, and I absolutely don't want that, because it's late.'

'There's no point in your going out now, Filip,' says Maja, 'they can go with us to the square, and then we can explain how to carry on.'

'There's no problem, Maja, thank you, but I really want to be in the air for a while.'

'OK, if you insist,' says Maja.

Jelena looks carefully at Filip: she knows him very well and he doesn't usually insist like this.

Unit 9

'How do you spend your time in Belgrade?' asks Jelena.

'I study a bit, I watch television a bit,' replies Dado.

'Do you do any sport?' asks Jelena.

'I like football a lot, but I don't know people here.'

'We can fix that!' says Jelena cheerfully, but Dado says nothing.

On the other side of the table, Filip is having a lively conversation with Sanja.

'Have you got time to get to know Belgrade?' he asks.

'Not a lot. Now it's not cold any more, but now I have to study and I haven't much time for looking round the city,' replies Sanja.

'We can change that!' says Filip. 'There are beautiful and interesting places in this big city. Do you want to get to know them?'

'Certainly,' replies Sanja. 'Dado has to get out more as well.'

'Agreed, then!' says Filip.

Unit 10

'Do you have a large family?' Maja asks Sanja and Dado.

'Our family is quite large,' replies Sanja. 'But now they are all scattered over the world. One aunt with her husband and sons is now in Canada, another is in France, while our uncle is in New Zealand.'

'We've got a distant relative, here in Belgrade,' says Dado.

'Yes, it's a bit complicated,' adds Sanja. 'He's our mother's brother-in-law, although he's not married to her sister any more. They were divorced two years ago, unfortunately. But we still all like him a lot, and he is very good to us.'

'He hasn't got children of his own, so he's adopted us in a way,' says Dado.

'Nice of him! Let's drink a glass of wine in honour of relatives!' suggests the always good-humoured Luka, as he takes Maja by the hand. 'I want Maja one day to be my wife and all of you to come to our wedding!'

Maja blushed a little, but she was obviously pleased.

Unit 11

Jelena is Filip's best friend. She sees that Sanja attracts him in a way that is new for him, and wants to help him. She decides to invite Dado to the cinema.

'What are you doing next Friday, Dado?' asks Jelena.

'Nothing particular, as far as I know,' he replies.

'There's a new Serbian film on in the cinemas. The reviews are excellent. Everyone's praising it.'

'Great. I like the cinema. I don't know what the others are doing . . .'

'I don't either, but I've got a friend who can give us two free tickets.'

'You've got good connections, then! Well I don't know, I'll have to see with Sanja.'

'I think Filip is planning to invite her somewhere. Come on, Dado, you don't have to be with her all the time!'

'I know I don't, but, we've been together so much these last months, I've got used to thinking of her always.'

'That's nice of you. But one day you have to separate a bit! Come on, this film is really interesting!'

It was clear to Jelena that Dado was embarrassed, but she still hoped that in the end he would decide to keep her company.

Unit 12

Filip invited Sanja to a concert of his favourite band. When they were approaching the Sava Centre there was a terrible crowd.

'I think it will be best if we hold hands. I don't want to lose you in this crowd,' said Filip.

'OK. I'm a bit afraid: I've never liked so many people,' said Sanja.

'Don't be afraid, just hold me tight! The band is very popular and young people in Belgrade are eager for good music, entertainment and enjoyment!'

'I understand. It's similar in Bosnia. Immediately after the war everyone began playing music from Serbia because of its unusual energy.'

'Music is after all a universal language, regardless of politics, isn't it?'

'I agree. But we're still very proud of our own local bands! Do you play anything?'

'I play the guitar, but not exactly brilliantly! I was in a band at secondary school. What about you?'

'I play the piano and I like it a lot. Unfortunately there isn't a piano at our relative's.'

'We'll find a way for you to play again. I think that there's a piano at Maja's. But now, we're going into the hall, hold me tight!'

Unit 13

After the concert, Filip suggests that they go somewhere for a drink.

'I don't know,' said Sanja, 'It's fairly late already.'

'It's only half past ten,' said Filip. 'We won't stay long. I know a great place not far from your house.'

'OK, but really for a short time.'

'Don't worry, you'll be home by midnight. On Fridays one can stay out a little later and you have to get to know Belgrade by night as well!'

'Thank you, but there's no need for you to make an effort around me. I don't lack anything.'

'Apart from a piano. All right, I won't exaggerate, but when I say that it will be a pleasure to show you my city, I mean it seriously. Presumably you see that I like you a lot?'

'Thank you for your attention, Filip. But I don't know whether I'm ready for a relationship.'

'Slowly, I just wanted to say that I like being with you and I want to see you again. Tomorrow there's going to be a party at Maja's and

I'd like you to come with me. You can have a look at the piano there and make a plan with Maja.'

'Thank you, I have to see what Dado's doing.'

'OK, I understand that you have to take him into account as well, but you need to think about yourself a bit as well!'

'All right, I shall! But now I really have to go.'

Unit 14

Dado and Jelena liked the film, and then they went to a nearby café for a drink.

'Did you go to the cinema often when you lived in Bosnia?' asked Jelena.

'It depends: fairly often, mostly in winter when it's otherwise cold and you can't be outside much. But in summer I preferred to do sport,' Dado replied.

'That's what I thought: you're very well built,' said Jelena. But then she quickly added: 'I mean, you're similar to Luka, who adores football. While Filip is more a bookish type: I've never heard him mention sport. Although he likes music a lot and dances very well.'

Dado said nothing, so Jelena went on: 'Yes, Filip is one of the best dancers I've ever seen. And as we're talking of that, Maja's having a party tomorrow, so if you feel like it, come.'

'Well, I don't know. I have to see what Sanja's doing.'

'Don't worry, I'm sure Filip will invite her. Come on, it'll be fun!'

'I don't know, I'll see. Can I see you home?' Just as they stood up, Maja and Luka came in. Dado obviously felt better immediately.

'Jelena, I've been trying for hours to get you on your mobile, but it seems it was switched off. Still, it's great that we've found you together, We wanted to invite Dado to the party tomorrow, but didn't know how to contact him. Filip has already invited Sanja, and we'll be pleased if you can come as well.'

'Thank you, all right,' said Dado, still a little confused.

Unit 15

Maja and Luka went with Jelena and Dado towards Jelena's house.

'On the way we can show you where Maja's house is,' said Luka.

'Why yes, it's not far from here,' observed Jelena. 'There, you see that street there, with the little supermarket on the corner? You go along that road to the first traffic lights, then turn left, my flat is in the first building on the right-hand side of that road, beside the video club,' said Maja.

'Just make a note of the address on this piece of paper, please,' said Dado.

'I'm giving you my mobile number as well – just in case.'

'OK, guys, we'll now go down this street,' said Luka, who was going to Maja's place as well.

'Good night! Till tomorrow,' said Maja cheerfully.

'Good night!'

Dado and Jelena continued on their way. 'Here, we've arrived, this is my building. Can I offer you a coffee, or something else?' asked Jelena.

'No, thank you,' said Dado quickly. 'It's high time I went home.'

'So, thank you for seeing me home.'

'You're welcome. Till tomorrow. Good night!' And Dado set off towards his part of the city.

Unit 16

Filip accompanied Sanja home. On the way they talked.

'I want to know as much as possible about you and your life, how you lived and what you occupied yourself with there in that Bosnia of yours,' said Filip.

'Well, we lived like young people everywhere ... I was actively involved in skiing. But, unfortunately, I stopped when the war began. Do you ski?' asked Sanja.

'Unfortunately, I have to confess that I'm not a sporty type: I prefer to sit in an armchair with a book. Was your house on a hill? Or maybe you don't want to talk about it?'

'It's all right, don't worry. I often think about that house of ours, so it seems normal to talk about it sometimes. Although I haven't done that up to now ... It wasn't especially nice, in a new settlement, but – it was ours.'

Filip felt the sadness in her voice, so he reached his hand towards hers and gently took it in his. 'I'm sorry, Sanja, about you, about the war, about everything ...'

Sanja held Filip's hand more tightly. 'Thank you, Filip, I know. It's all right. But maybe it's better after all not to talk about it, at least for now.'

'Agreed. Do you see that shop window with the lights on over there? That's the best confectioner's in Belgrade. Let's go and treat ourselves to something sweet.'

Unit 17

On Saturday the whole gang met up at Maja's place. Luka was the host and he offered each guest a drink.

'What a beautiful flat you have!' said Sanja as soon as they entered.

'I'm lucky: this is our family home, in which I grew up. Unfortunately my parents were killed in a traffic accident two years ago, so that I've remained here on my own.'

'Oh, I'm really sorry,' said Sanja, touched: she and Dado had their problems, but at least their parents were alive.

'Would you like me to show it to you? This is the dining room, but it's rarely used except when there are guests. I prefer to eat in the kitchen, which is quite large enough even for a group of 5 to 6 people. The living room is even larger: that's where the piano is that Filip told you about. On one side of the corridor there are two bedrooms with a bathroom, and on the other side another two, of which the biggest and nicest is mine. My room has a large balcony with a wonderful view of Vračar.'

'It's beautiful,' said Sanja. 'I've never been in a flat like this before.'

Suddenly Maja turned to her, her face joyful.

'You know what, Sanja, I've just had a brilliant idea! How would it be if you and Dado moved here to my place?'

Sanja stopped, her eyes wide open. 'Sorry?' she said.

'Why yes! I don't know how I didn't think of it immediately. I'm here on my own. OK, Luka is often here, but that doesn't matter: he sleeps in my room in any case. There really is a lot of space. And you can play the piano as much as you like! Say you agree that the idea is perfect!'

'I really don't know what to say. It's infinitely good of you to propose such a thing. You hardly know us ...'

'Think about it, ask Dado. But, please, I mean it most seriously. I'm certain that we will get along excellently.'

'I'll look for Dado at once. Then we have to come to an arrangement about money.'

'Slowly. First see what Dado says.'

Unit 18

At the party, Dado was looking out of the window at the illuminated city.

'Dado,' Jelena came up to him. 'Come over here.'

'OK,' he said, a little embarrassed, as always in her company.

'I want to introduce you to my boyfriend,' she explained.

Suddenly Dado felt better. 'I'm coming,' he said, with a smile.

'Here he is. Vedran, this is our new friend, Dado, who I told you about. Dado, I think that you'll get along excellently with Vedran, because he likes sport a lot as well. Don't you, Vedran?'

'Absolutely. You have to come and play football with my mates,' said Vedran.

'That would be great,' said Dado, whose smile was becoming ever broader. 'How come I haven't met you earlier?' he asked.

'I was away on business,' explained Vedran.

'Vedran, offer Dado something to drink: his glass is empty,' said Jelena.

'Here you are.' Vedran handed Dado a glass of wine. 'And now, let's go and dance, Jelena!'

An unknown black-haired girl with lively eyes and a bright smile came up to Dado.

'Hi,' she said, 'I'm Ivana. You must be Dado from Bosnia, Sanja's brother.'

'That's right,' he said and shook her hand. 'Pleased to meet you. I haven't seen Sanja for ages.'

'There she is, see, I've just been with her. But don't let's interrupt them: I think she's having an important conversation with Filip.'

'OK,' Dado laughed. 'Do you like dancing?'

'Lots!'

'Then, let's go and dance!' And they set off towards the dining room and the music.

Unit 19

Immediately after her conversation with Maja, Sanja had a talk with Dado. He was delighted at the idea of their moving to this beautiful, spacious flat. They arranged with Maja that they would get in touch with her as soon as they had a chance to have a chat with Branko.

Filip had followed their conversation from the other side of the room. When Dado went away to find Ivana to invite her to dance again, he went up to Sanja.

'It would be really wonderful, if you were here!' he said.

'I know, the more I think about it, the more I like the idea. I would really be able to devote myself to playing, which I haven't done for years now. And Dado would be with people who are involved in sport . . .'

'That's all true. But I know what will be the greatest advantage for me.'

Sanja knew roughly what he was going to say, but she didn't say anything. She waited for Filip to express himself.

'I think you already know,' Filip began. 'It's important for me because I would feel freer, if you weren't at Branko's any more. I know that he's exceptionally kind, but all the same, I can't see you at any time.'

'Who said you could "at any time" even if we were here!' Sanja laughed.

'You know what I mean,' said Filip. 'I want to be with you as often as possible for as long as possible – as long as that's what you want as well, of course.'

'Come on, Filip, you've talked enough. Do you want to dance?'

'Yes! Let's go!'

Unit 20

They all agreed that the party was brilliant and it was quite late when they all dispersed. The next morning, the telephone rang at Branko's – Sanja and Dado's relative's – place. It was Vedran inviting them to come with the rest of the gang to spend the rest of the day on his barge on the Sava, near Ada Ciganlija. It was a sunny, bright day, so Sanja and Dado quickly got ready.

'Hi, guys!' they called when they reached the shore.

'Hey, welcome!' said Vedran and helped Sanja to climb onto the boat. Dado was especially pleased when he saw that Ivana was among the friends. And Filip was obviously glad that Sanja had come.

'What a wonderful boat you have!' said Sanja.

'Do you live here?' asked Dado, also delighted.

'Why yes, this is my home,' replied Vedran. 'I travel a lot, on business, and then I sleep in various hotels, so I really enjoy it whenever I come back here to such a simple and relaxed way of life.'

'In the winter, he sometimes shows up at friends' houses!' Jelena laughed. 'What do you want to drink? The beer is cooling in the river, and of course there's wine and all sorts.'

'Luka and Maja are busy with the grill. There they are, under the trees,' said Filip. 'And I'm in charge of the salad.'

'Can I help you?' Sanja offered.

'If you don't mind, you can. Thanks for the offer. It'll be ready sooner.' He led her down to the little kitchen.

'Great, there's everything we need here,' said Sanja.

'Yes, all that's lacking is a little more space! But it doesn't matter. Can you chop these tomatoes? I'll give you a board.'

They worked quietly, and then Filip stopped and looked at Sanja. 'I'm really enjoying this, being here with you, working together in the kitchen, as though we're a real couple.'

'Filip, please, don't exaggerate! Let's enjoy ourselves today, there's time for all those things,' said Sanja decisively.

They all spent a wonderful day together and in the end they parted happy, rested and ready for Monday: some for work and others for university.

Serbian–English glossary

The glossary does not contain every word introduced in the units, but all the more common ones are here. The unit number where each word first appears is given in square brackets. If you need to look a word up, put a small dot beside it. Once there are three dots, you will see that it is a common word and you should memorize it! From time to time, try reading through sections of the glossary, to familiarize yourself with groups of related words.

A

a	and/but [1]
aerodrom	aiport [1]
akcija	campaign [17]
ako	if [4]
ali	but [2]
ambulanta	clinic [18]
apoteka	chemist [1]
atentat	assassination [20]
autobus	bus [2]
automobil	car [1]

B

baka	grandmother [5]
balkon	balcony [6]
barem	at least [4]
baviti se (imp.)	to occupy oneself with [9]
baš (emph. part.)	just, right, really [2]
beba	baby [11]
beleška	note [20]
beli luk	garlic [17]

beo, bela	white [5]
beskrajan	endless, infinite [17]
besplatan, -tna	free (gratis) [11]
bez obzira na (+A)	without regard to, regardless of [12]
bilo kakav	of whatever kind [16]
bioskop	cinema [9]
bitan, -tna	fundamental [13]
bitka	battle [18]
bivši	former [11]
blag	gentle [17]
blizak, -ska	near [14]
blizu (+G)	near [4]
bluza	blouse [14]
bogat	rich [13]
boja	colour [5]
bojati se (imp. bojim se)	to be afraid [12]
boleti (imp. bolim)	to hurt [18]

bolje te našao!	(used as a response to **dobro došao**) [1]	**čestitati** (imp.)	to congratulate [2]
		često	often [4]
		četvrtak	Thursday [13]
bombon	sweet [17]	**čiji**	whose [16]
brat (pl. **braća**)	brother [3]	**čika** (informal)	uncle [3]
brat/sestra od strica	cousin [11]	**čim**	as soon as [16]
		čitalac	reader [14]
brdo	hill [15]	**čitati** (imp.; **pročitati**)	to read [10]
breskva	peach [17]		
brinuti (imp. **brinem**)	to worry [13]	**čitav**	whole [19]
		član	member [14]
brod	boat [20]	**članak**	article [19]
broj	number [7]	**čokolada**	chocolate [17]
brojan, -jna	numerous [20]	**čudan, -dna**	strange [16]
brz	quick, fast [9]	**čuditi (se)** (imp.)	to surprise (be surprised) [10]
bučan	noisy [6]		
buran, -rna	stormy [20]	**čudo**	surprise, wonder [20]

C

cena	price [18]	**čuti** (imp. **čujem**)	to hear [10]
centar	centre [5]	**čuven**	famous [18]
ceo, cela	whole [12]	**čvrst**	firm [12]
cipele	shoes [14]	**ćao**	hi, bye [1]
crkva	church [9]		
crkveni	church (adj.) [13]	**Ć**	
crn	black (of wine: red) [3]	**ćerka**	daughter [11]
		ćošak	corner [7]
crnokos	black-haired [18]	**ćutati** (imp. **ćutim**)	to be silent [9]
crven	red [14]		
cveće (n., coll.)	flowers [6]	**D**	

Č

		da	yes [1]
čaj	tea [8]	**da**	to, in order to [2]
čak	even [11]	**da li**	whether [2]
čarape	socks, stockings [14]	**dakle**	therefore [9]
		daleki;	far, distant [6];
čast (f.)	honour [10]	**daleko od toga**	far from it [13]
častiti (se) (imp.)	to treat, pay [2]		
čaša	glass [3]	**dan**	day [1]
čekati (imp.)	to wait [1]	**danas**	today [2]
čelo	head (lit. forehead) [18]	**davati** (imp. **dajem**; **dati**)	to give [3]

deca (pl. of children [3]
dete; f. sing.)
deda grandfather [11]
deka (abbrev. 10 grammes [17]
of dekagram)
delo work, deed [8]
delovati (imp. to act [18]
delujuem)
desetak roughly ten, ten
or so [13]
desiti se (pf.) to happen [8]
desni right [15]
dešavati se (imp.) to happen [2]
dimnjak chimney (dim
smoke) [6]
dirnut touched [17]
divan, -na wonderful [4]
dizati se (imp. to rise [18]
dižem)
dnevna soba living room [6]
dnevnik diary [19]
do (+G) beside [1], to,
up to [3]
do viđenja goodbye [9]
dobar, dobra good [1]
dobiti to acquire [5]
(pf. dobijem)
dobrodošlica welcome [12]
dočekati to wait for,
(pf. dočekivati) greet [17]
doći (pf.; dođem; to come [10]
dolaziti)
dodatan, -tna additional [20]
dodati (pf.) to add [14]
dodavati to add [10]
(imp. dodajem)
dodir contact, touch
[19]
događaj event [13]
dogovarati se to arrange, agree
(imp.; [4]
dogovoriti se)
dogovoreno agreed [9]
dogovoriti se [13] see dogovarati se

dok while [2]
dokaz proof [20]
dolaziti (imp.; to come [1]
doći, dođem)
dole down, below [20]
dom home [20]
dom zdravlja health centre
[18]
domaći local, home-
made [6]
domaćin host [17]
doneti (pf. to bring [8]
donesem)
donje rublje underwear [14]
dopisnik correspondent
[19]
doručak breakfast [8]
(G doručka)
dosta enough, quite
[10]
dostići to reach [15]
(pf. dostignem)
dotle until then [16]
dovesti to bring [10]
(pf. dovedem,
dovoditi)
dovoljan, -jna sufficient [6]
dozvoliti (pf.) to allow [8]
dozvoljen permitted [15]
dragocen precious [17]
drugačiji different [10],
also drukčiji
[18]
drugar friend, 'mate'
(informal) [2], also drug
drugi other [9]
društven social [13]
društvo society, company,
friends [14]
drveće (coll.) trees [11]
drveni wooden [6]
držati (imp. to hold [12]
držim)
država state [15]

duboko	deeply [7]	**gladan, -dna**	hungry [1]
dugačak, -čka	long [16]	**glas**	voice [16]
dugo	long [13]	**glava**	head [18]
dugotrajan, -jna	lengthy [18]	**glavni**	main [4]
dugovati (imp.	to owe [20]	**glavobolja**	headache [14]
dugujem)		**gledati** (imp.)	to watch, look
dušek	mattress [6]		[6]
duvati (imp.)	to blow [19]	**glumac**	actor [9]
dužan, -žna (biti)	to owe [7]	(G **glumca**)	
dva, dve	two [6]	**go, gola**	naked [18]
dvoje	two (mixed	**godina**	year [10]
	gender) [4]	**gospodin**	Mr, sir [3]
dvorište	yard, garden [11]	**gospođa**	Mrs, madam [3]
dvospratnica	two-storey house	**gost**	guest [7]
	[6]	(G pl. **gostiju**)	
		gostoprimljiv	hospitable [20]
Dž		**gostujući**	visiting [12]
džamija	mosque [17]	**gotovina**	cash (ready
džemper	jumper [14]		money) [20]
džigerica	liver [17]	**govoriti** (imp.)	to speak [1]
		grad	town [3]
E		**graditi** (imp.)	to build [11]
eksponat	exhibit [6]	**gradski** (adj.)	urban, town [13]
engleski	English [1]	**granica**	limit, border [19]
Englez	an English	**grejalica**	heater [6]
	person [1]	**grejanje**	heating [6]
epski	epic [13]	**grejati**	to heat [19]
eventualno	possibly [14]	(imp. **grejem**)	
		grešiti (imp.)	to be mistaken
F			[3]
faliti (imp.)	to be lacking 13]	**grozan, -zna**	horrible,
farmerke	jeans [17]		dreadful [19]
fioka	drawer [6]	**grožđe** (coll.)	grapes [17]
fleka	mark, stain [14]	**grob**	grave [19]
formular	form [7]	**grupa**	band, group
fotelja	armchair [6]		(musical) [12]
freska	fresco [7]	**gubiti** (imp.)	[17] *see* **izgubiti**
frizer	hairdresser [7]	**gust**	dense [20]
frižider	fridge [6]	**gužva**	crowd [12]
		gužvati se (imp.)	to crush [14]
G			
garsonjera	bachelor flat [6]	**H**	
gazdarica	landlady [15]	**haljina**	dress [14]
gde	where [1]	**hladan, -dna**	cold [9]

hladiti se (imp.) to get cool [20]
hladovina shade, cool [12]
hleb bread [7]
hodati (imp.) to go (on foot) [17]
hodnik corridor, hall [6]
hvala thank you [1]
hvala bogu thank goodness, God [7]
hvaliti (imp.) to praise [11]

I

i and [3], also [4], even [10]
iako although [4]
idući next, the coming [11]
igrani film feature film [11]
igrati (imp.) to dance [14]; *also* **igrati se**: to play
ikada ever [19]
ili or [2]
ima there is/ there are [3]
imati (imp., pf.) to have [4]
imati (nešto) na umu to bear in mind [14]
imati smisla to have a point, make sense [19]
ime name [3]
inženjer engineer [1]
interesovati (imp. to interest [10]
interesujem)
ionako in any case [14]
ipak nevertheless [11]
isključen switched off [14]
ispeći to bake [17]
(pf. **ispeknem**)
isplatiti se (imp.) to be worth (doing something) [19]

ispred (+G) in front of [4]
ispričati (pf.) to relate [19]
ispunjen filled [11]
istok east [12]
istorija history [6]
iz (+G) from, out of [1]
iza (+G) behind [11]
izabrati to choose [19]
(pf. **izaberem**)
izaći (pf. **izađem**; to go out [8]
izlaziti)
izbegavati (imp.) to avoid [18]
izbor choice [17]
izdaleka from a distance [5]
izdavač publisher [14]
izgleda (impers.) it seems [11]
izgoreti to burn down [9]
(pf. **izgorim**)
izgrađen built [9]
izgubiti (se) (pf.) to lose; get lost [8]
izgubljen lost [17]
(pass. part.)
izjasniti se to express oneself [19]
izlaz exit [15]
izlaziti (imp.) *see* **izaći** [1]
izlog shop window [16]
izložba exhibition [13]
izložbeni exhibition (adj.) [13]
izložen laid out, displayed [17]
iznad (+G) above [16]
iznajmiti to hire [18]
(pf. **iznajmljivati**)
iznenaditi se to be surprised [14]
(pf.)
izostaviti (pf.) to leave out, omit [20]
izuzetan, -tna exceptional [18]
izvaditi (pf.) to take out [3]

izvanredan, -dna	exceptional [7]	
izviniti (pf.)	to excuse [3]	
izvolite	please, here you are [3]	
izvor	source, spring [12]	
izvoz	export [18]	

J

ja	I [1]
jabuka	apple [8]
jaje	egg [8]
jak	strong [16]
jako	very [12]
jasan, -sna	clear [11]
jastuk	pillow [6]
javljati se (imp.)	to contact, get in touch with [1]
javno	publicly [15]
jedini	single, only [16]
jedinstven	unique [7]
jednospratnica	one-storey house [6]
jednostavno	simply [9]
jedva	barely, hardly [12]
jelo	dish, meal [8]
jelovnik	menu [8]
jer	because [8]
jesen (f.)	autumn [13]
jezero	lake [12]
jezik	language, tongue [1]
jogurt	yogurt [17]
jorgan	duvet [6]
još ne	not yet [1]
još uvek	still [5]
juče	yesterday [5]
jug	south [18]
jutro	morning [4]
južni	southern [16]

K

kafa	coffee [2]
kafana	café, restaurant, 'pub' [4]
kafić	café [1]
kajsija	apricot [17]
kako da ne	of course [8]
kako kad	sometimes, it depends when [14]
kako	how [1]
kalendar	diary [13]
kamen (n., adj.)	stone [17]
kamerni	chamber [13]
kao i	as also [12]
kapućino	cappuccino [17]
karta	ticket; map [9]
kasa	till, cash desk [17]
kaseta	cassette [7]
kasniti (imp.)	to be late [7]
kasno	late [8]
kazati (imp. **kažem**)	to say [2]
kašika	spoon [6]
kesica	bag [17]
kiselo mleko	sour milk (thicker than **jogurt**, which is really a drink) [17]
kiša	rain [18]
kišobran	umbrella [3]
klasičan	classical [12]
klavir	piano [12]
klisura	gorge [20]
ključ	key [3]
klub	club [1]
knjiga	book [6]
knjižara	bookshop [1]
književni	literary [15]
književnik	author [14]

ko	who [1]	kroz (+A)	through [5]
kobasica	sausage [17]	kuća	house [3]
kod (+G)	at (French	kući	(to) home [8]
	'chez') [5]	kuhinja	kitchen [6]
kod kuće	at home [6]	kula	tower [18]
kofer	suitcase [14]	kulturni	cultural [1]
koji (f. koja)	which [4]	kupaći kostim	swimming
kola (n. pl.)	car [2]		costume [14]
kolač	cake [6]	kupati se (imp.)	to bathe [19]
kolega	colleague [3]	kupatilo	bathroom [3]
koliko	how much,	kupiti (pf.)	to buy [2]
	how many,	kupovati (imp.	to buy [9]
	as far as [8]	kupujem)	
komad	piece [15]		
kombi	minibus [2]	**L**	
komplikovan	complicated [9]	lak	light, easy [14]
konačno	finally [9]	lakat (G lakta)	elbow [18]
konzerva	tin (of food)	laku noć	goodnight [15]
	[17]	ležati	to lie, go to bed
kopija	copy [7]	(imp. ležim)	[13]
koristiti (pf.)	to use [17]	lek	medicine [18]
kosa	hair [7]	lekar, lekarka	doctor [18]
kostim	costume [9]	lep	nice, beautiful
koštati (imp.)	to cost [2]		[2]
košulja	shirt [14]	lepo se	have a good
koverta	envelope [7]	provedite!	time! [4]
kraj	area, region [6];	lepota	beauty [7]
	end [8]	leti	in summer [13]
krajnje vreme	high time [15]	leto	summer [13]
kralj	king [19]	letos	this summer [11]
kraljevina	kingdom [18]	levo	left [5]
krastavac	cucumber [17]	li (interrog. part.)	[1]
(G krastavca)		lice	face [17]
kratak, -tka	short [11]	liker	liquer [8]
krenuti	to set off [15]	lonac	pot, pan [6]
(pf. krenem)		loš	bad [1]
kretati	to move, set off	lubenica	water melon [17]
(imp. krećem)	[5]	luk	onions [17]
krevet	bed [6]		
kritika	criticism, review	**Lj**	
	[11]	ljubaznost (f.)	kindness [3]
krivudav	winding [19]	ljubičast	mauve [14]
krompir	potatoes [17]	ljubitelj	lover, fan [11]
krov	roof [6]	ljudi	people [8]

M

majica	T-shirt [14]
majka	mother [10]
majstor	mechanic, workman [16]
mali	small [2]
maramica	handkerchief [17]
marka	postage stamp [7]
mast (f.)	ointment [18]
mašina za pranje suđa	dishwasher [6]
mašina za pranje veša	washing machine [6]
međunarodni	international [12]
međutim	however [10]
mejl	email [20]
mesar	butcher [16]
mesec	month, moon [11]
mesečnik	monthly [19]
meso	meat [8]
mesto	place, space [3]
mešan	mixed [8]
miran, -na	peaceful [6]
misliti (imp.)	to think [2]
mlad	young [12]
mlečni (adj.)	milk [17]
mlekara	dairy [12]
mleko	milk [8]
mleven	ground, minced [17]
mnogo	much, many [4]
mnogo toga	a lot of things [2]
modar, -dra	deep blue [14]
moderan	modern, contemporary [6]
moć (f.)	power [15]
moćan, -ćna	powerful [18]
moći (imp., pf. mogu, možeš, može, možemo, možete, mogu)	to be able [2]

moguće	possible [7]
molim	please (lit. 'I pray') [3]
moliti (imp.)	to ask for [1]
momak (G momka)	boy, young man [18]
momenat	moment, event [6]
morati (imp.)	to have to [3]
more	sea [3]
motor	engine [16]
možda	perhaps [13]
može	all right [8]
mrzeti (imp. mrzim)	to hate (mrzi me I can't be bothered) [20]
muslimanski	Muslim (adj.) [14]
muzika	music [7]
muž	husband [1]

N

na (+L or A)	at, on [1]
na miru	in peace [19]
na primer	for example [10]
na raspolaganju	at one's disposal [13]
na sreću	luckily [6]
na tapetu	on the agenda [14]
nažalost	unfortunately [1]
na žaru	grilled (on the grill) [8]
način	way [8]
naći (pf. nađem)	to find [2]
nadati se (imp.)	to hope [10]
nadoknaditi (pf.)	to make up for [13]
nađen (pass. part. of naći)	found [17]
naglasak	accent [10]
najbolje	best [4]
najlon kesica	plastic bag [17]
nakit	jewellery [17]

nalaziti se (imp. **naći se**)	to be found, situated; *also* to meet [3]	**nema na čemu!**	you're welcome! [4]
nameštaj	furniture [6]	**nema problema!**	no problem! [3]
napisati	to write [7]	**nema smisla**	there's no point [8]
(pf. **napišem**)		**nema veze**	it doesn't matter [11]
naporan, -rna	arduous, hard [13]	**nema**	there is not [4]
napolju	outside [14]	**nemati**	not to have [7]
napraviti (pf.)	to make [2]	(neg. of **imati**)	
naravno	of course [7]	**neobičan, -čna**	unusual [8]
narodni	national [6]	**neposredno**	directly [18]
naročito	in particular [11]	**nesreća**	accident, misfortune [17]
naručiti (pf.)	to order [2]	**nešto**	something [7]
naselje	settlement, estate [16]	**neverovatan, -tna**	unbelievable, incredible [10]
naseljen	inhabited [20]	**nezaposlen**	unemployed [14]
nasmejati se (pf. **nasmejem se**)	to laugh [16]	**nezavisan, -sna**	independent [7]
nastati (pf.)	to emerge, come into being [11]	**nezgodan, -dna**	awkward, uncomfortable [14]
nastaviti (pf.)	to continue [8]	**nežan, -žna**	tender [16]
naš	our [5]	**nikada(a)**	never [12]
natrag	back [16]	**nikako**	no way, not at all [8]
navika	habit [19]	**niko**	no one [7]
navikao, -kla	accustomed [11]	**ništa**	nothing [1]
naviknuti se (pf.)	to get used [19]	**niz** (+A)	down, along [19]
nedaleko od	not far from [6]	**niz**	series [19]
nedavno	recently [17]	**nizak, niska**	low [16]
nedeljnik	weekly magazine [19]	**nizbrdo**	downhill [12]
nećak	nephew [14]	**noć** (f.)	night [3]
nečiji	someone's [16]	**noga**	leg, foot [18]
negde	somewhere [2]	**nošnja**	costume [6]
nego	but, then [12]	**notes**	notebook [17]
neki	some [6]	**nov**	new [3]
nekoliko	a few [2]	**novac**	money [17]
nekud	somewhere (with motion) [11]	**novinar**	journalist [1]
		novine (fem. pl.)	newspaper(s) [2]
		nož	knife [6]
		nuditi (**nekoga nečim**)	to offer [7]

O

o (+L)	about [10]
oba (m. **obe**;	both [15]
f. **oboje**; n.,	
mixed gender)	
obala	shore, bank [8]
obavestiti (pf.)	to inform [13]
obećati (pf.) (+D)	to promise [16]
običaj	custom [10]
obično	usually [11]
obići (pf. **obiđem**;	to go round,
obilaziti)	visit [12]
obilan, -lna	abundant [8]
obilazak	visit, lit. 'going
	round' [7]
obližnji	nearby [7]
objasniti (pf.)	[8] see
	objašnjavati
objašnjavati	to explain [2]
(imp. **objasniti**)	
oblačan, -čna	cloudy [19]
oblak	cloud
oblast (f.)	area [6]
obližnji	neighbouring
	[7]
obnavljati (imp.)	to renew [13]
obnova	renewal [17]
obožavati (imp.)	to adore [14]
obraćati se (imp.)	to turn to [6]
obratiti se (pf.)	to turn to [17]
obradovati (se)	to make happy
(imp. **obradujem**;	[20]
obraditi)	
obrok	meal [9]
obući	to put on
(pf. **obučem**;	(clothes) [14]
oblačiti)	
obuti	to put on/
(pf. **obujem**)	wear shoes [14]
očajan, -jna	desperate,
	terrible [7]
očigledan, -na	evident [7]
očuvan	preserved [19]

očuvanje	protection,
	conservation
	[10]
odakle	from where [4]
odatle	from there [4]
odavde	from here [4]
odgovarati (imp.)	to reply [2]
odjednom	suddenly [17]
odlaziti (imp.)	to go, leave [1]
odličan, -čna	excellent [2]
odlučan, -čna	decisive [20]
odlučivati se	to decide [11]
(imp. **odlučujem**;	
odlučiti)	
odmah	immediately [4]
odmor	rest, holiday [19]
odmoran, -rna	rested [20]
odmoriti se (pf.)	to rest [12]
odneti	to take (away)
(pf. **odnesem**)	[3]
odnos	relationship [13]
odrastao, odrasla	grown up [17]
odrasti	to grow up [11]
(pf. **odrastem**)	
određen	specific, fixed
	[19]
odrezak	cutlet [17]
održati (pf.)	to maintain,
	to be held [13]
održavati se	to be held (up)
(imp.)	[10]
odspavati (pf.)	to take a nap
	[19]
oduševljen	delighted [9]
odvesti	to take, lead
(pf. **odvedem**)	(away) [7]
odvojiti se (pf.)	to part, separate
	from [11]
ofarbati (pf.)	to colour, dye [7]
ogledalo	mirror [6]
ogroman, -mna	huge [13]
ohladiti (se) (pf.)	to cool [8]
ojačati (imp.)	to strengthen
	[19]

oko (N; pl. **oči**; G pl. **očiju**) — eye [17]
oko (+G) — around [11]
okolina — surroundings [15]
okružen — surrounded [8]
okvir — framework [18]
olakšati (pf.) — to ease, become easier [18]
omiljen — favourite [12]
onda — then [4]
opet — again [9]
opisati (pf. **opišem**) — to describe [17]
oporaviti se (pf.) — to recover [18]
opremljen — equipped [13]
oprostiti (pf.) — to forgive, excuse [3]
opušten — relaxed [20]
orah (pl. **orasi**) — walnut [8]
organizovan — organized [10]
orman — wardrobe [6]
osetiti (pf. **osećati**) — to feel [16]
osim (+G) — apart from [12]
osmeh — smile [6]
osnivati (imp. **osnujem**) — to found [15]
osnovan — founded [7]
ostajati (imp. **ostajem**) — to stay [2]
ostali — the others [6]
ostatak — remainder [18]
ostati (pf. **ostanem**) — stay, remain [2]
ostaviti (pf.) — to leave, abandon [16]
osvežiti (se) (pf.) — to freshen up [17]
osvetljen — lit [16]
ošišati se (pf.) — to have one's hair cut [7]
otac (G **oca**; pl. **očevi**) — father [11]

otići (pf. **odem**; **odlaziti**) — to go (away) [2]
otkad — since when [5]
otplatiti (pf.) — to pay off, repay [20]
otpratiti (pf.) — to accompany, see home [8]
otprilike — roughly [18]
otvoriti (se, pf.) — to open [16]
ovakav — this kind of [8]
ovamo — here (with motion) [1]
ovde — here [2]
ovo — this (n.) [1]
ozbiljan, -jna — serious [13]
oženjen — married (of man) [10]

P

pa — then, so [4]
padati, pasti na pamet — to occur to [11]
padina — slope [7]
pakovati se (imp. **pakujem**; **spakovati**) — to pack [14]
palačinka — pancake [8]
paliti (imp.) — to light, switch on [6]
pametan, -tna — clever, intelligent [14]
pantalone — trousers, slacks [14]
paprika — green, red pepper [17]
par — couple [11]
pas (G **psa**; pl. **psi**) — dog [8]
pasoš — passport [3]
pašteta — paté [17]
patlidžan — aubergine [17]
pažljiv — careful, attentive [8]
pažnja — attention, care [13]

pecivo	roll [17]		pod	floor, ground [7]
pejzaž	landscape [18]		pod vedrim	in the open air
pekara	baker's shop [17]		nebom	(lit. 'under the clear sky') [17]
pesma	song, poem [13]		podne	noon [13]
pesnik, pesnikinja	poet [15]		podsećati (imp.; podsetiti)	to remind [14]
peške, pešice	on foot [4]		podstanar, -ka	lodger [15]
peškir	towel [14]		poginuti	to perish [17]
petak	Friday [13]		(pf. poginem)	
pevač	singer [13]		pogledati (pf.)	to take a look [3]
pevati (imp.)	to sing [13]			
piće	drink [2]		pogoditi (pf.)	to guess, hit, affect [10]
pijaca	market [17]		pogotovo	particularly [10]
pisac	writer [14]		pogrešiti (pf.)	to be mistaken [20]
pisanje	writing [15]			
pitanje	question [10]		pojaviti se	to appear [17]
pitati (imp.)	to ask (question) [2]		(pf.; pojavljivati)	
piti (imp. pijem)	to drink [3]		pojedini	individual [9]
pitom	tame [20]		pokazati	to show [6]
pivo	beer [3]		(pf. pokažem)	
plaćati (imp. platiti)	to pay [6]		pokazivati (imp. pokazujem)	to show [3]
planina	mountain [12]		poklon	present, gift [11]
plata	pay, salary [14]			
platiti (pf.)	[17] see plaćati		pokrenuti	to launch, set in
plav	blue [14]; blond (of hair) [17]		(pf. pokrenem)	motion [17]
plesti (imp. pletem)	to knit [10]		pokriven	covered [16]
			pokupiti (pf.)	to collect [17]
pletenje	knitting [10]		pokušavati (imp.; pokušati)	to try [9]
plin	gas [6]		pokvariti se (pf.)	to spoil [17]
plivati (imp.)	to swim [20]		polako	slowly [5]
plodan, -dna	fertile [13]		polica	shelf [6]
po (+L)	through, round [2]		polje	field [12]
pocrveneti (pf.)	to blush [10]		polomiti (pf.)	to break [18]
početak	beginning [5]		položaj	position [8]
početi (pf. počnem; počinjati)	to start [10]		pomagati (imp. pomažem)	to help [5]
počinjati (imp.)	see početi		pomalo	a bit [10]
poći nekom za rukom	to succeed [16]		pomoć (f.)	help [5]
			pomoći (pf. pomognem)	to help [7]

pomoću (+G)	with the help of, thanks to [18]	**poslužiti** (pf. **služiti**)	to serve [5]
ponedeljak	Monday [13]	**postajati** (imp)	[18] *see* **postati**
ponekad	sometimes [2]	**postati**	to become [11]
poneti (pf. **ponesem**)	to take, carry [5]	(pf.; **postanem**; **postajati**,	
ponoć (f.)	midnight [13]	**postajem**)	
ponosan, -na	proud [12]	**postaviti pitanje**	to ask a question [19]
ponovo	again [9]		
ponuda	offer [20]	**posteljina**	bed linen [6]
ponuditi (pf. **nekoga nečim**)	[15] *see* **nuditi**	**postojati** (imp. **postojim**)	to exist [11]
ponuditi se (pf.)	to offer oneself [14]	**posvetiti se** (pf.)	to devote oneself to [19]
popeti se (pf. **popnem**)	to climb [20]	**pošta**	post office [1]
		pošto	since [16]
popiti (pf. **popijem**)	to have a drink, drink up [10]	**potpun**	complete [16]
		potražiti (pf.; **tražiti**)	to look for [17]
popraviti (pf.)	to mend, put right [9]	**potreba**	need [13]
popraviti (se) (pf.)	to improve [19]	**potreban, -bna**	necessary [14]
		potruditi se (pf.; **truditi se**)	to try [11]
popravka	repair [17]	**potvrditi** (pf.)	to confirm [13]
popuniti (se) (pf.)	to fill, complete; be filled up [7]	**povezan**	linked [15]
pored (+G)	beside [5]	**povrediti** (pf.)	to injure [18]
porodični	family (adj.) [11]	**povrće** (coll.)	vegetables [16]
		pozdrav	greeting [3]
porodica	family	**pozdraviti** (pf.; **pozdravljati**)	to greet [20]
posao (G **posla**)	work [19]	**pozivati** (imp.; **pozvati**, **pozovem**)	to invite [6]
posebno	especially [8]		
posedeti (pf.)	to sit for a while [6]	**pozivni broj**	area code [7]
poseta	visit [12]	**poznat**	well-known, famous [10]
posetiti (pf.)	to visit [16]		
poslastičarnica	confectioner's [16]	**poznavati** (imp. **poznajem**; **poznati**)	to know (be acquainted with) [7]
poslati (pf. **pošaljem**)	to send [7]	**pozorište**	theatre [1]
posle (+G)	after [12]	**pozvan**	invited [7]
posle podne	afternoon [13]	**pozvati** (pf.)	to invite [7]
poslednji	last [11]	**poželjan, -jna**	desirable [19]
poslovni put	business trip [18]	**požuriti** (pf.)	to hurry [18]

prababa	great-grand-mother [11]	**predstavljati** (imp.;	to introduce, represent [3]
pradeda	great-grandfather [11]	**predstaviti**)	
		predstojeći	forthcoming [16]
prašak	powder [18]	**predug**	too long [7]
(G **praška**)		**pregledati** (pf.)	to examine [18]
pratiti (imp.)	to follow, accompany [10]	**pregovor**	negotiation [18]
		prekinuti	to interrupt [18]
pratnja	company, accompaniment [6]	(pf. **prekinem**)	
		prekjuče	the day before yesterday [10]
pravac	direction [5]	**preko** (+G)	through, across; more than [10]
pravi	real, true [4]		
praviti	to make [4]	**preko puta**	opposite (adv.)
praviti (**nekome**)	to keep (some-	**prekoputa**	[3]
društvo	one) company [11]	(+G) (prep.)	
		prekrasan, -na	beautiful [6]
pravo;	right; straight [5]	**prelaziti** (imp.)	to cross [5]
u pravu [3];	right	**prema** (+L)	towards [5]
imati pravo	to be right	**premijera**	first night (new show) [12]
pravoslavan	Orthodox [7]		
prazan, -zna	empty [18]	**preporučivati**	to recommend
pre (+G)	before [14]	(imp.	[2]
pre nego što	before [15]	**preporučujem**)	
preći	to cross [16]	**preporučeno**	registered [7]
(pf. **pređem**)		(**pismo**)	
pred (+I)	in front of [11]	**prepun**	very full [7]
predati (pf.)	to hand over [20]	**prerano**	too early [17]
		preseliti se (pf.)	to move [17]
predivan, -vna	wonderful [15]	**presladak,**	very sweet [11]
predjelo	starter [8]	**preslatka**	
predlagati	to suggest [4]	**prespavati** (pf.)	to spend the night [12]
(imp. **predlažem**;			
predložiti)		**prestajati**	to stop [10]
predlog	suggestion [6]	(imp. **prestajem**)	
predložiti	[13] *see* **predlagati**	**preterivati** (imp. **preterujem**)	to exaggerate [13]
		prethodno	in advance [19]
prednost (f.)	advantage [16]	**pretpostaviti** (pf.;	to suppose
predsednik	president [3]	**pretpostavljati**)	[17]
predsoblje	vestibule [6]	**previše**	too much [12]
predstava	performance, production [9]	**prevod**	translation [14]
		prevodiv	translatable [11]
predstaviti	*see* **predstavljati**	**prezime**	surname [3]

prezivati se	to be called (surname) [3]	**proći** (pf.; **prođem**;	to go through [7]
pri ruci	to hand [14]	**prolaziti**)	
približiti se (pf.;	to approach,	**prodati** (pf.)	to sell [10]
prebližavati se)	draw near [12]	**prodavati** (imp. **prodajem**)	to sell [10]
pribor za jelo	cutlery [6]	**prohodati** (pf.)	to start to walk [16]
priča	story [13]		
pričati (imp.)	to talk [9]	**proizvod**	product [10]
pričekati (pf.)	to wait a moment [17]	**proizvoditi** (imp.)	to produce [14]
prići (pf. **priđem**)	to approach, come up to [18]	**proleće**	spring [13]
		promeniti (pf.; **menjati**)	to change [19]
prihvatiti	to accept [15]	**pronaći**	to find [14]
prijatan, -na	pleasant [3]	(pf. **pronađem**)	
prijatno!	enjoy! bon appetit [8]	**prostor**	space [17]
prijatelj	friend [1]	**prostorija**	premises, room [7]
prijateljstvo	friendship [5]	**prostran**	spacious [6]
prijati (nekome, imp.)	to please, appeal to [16]	**protekao, -kla**	past [10]
prijaviti (pf.)	to register [12]	**protiv** (+G)	against [14]
priličan, -čna	considerable [14]	**proveriti** (pf.)	to check [12]
prilično	fairly [10]	**provesti**	[13] see **provoditi**
prilika	opportunity [13]	**provod**	entertainment, fun [7]
primerak	example, copy [12]	**provoditi** (imp.; **provesti**, **provedem**)	to spend (time) [7]
primetiti (pf.)	to notice, observe [14]	**prozor**	window [6]
primiti (pf.)	to receive [17]	**prtljag**	luggage [3]
pripremati (imp. **pripremiti**)	to prepare [3]	**pružiti** (imp.)	to offer, extend [16]
priredba	performance [13]	**prvi**	first [2]
priroda	nature, country-side [10]	**ptica**	bird [19]
		publika	audience [15]
pristojan, -jna	decent [18]	**pun**	full [6]
prisutan, -tna	present [10]	**puno**	a lot of, much, many [8]
privlačiti (imp.)	to attract [11]		
priznati (pf.; **priznavati**)	to confess [16]	**pustiti** (pf.)	to leave, let go; show [11]
probati (imp.)	to try [7]	**pustolovina**	adventure [18]

put journey; path, way; *also* time [2]
putnik traveller [3]
putokaz signpost [15]
putovati to travel [2]
(imp. **putujem**)

R

račun bill, account [6]
raditi (imp.) to do; work [1]
radi se (o+L) it's about … [11]
radnja shop [5]
radni (dan) working (day) [13]
rado gladly [3]
radostan, joyful [17]
radosna
radovati (se) to be glad [20]
(imp. **radujem**)
rakija brandy [13]
rani early [12]
raskrsnica crossroads [15]
raspad disintegration, collapse [18]
raspoložen in a good mood; in the mood [10]
rastvoriti (se) to disintegrate (pf.) [18]
rat war [12]
razni various [13]
razaranje destruction [18]
razbacan scattered [10]
razgledati (pf.) to look over [7]
razgledavati to examine,
(imp.; **razgledati**) look over [11]
razglednica postcard [7]
razgovarati to talk, converse
(imp.) [2]

razgovor conversation [9]
razići to part, disperse
(pf. **raziđem**) [19]
različit various [6]
razmisliti (pf.) [17] *see*
razmišljati
razmišljati to reflect,
(imp.; **razmisliti**) consider [13]
razni various [8]
raznovrsnost variety [19]
razonoda entertainment [12]
razumeti (imp.) to understand [1]
razveden divorced [10]
razvedriti se (pf.) to clear up [19]
razvijen developed [10]
razvitak development
(G **razvitka**) [16]
realan, -lna realistic [19]
recept prescription [18]
redovno regularly [12]
rečnik dictionary [2]
reći (pf. **reknem**) to say [2]
rerna oven [6]
rešenje solution [16]
rešiti (pf.) to decide [12]
retko rarely [17]
(**redak, retka**)
rezervni deo spare part [16]
režija staging, production [9]
roditelj parent [5]
rođak relative [10]
rođendan birthday [2]
roštilj charcoal grill, barbecue [16]
ručak lunch [8]
ruka hand, arm [10]
rukav sleeve [18]
rukovati se (imp. to shake hands
rukujem se) [18]

S

s, sa	with [6]
s obzirom na+A	with regard to, given [14]
sad(a)	now [1]
sagraditi (pf.)	to build [11]
sagrađen	built [16]
sako	jacket [14]
sala	hall, auditorium [6]
sam	oneself, itself etc., alone [8]
samo	only [12]
samoposluga	supermarket [15]
samostalan, -lna	independent [18]
saobraćajni	traffic (adj.) [17]
sarađivati (imp. **sarađujem**)	to cooperate [18]
sastati se (pf. **sastanem**)	to meet (by arrangement) [2]
sasvim	quite, completely [17]
savremen	contemporary [8]
savršen	perfect [17]
saznati (pf.)	to get to know [10]
scena	stage [12]
sećati se (imp.; **setiti se**) (+G of thing remembered)	to remember [8]
sedeti (imp. **sedim**)	to sit (be sitting) [3]
sedište	seat [12]
seljak (m), **seljanka** (f.)	villager, peasant [10]
selo	village [3]
semafor	traffic lights [9]
seoski	village (adj.) [6]
servis	garage (repairs) [16]
sesti (pf. **sednem**)	to sit down [9]
sestra	sister [10]

setiti se	to remember, have an idea [17]
sever	north [12]
sići (pf. **siđem**)	to go/come down [6]
sićušan, -šna	tiny [18]
siguran, -na	certain [5]
silaziti (imp.)	to get off (go down) [5]
simpatičan, čna	charming, nice [11]
sin	son [10]
sinuti (pf.)	to flash [17]
sipati (imp.)	to pour [5]
sir	cheese [7]
sitniš	change, loose coins [17]
siv	grey [14]
sjajan, -jna	brilliant [7]
skratiti (pf.)	to shorten [7]
skrenuti (pf. **skrenem**; **skretati, skrećem**)	to turn [5]
skroman, -mna	modest [13]
skulptura	sculpture [6]
skup	expensive [2]
skupljati (se) (imp.)	to gather, meet up [6]
sladak, slatka	sweet [8]
sladoled	ice cream [17]
slagati se (imp. **slažem**)	to agree [2]; go (well) together [14]
slanina	bacon [17]
slaviti (imp.)	to celebrate [2]
sledeći	next [4]
sličan, -čna	similar, like [12]
slika	picture, painting [6]
slikar	painter [8]
slikarstvo	painting [16]
slobodan, -dna	free [19]
složiti se (pf.)	to agree [15]

slučaj	case [14]	sredina	centre, surround-
slučajno	by chance [16]		ings, milieu
slušati (imp.)	to listen [13]		[18]
služiti (imp.)	see **poslužiti**	srediti (pf.)	to organize, sort
	to serve [6]		out [12]
smanjiti se	to be reduced	srednja škola	secondary school
	[18]		[12]
smatrati (imp.)	to consider [6]	srednjevekovni	medieval [15]
smeđ	brown [14]	sredstvo	means, funds
smena	shift [19]		[14]
smeštaj	accommodation	sresti (se)	to meet
	[12]	(pf. **sretnem**)	[18]
smetati	to disturb [17]	stajati (imp.)	to stand, stop
(imp.+D)			[4]
smeti (imp.)	to dare, be	staklo	glass [9]
	allowed [13]	stalno	constantly [6]
snaja	daughter-in-law,	stalo je (**nekome**)	(someone) cares
	sister-in-law	(**do nečega,**	(about some-
	[11]	**nekoga**)	thing, some-
snimati (imp.)	to record, shoot		body) [20]
	(of film) [11]	stambena	block of flats,
so (f. G **soli**)	salt [12]	zgrada	apartment
soba	room [3]		block [6]
sopstven	one's own [7]	stan	flat, apartment
spanać	spinach [17]		[5]
spavaća soba	bedroom [6]	stanovati	to live, reside [6]
spavanje	sleeping [3]	(imp. **stanujem**)	
splav	barge [20]	stanovništvo	population [14]
spomenuti	to mention [14]	stari	old [5]
(pf. **spomenem**)		starinski	ancient, old-
spominjati	to mention [19]		fashioned [13]
(imp. **spominjem**)		stati (pf. **stanem**)	to stop [16]
sprat	storey, floor [6]	staviti (pf.)	to place [18]
spreman, -mna	ready, prepared	steći	to achieve,
	[6]	(pf. **steknem**)	acquire [14]
spustiti se (pf.)	to go down	stići	to arrive, reach
	[19]	(pf. **stignem**)	[4]
srdačan, -čna	warm (cordial)	stizati	to arrive [3]
	[15]	(imp. **stižem**)	
sreća;	luck, happiness;	sto (G **stola**)	table [3]
imati sreće;	to be lucky [6];	stolica	chair [6]
srećan, srećna	happy	stradati (imp.)	to suffer, be
srećom	luckily [19]		killed [18]
sreda	Wednesday [13]	strana	side [9]

stranac	foreigner,	svetao, -la	light, bright [6]
(G stranca)	stranger [10]	svetski	international [10]
stranka	(political) party	sveukupno	altogether [12]
	[18]	svež	fresh, cool [7]
strastven	passionate [14]	svi	all, everyone [3]
strašan, -na	terrible [12]	sviđati se (imp.;	to appeal to [8]
stric	uncle [11]	svideti se,	
strog	strict, severe	svidim)	
	[19]	svirati (imp.)	to play (music)
strpati (imp.)	to squeeze,		[12]
	shove into [16]	svoj	one's own [10]
struja	electricity (lit.	svratiti (kod, pf.)	to visit, call on
	'current') [6]		[14]
student,	student [1]	svuda	everywhere [16]
studentkinja		**Š**	
stupiti (pf.)	to step [20]		
stvar (f.)	thing [3]	šalter	counter [7]
stvarno	really [11]	šećer	sugar [13]
subota	Saturday [9]	šetalište	place to walk [8]
suditi (imp.)	to judge [20]	šetati se (imp.)	to walk, go for a
suknja	skirt [14]		walk [8]
suma	sum (of money)	šetnja	walk [4]
	[17]	širok	wide [11]
sumnjati (imp.)	to doubt, suspect	škola	school [7]
	[19]	šljivovica	plum brandy [17]
sunce	sun [18]	šminka	make-up [17]
supa	soup [8]	šolja	cup [6]
super	great [2]	šorc	shorts [14]
suprug	husband [18]	šporet	cooker [6]
	(supruga wife)	šta	what [1]
susedni	neighbouring	štampa	press [19]
	[12]	što se tiče ...	as far as ... is
sutra	tomorrow [5]		concerned [14]
suv	dry [17]	šuma	woods, forest
suviše	too [9]		[12]
svakako	certainly [3]	šumica	copse (šuma
svaki	every, each [10]		wood) [15]
svaki čas	at any time [19]	šunka	ham [17]
svakodnevni	everyday [19]	**T**	
svakojaki	of all kinds [18]		
sve	everything [7]	tačan, -čna	accurate, exact
svega i svačega	all sorts [14]		[7]
svejedno	all the same [8]	taj (m.)	that [5]
svet	world, people [5]	tako	so [2]

takođe	also, likewise [4]	**U**	
tamo	there [1]	u (+L or A)	to, into [1]
tanjir	plate [6]	u inostranstvu	abroad [19]
tapete (f. pl.)	wallpaper [6]	u međuvremenu	in the meantime
teget	navy blue [14]		[14]
tek	only, just [13]	u pravu	in the right [3]
telefon	telephone [6]	u redu	OK [16]
televizor	television set [6]	u svakom	in any case [14]
tepih	carpet [6]	slučaju	
tetka	aunt [10]	učestvovati (imp.	to participate
teškoća	difficulty [18]	učestvujem)	[10]
težak (f. teška)	difficult [10]	učiniti uslugu	to do (someone)
tiraž	print-run, edition	(pf.)	a favour [20]
	[14]	učiti (imp.)	to learn, study
tokom (+G)	during [11]		[1]
topao, -pla	warm [8]	učtivost	politeness [14]
torba	bag, handbag	ući (pf. uđem)	to enter [12]
	[3]	udaljen	distant [12]
trag	trace [20]	udoban, -na	comfortable
trajati	to last [7]		[6]
(imp. trajem)		ugao (G ugla)	corner [6]
tražiti (imp.)	to seek, ask for,	ugasiti (se) (pf.)	to extinguish
	look for [6]		[18]
trčati	to run [12]	uglavnom	on the whole
(imp. trčim)			[11]
treba (impers.)	(one etc.) should	ugledan, -dna	respected [14]
	[2]; need [7]	ugurati	to push into
trenutak	moment [17]		[18]
(G trenutka)		ujak	uncle (mother's
trenutno	at the moment		brother) [10]
	[11]	ujedno	at the same time
trg	square [4]		[14]
trosoban, -na	three-room [6]	ujutru	in the morning
trošak	expense [19]		[15]
(pl. troškovi)		uključiti (pf.)	to plug in [6]
trpezarija	dining room [3]	uklopiti se (pf.)	to be included,
truditi se (imp.)	to try, make an		integrate [13]
	effort [9]	ukusan, -sna	tasty, delicious
tu	here [3]		[8]
tuga	sadness [16]	ulazna vrata	front door [6];
turski	Turkish [5]	ulaz	entrance
tvorevina	creation [18]	ulica	street [4]
tvrd	hard [7]	uloga	role [7]
tvrđava	fortress [5]		

umesiti (pf.)	to bake (cake, bread) [6]	**uvesti** (pf. **uvedem**)	to bring into [9]
umetnički	artistic [6]	**uvrediti** (pf.)	to hurt, offend [19]
umetnik	artist [13]	**uz** (+A)	together with, alongside [8]
umoran, -na	tired [1]		
unuk	grandson (granddaughter **unuka**) [11]	**uzak, uska**	narrow [16]
		uzbudljiv	exciting [19]
unutra	inside [16]	**uzbuđen**	excited [15]
uočiti (pf.)	to catch sight of [15]	**uzeti** (pf. **uzmem**)	to take [8]
		uzgajan	raised [16]
uopšte	in general, at all [14]	**uzgred budi rečeno**	incidentally [20]
upečatljiv	indelible [20]	**uzimati** (imp.)	to take [10]
upoznati (pf.)	to get to know [2]	**uživanje**	enjoyment [12]
upozoriti (pf.)	to warn, point out [14]	**uživati** (imp.)	to enjoy (+**u**+L) [7]
uputstvo	instruction [15]	**V**	
uskoro	soon [3]		
uslov	condition [19]	**valjda**	presumably [12]
usluga	favour, service [8]	**vazduh**	air [8]
		važan, -na	important [6]
uspeh	success [10]	**važi**	OK, agreed [1]
uspeti (pf.)	to succeed [12]	**važnost** (f.)	importance [16]
uspešan, -na	successful [18]	**veče**	evening [3]
uspeti (pf.)	to succeed [12]	**večera**	dinner [3]
uspomena	memory, memento [20]	**večeras**	this evening [15]
		večerati (imp.)	to have dinner [3]
usput	on the way [5]		
ušće	confluence [5]	**već**	already [17]
ustanak	uprising [18]	**većina**	majority [19]
ustanoviti (f.)	to ascertain, establish [17]	**vedar, vedra**	bright [18]
		vek	century [15]
ustati (pf. **ustanem**)	to get up [6]	**velik**	large [6]
		veoma	very [4]
usvojiti (pf.)	to adopt [10]	**veran, -na**	faithful [7]
utisak	impression [7]	**verovatan, -tna**	probably [16]
utorak	Tuesday [13]	**verovati** (imp. **verujem**+D)	to believe [5]
uvažen	respected [15]		
uveče	in the evening [9]	**veseo, vesela**	cheerful [6]; fun [14]
uvek	always [11]	**veza**	connection [11]; relationship [13]
uverljiv	convincing [9]		

videti	to see [2]	**vrlo**	very [2]
(imp. **vidim**)		**vruć**	hot [8]
vikendica	holiday home [16]	**vuneni**	woollen [10]
viknuti	to shout [20]	**Z**	
(pf. **viknem**)		**za** (+A)	for [3]
viljuška	fork [6]	**za svaki slučaj**	just in case [14]
vino	wine [3]	**za vreme** (+G)	during [15]
vinska karta	wine list [8]	**zabeležiti** (pf.)	to note, make a
više voleti	to prefer [3]		note [19]
više	more [5]; several [6]	**zaboraviti**	to forget [13]
vladavina	rule [18]	(pf.; **zaboravljati**)	
vlasnik	owner [16]	**zadovoljan, -ljna**	pleased [2]
vlast (f.)	power, government [18]	**zadovoljstvo**	pleasure [13]
		zadržati se	to stay [14]
voće (coll.)	fruit [7]	(pf. **zadržim**)	
voda	water [1]	**zadržavati se**	to stay, be held
vodič	guide [20]	(imp.)	up [13]
voditi (imp.)	to lead, take [1]; *also* wage [18]	**zadužen**	in charge of, responsible for [20]
voditi računa (**o nekome, nečemu**) (imp.)	to take account of somebody/ something [13]	**zagrliti** (pf.)	to embrace, hug [20]
voditi razgovor	to carry on a conversation	**zahvaliti se** (pf.)	to thank [20]
		zaista	really [17]
vođa	leader [18]	**zajednički**	common, shared [11]
voz	train [3]		
vozilo	vehicle [4]	**zajedno**	together [4]
voziti (se) (imp.)	to drive [2]	**zamisliti** (pf.)	to imagine [16]
vožnja	drive [18]	**zamoliti** (pf.)	to ask (a favour etc.), request [8]
vrata (n. pl.)	door [6]		
vraćati (se) (imp.)	to return [7]	**zanimati** (imp.)	to interest [7]
vratiti (se) (pf.)	[13] *see* **vraćati (se)**	**zanimanje**	job, occupation [1]
vredeti	to be worth [16]	**zanimljiv**	interesting [5]
(imp. **vredim**)		**zapad**	west [12]
vredi	it is worth [5]	**zapanjen**	astonished [15]
vrednost (f.)	value [17]	**zaposlen**	employed [7]
vreme	time [9]	**zapravo**	in fact, actually [14]
(G **vremena**)			
vrh	top, tip [19]	**zar**	(introduces negative question) [1]
vrhunac	height [15]		

zar ne?	aren't you, isn't it? etc. [1]	**znamenitost** (f.)	sight, thing of interest [4]
zaraditi (pf.)	to earn [19]	**znatan, -na**	significant, considerable [12]
zarađivati (imp. **zarađujem**)	to earn [19]	**znati** (imp.)	to know [2]
zaslužiti (pf.)	to deserve [17]	**zub**	tooth [14]
zatim	then, next [8]	**zvati (se)** (imp. **zovem**) **(se)**	to call, be called [1]
zato	for that reason [10]	**zvezda**	star [14]
zatvarati (se) (imp.; **zatvoriti**)	to shut [18]	**zvučati** (imp. **zvučim**)	to sound [2]
zaustaviti (se) (pf.; **zaustavljati**)	to stop [16]	**zvuk**	sound [16]
zauzet	busy, occupied [7]	**Ž**	
zavesa	curtain [6]	**žaliti se**	to complain, regret [17]
završiti (pf.)	to finish [17]	**žao mi je**	I'm sorry [7]
zašto	why [1]	**želeti** (imp. **želim**)	to want [2]
zbog (+G)	because of [13]	**železnička stanica**	railway station [19]
zbuniti se (pf.)	to be confused, embarrassed [11]	**železnički**	railway (adj.) [9]
zbunjen	confused, embarrassed [14]	**željan, -ljna**	eager for [12]
zbunjivati se (imp. **zbunjujem**) [15]	to be confused	**žena**	wife [1]
zdrav	healthy [12]	**ženski**	women's [13]
zdravo	hello [1]	**žestok**	cruel, vicious [18]
zelen	green [8]	**žica**	string, wire [13]
zemlja	country, ground, soil [11]	**živ**	alive, lively [9]
zet	son-in-law, brother-in-law [10]	**živahan**	lively [9]
		živahnost	liveliness [7]
zgodan, -dna	convenient [2]; *also* good-looking	**živeo, -la, -li!**	cheers! (lit. 'long live') [5]
zgrada	building [5]	**živeti** (imp. **živim**)	to live [2]
zid	wall [7]	**živopisan, -sna**	picturesque [20]
zidina	wall (of city) [18]	**život**	life [1]
zima	winter [5]	**životinja**	animal [12]
zimi	in winter [13]	**žurka**	party [13]
značiti (imp.)	to mean [11]	**žuriti (se)** (imp.; **požuriti**)	to hurry [13]
		žustro	briskly [15]
		žut	yellow [14]

English–Serbian glossary

A

to be able	**moći** (imp. and pf.)
abroad	**inostranstvo**
to accept	**primati** (imp.), **primiti**
accident	**nesreća**
aeroplane	**avion**
after	**posle** (+G)
afternoon	**posle podne** (G **poslepodneva**)
although	**mada, iako**
always	**uvek**
and	**i** (sometimes **a** if there is a slight element of contrast)
arrival	**dolazak**
to arrive	**dolaziti** (imp.), **doći** (**dođem; došao**)
to ask	
(a question)	**pitati** (imp.);
(a favour)	**moliti** (imp.), **zamoliti**

B

bag	**torba**; handbag **tašna**
to bathe	**kupati se** (imp.), **okupati se**
bathroom	**kupatilo**
beautiful	**lep, prekrasan**
because	**zato što, jer**
bed	**krevet**
bed linen	**posteljina**
beer	**pivo**
before	**pre** (+G); **ranije**
to begin	**počinjati** (imp. **počinjem; početi** (pf. **počnem**)
behind	**za** (+I), **iza** (+G); **pozadi** (adv.)
to believe	**verovati** (imp. **verujem**+D)
big	**veliki**
bill	**račun**
birthday	**rođendan**
black	**crn**
boat	**brod; čamac** (small motor or rowing boat)
bonnet (of car)	**hauba**
book	**knjiga**
bread	**hleb**
breakfast	**doručak** (**doručkovati, doručkujem**: to have breakfast)
to bring	(carry) **donositi** (imp. **doneti; dovoditi** (imp.), **dovesti**

bus	**autobus**	daughter	**ćerka**
busy	**zauzet, u poslu**	day	**dan**
		dear	**drag; mio, mila**
C		to decide	**odlučiti (se)** (pf.)
café	**kafana,** *also* **kafić**		**odlučivati (se)**
to call	**zvati (zovem);**	I'm delighted	**drago mi je**
	be called **zvati se**	to depart	**odlaziti** (imp.),
	(imp. **zovem se**)		**otići (odem)**
car	**automobil, kola**	departure	**odlazak**
	(n. pl.)		(G **odlaska**)
to be careful	**paziti** (imp.)	dictionary	**rečnik**
to carry	**nositi** (imp.)	difficult	**težak, teška**
to celebrate	**slaviti** (imp.)	dinner	**večera**
certain	**siguran, sigurna**	direction	**pravac**
chair	**stolica**		(G **pravca**)
cheap	**jeftin**	dirty	**prljav**
cheese	**sir**	divorced	**razveden**
chemist	**apoteka**	doctor	**lekar, lekarka**
child	**dete** (G **deteta**;	dog	**pas** (G **psa**)
	pl. **deca**, f. sing.	door	**vrata** (n. pl.)
	takes pl. verb)	double	**dvokrevetna soba**
choice	**izbor**	room	
cinema	**bioskop**	dress	**haljina**
clean	**čist**	drink	**piće**
clear	**jasan, jasna**	to drink	**piti** (imp. **pijem**),
clinic	**ambulanta**		**popiti**
clothes	**odeća;** (underwear,	dry	**suv;** to dry **sušiti**
	washing) **rublje**		(imp.)
	(both coll. nouns)	early	**rani**
coast	**obala**	East	**istok, istočni** (adj.)
coffee	**kafa**	easy	**lak**
cold	**hladan, hladna;**	to eat	**jesti** (imp. **jedem;**
I am cold	**hladno mi je**		**pojesti**)
to come	**dolaziti** (imp.),	end	**kraj**
	doći (dođem)	engine	**motor**
comfortable	**udoban, -bna**	England	**Engleska**
completely	**potpuno**	English	**engleski**
crossroads	**raskrsnica**	English	**Englez, Engleskinja**
		person	
D		enough	**dosta**
		entrance hall	**predsoblje**
dangerous	**opasan, -sna**	envelope	**koverat**
date	**datum**	evening	**veče** (n.)
		excellent	**odličan, -čna**

excuse me	**oprostite**		to greet	**pozdravljati** (imp.),
expensive	**skup**			**pozdraviti**
to explain	**objašnjavati**		guest	**gost**
	(imp.), **objasniti**			

F

H

			hair	**kosa**
family	**porodica** (f.)		happy	**srećan, srećna**
far	**dalek**		to have	**imati** (imp.)
father	**otac** (G **oca**; pl.		to have to	**morati** (imp.)
	očevi)		he	**on**
fast	**brz**		head	**glava**
to find	**nalaziti** (imp.)		to hear	**čuti** (imp. **čujem**)
	naći, nađem		help	**pomoć** (f.)
to finish	**završiti** (pf.)		to help	**pomagati** (imp.
first	**prvi**			**pomažem; pomoči,**
floor (storey)	**sprat**			**pomognem**) +D
food	**hrana, jelo**		her	**njen**
(prepared dish)			here	**ovde, tu**
football	**fudbal**		to hide	**kriti (se)** (imp.
foreigner	**stranac, strankinja**			**krijem; sakriti (se)**
to forget	**zaboravljati**		hill	**brdo**
	(imp.), **zaboraviti**		to hire	**iznajmljivati** (imp.
friend	**prijatelj,**			**iznajmiti** (pf.)
	prijateljica		his	**njegov**
in front of	**pred** (+I), **ispred**		holiday	**odmor**
	(+G)		to hope	**nadati se** (imp.)
fruit	**voće** (n. coll.)		hospital	**bolnica**
			house	**kuća**

G

			hot	**vruć; topao, topla;**
garden	**bašta**		I am hot	**toplo mi je**
to get on	**slagati se** (imp.		how much	**koliko**
(well)	**slažem se**)		hungry	**gladan, gladna**
girl	**devojka**		to hurt	**boleti** (imp. **bolim;**
to give	**davati** (imp.			usually used in the
	dajem), **dati**			3rd pers.: **boli me**
	(**dam**)			**glava** I have a
to go	**ići** (imp. and pf.			headache)
	idem)		husband	**suprug, muž**
gladly	**rado**			
good	**dobar, dobra**		**I**	
good-looking	**zgodan, zgodna**		I	**ja**
grammar	**gramatika**		ice cream	**sladoled**
book			if	**ako**
grapes	**grožđe** (n. coll.)		immediately	**odmah**

impossible	**nemoguć**
in	**u** (+L), into **u** +A
injured	**povređen**
inside	**unutra**
to interest	**zanimati** (imp.);
that interests me	**to me zanima**
international	**međunarodni**
to invite	**pozivati** (imp.), **pozvati**

J

jewellery	**nakit**
journey	**put, putovanje**
jumper	**džemper**

K

key	**ključ**
kind	**ljubazan**
kitchen	**kuhinja**
to know	**znati** (imp.)

L

language	**jezik** (tongue)
last	**poslednji**
last year	**prošla godina**
late	**kasni** (to be late: **kasniti**, imp. **zakasniti**)
to laugh	**smejati se** (imp. **smejem**)
lavatory	**WC, toalet**
to leave (abandon) (depart)	**ostaviti** (pf.), **ostavljati**; **odlaziti, otići**
left (hand)	**levi**
letter	**pismo**
life	**život**
to like	**voleti** (imp. **volim**); **sviđati se nekome**
to live	**živeti** (imp. **živim**)
living room	**dnevna soba**
little	**malen, mali**

local	**domaći**
to look	**gledati** (imp.);
look for	**tražiti** (imp.), **potražiti**;
look after	**čuvati** (imp.) **sačuvati**
to lose	**gubiti** (imp.), **izgubiti**
to love	**voleti** (imp. **volim**)
to be in love	**biti zaljubljen**
lucky you!	**blago vama/tebi!**
luggage	**prtljag**

M

to marry	**ženiti se** (imp.), **oženiti se** (of man); **udavati se** (imp. **udajem se**), **udati se** (of woman)
meat	**meso**
to meet	**sresti (se)** (pf. **sretnem**); **naći se** (pf.)
menu	**jelovnik**
moment	**čas, časak, trenutak**
month	**mesec**
more	**više**
morning	**jutro**
mother	**majka**
much	**mnogo** (+G)
my	**moj**

N

near	**blizu**, prep.+G
never	**nikad**
new	**nov**
newspaper	**novine** (pl.)
next	**sledeći**
night	**noć** (f.)
no	**ne**
north	**sever**; adj. **severni**

to notice	primećivati (imp. primećujem; primetiti	to read	čitati (imp.) pročitati
now	sad	ready	gotov; spreman, spremna
O		relation	rođak, rođakinja
of course	naravno	to remain	ostajati (imp.), ostati (ostanem)
often	često	to remember	sećati se, setiti se
old	star		(imp. +G of thing
on	na+L;		remembered)
onto	na+A	rest	odmor
our	naš	to rest	odmarati se (imp.), odmoriti se
outside	napolje	to return	vraćati (se) (imp.), vratiti (se)
P			
parent	roditelj	right-hand	desni
to park	parkirati se (imp.)	river	reka
to pay	plaćati (imp.), platiti	road	put, ulica
peach	breskva	room	soba
perhaps	možda	round	iza (ugla)
piece	komad (also play, drama)	(a corner)	
pillow	jastuk	**S**	
place	mesto	stamp	marka
to play	igrati se (imp.)	to say	reći (pf. past part.:
pleasant	prijatan, -tna		rekao, rekla),
please	molim (lit.: 'I pray')		kazati (imp. kažem)
to prefer	više voleti	school	škola
possible	moguć	sea	more
postcard (picture)	razglednica	second	drugi
post office	pošta	to see	videti (imp., pf. vidim)
probably	verovatno	to sell	prodavati (imp. prodajem), prodati
to put	stavljati (imp.) staviti	to send	slati (imp. šaljem), poslati
Q		to set off	polaziti (imp.), poći (pođem)
quiet	tih	shade	hlad
R		she	ona
rain	kiša;	shirt	košulja
to rain	padati kiša		

shop	**radnja, prodavnica**	to talk	**govoriti, razgo-**
shop window	**izlog**		**varati** (imp.),
to sing	**pevati** (imp.)		**razgovoriti**
sister	**sestra**	tea	**čaj**
to sit (down)	**sesti**	teacher	**nastavnik**
to be sitting)	**sednem** (pf.)		(primary);
	sediti (imp.)		**profesor**
slacks	**pantalone** (f. pl.)	thank you	**hvala**
small	**malen, mali**	theatre	**pozorište**
to sleep	**spavati** (imp.)	their	**njihov**
to smoke	**pušiti** (imp.),	there	**tamo**
	popušiti	they	**oni** (m.), **one** (f.),
some	**neki**		**ona** (n.)
someone	**neko**	thing	**stvar** (f.)
something	**nešto**	to think	**misliti** (imp.),
somewhere	**negde**		**pomisliti**
son	**sin**	through	**kroz** (+A)
song	**pesma** (*also*	tin (of food)	**konzerva**
	poem)	today	**danas**
soon	**uskoro**; as soon	tomorrow	**sutra**
	as **čim**	town	**grad**
to speak	**govoriti** (imp.)	train	**voz**
spring	**proleće**	to travel	**putovati** (imp.
to stand	**stajati** (imp.		**putujem**)
	stajem), **stati**		n. **putovanje**
	(**stanem**)	to try	**probati** (imp., pf.);
station	**stanica**		**pokušavati**
to stay	**boraviti** (imp.)		(imp.), **pokušati**
(sojourn)			
stop	**stanica**	**U**	
(bus etc.)		to understand	**razumevati** (imp.),
storm	**oluja**		**razumeti**
straight	**prav; ravan, ravna**		(**razumem, oni**
soup	**supa;**		**razumeju**)
thick soup	**čorba**	unfortunately	**nažalost**
south	**jug, južni** (adj.)	usually	**obično**
suitcase	**kofer**	**V**	
summer	**leto**		
sun	**sunce**	vegetables	**povrće** (coll.)
T		very	**jako, vrlo,**
			veoma
table	**sto** (G **stola**)	view	**pogled**
to take	**uzimati** (imp.),	visit	**poseta**
	uzeti (**uzmem**)		

W

to walk	**hodati** (imp.); **šetati** (to go for a walk) (imp.) **prošetati**
to want	**želeti** (imp. **želim**)
to wash	**prati** (imp. **perem**), **oprati**
washbasin	**lavabo**
way	**način**; direction **put**
we	**mi**
weather	**vreme** (G **vremena**)
week	**nedelja**
welcome	**dobro došao** (**došla, došli** etc.)
west	**zapad, zapadni** (adj.)
wet	**mokar, mokra**
when	**kad**
where	**gde**; **kuda, kamo** (with movement)
white	**beo, bela**
who	**ko**

why	**zašto**
wife	**supruga, žena**
wind	**vetar** (G **vetra**)
window	**prozor**
wine	**vino**
winter	**zima**
with	**s, sa** (+I)
without	**bez** (+G)
woman	**žena**
work	**posao** (G **posla**)
to work	**raditi** (imp.)
world	**svet**
to write	**pisati** (imp. **pišem**), **napisati**

Y

year	**godina**
yes	**da**
yesterday	**juče**
you	**ti** (familiar), **vi** (formal, pl.)
young	**mlad**
your	**tvoj** (sing. familiar), **vaš** (pl. formal)

Subject index

The numbers given against each entry refer to the unit(s) where the relevant information is given.